esse málaga

A Concise Guide to Spain's Most Hospitable City

Thomas Martin

FAROLA BOOKS

For my parents, who love Málaga

*In none of the Spanish towns have I been
so happy, so entirely at home, as here in Málaga.
I like the manners of the people. Good scenery,
and the open sea, both indispensable to me,
I have found here, and, what is still of more
consequence, I have found most amiable people.*

Hans Christian Andersen
(In Spain, 1863)

Published by Farola Books
farolabooks@gmail.com

First published 2023
Copyright © Thomas Martin, 2023

ISBN: 978-1-7395074-2-8

By the same author:

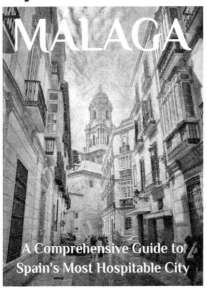

Málaga: A Comprehensive Guide to Spain's Most Hospitable City

This guide is far more than a list of bars, restaurants and museums. Written to be used alongside your mobile, this book uses QR codes and an online map to link with your smartphone. With more than 600 pages, it explores in detail Málaga's history, gastronomy, viticulture, language, religion, arts, celebrations, transport, politics and culture. It also contains information about the Province of Málaga — from the well-worn charms of Marbella to the delights of Romantic Ronda.

Reviews of 'Málaga: A Comprehensive Guide to Spain's Most Hospitable City':

> 'An unbeatable insider's guide from someone who loves the city and really knows its history, culture and daily life, not least its food and drink. I learnt a lot from it – and enjoyed the trip.' **Christopher Howse, author of *A Pilgrim in Spain***

> 'A fascinating guide to one of Spain's most charming cities. Highly recommended.' **Professor Carl Baudenbacher, President of the European Free Trade Area Court (2003–2017)**

 ISBN: 978-1-7395074-0-4

Contents

Introduction

'A couple of days is enough for Málaga.' (Hand-book for
Travellers in Spain, *Richard Ford, 1845*)

This book is a very concise version of *Málaga: A Comprehensive Guide to
Spain's Most Hospitable City*. That book explores the history, culture, gastronomy and daily life of Málaga in considerable detail, as well as exploring other places worth visiting in the Province of Málaga. It is the ideal
volume if you are spending a week or more in Málaga, or if you are a regular visitor. This short book, on the other hand, is a brief guide intended
for those on a short visit, or visiting for the first time.

Even so, I hope that this book will persuade you that Richard Ford — who
was as enamoured with Spain as he was (often) contemptuous of it —
was wrong about Málaga. Every year, more than 18 million travellers (a
quarter of them from the United Kingdom) touch down at Málaga–Costa
del Sol Airport. The overwhelming majority then hire a car, take a coach,
or board a local train to head for the resorts of Torremolinos, Benalmádena, or Fuengirola.

Málaga is often overlooked as a destination in its own right, just as the
charming city of Alicante is ignored in the stampede towards Benidorm.
The sun-worshippers heading towards the all-inclusive hotels of Fuengirola don't think of Málaga as a 'resort'. Maybe those *en route* to the
pueblos blancos or the great city of Granada with its magnificent Alhambra imagine Málaga to be uncultured, dull and mercantile. And many
more snootily ignore the Costa del Sol entirely, preferring the well-worn
charms of hip Barcelona, romantic Sevilla, or elegant Madrid.

In fact, Málaga has something to offer almost any type of visitor. If you're
the sort of person who likes the beach but wants to enjoy some local culture and cuisine as well, then Málaga is ideal. If culture is your thing,
then Málaga's dozens of museums could keep you busy for several days.
History buffs will find evidence of Phoenician, Roman and Moorish civ-
ilizations alongside baroque and Renaissance churches, ghosts of the
Civil War, and reminders of the city's industrial past. If it's culinary culture you're after, then Málaga offers some of the finest food and wine in
Spain. If you're an *aficionado* of the city-break, then whilst Málaga may

1

not be in quite the same league as Venice, Prague or Sevilla, it's no provincial backwater either.

Excellent transport links (by air, road and rail) mean that it is also easy to combine a stay in Málaga with another destination. If you are visiting Gaucín, Granada or Torremolinos, then why not spend a day or two in Málaga as well? Flights between the United Kingdom and Málaga are frequent and, due to the popularity of the Costa del Sol, relatively cheap, even from regional airports. Although it is possible to find direct flights to cities like Granada and Sevilla from some UK airports, they are often expensive, less than daily, and rarely available outside high season. Get a cheap flight to Málaga instead and approach these cities by rail. Combining a visit to Málaga with cities even further afield is also possible. You can leave Málaga after breakfast and, thanks to Spain's network of high-speed trains, be in Barcelona (or Madrid) in time for lunch (or elevenses).

Whatever sort of traveller you are, I hope this guide will encourage you to consider Málaga as more than simply an airport — either as a holiday destination in itself or as a place to spend an enjoyable day (or a few days) as part of a longer holiday.

¡Buen viaje!

T. Martin

Before You Go

When planning your trip, you should be aware that a number of the attractions mentioned in this guide are extremely popular and some will be fully booked weeks ahead.

Booking ahead — as far ahead as possible — is **essential** if you want to visit the **Alhambra** (Granada) or the **Caminito del Rey**. If you want to visit **Córdoba**, then it's advisable to book your train ticket ahead of time to get the cheapest price and book a timed-entry ticket for the **Mezquita-Catedral** at the same time. Booking ahead is also strongly advised if you wish to visit any fine-dining restaurants (the sort that serve tasting menus).

Finally, when planning your itinerary, bear in mind that **all municipal** museums and galleries in Spain are **closed on Mondays**.

 Every location (sightseeing attraction, restaurant, bar, shop, etc.) mentioned in this guide is shown on a companion Google Map. Scan the QR code or consult it here: **bit.ly/MalagaMap**

On a mobile device, you will need to use the **LEGEND** label to display the relevant 'layers' (travel, restaurants, shopping, etc. — day trips outside Málaga city also have their own layers).

⊕ Websites and Online Resources

A very useful website is **malagatop.com** 🔖 ⊕ run by Alejo Tomás, a native of Málaga. His site is comprehensive and regularly updated. Alejo is a great ambassador for his city and a trustworthy source of information (the website is in Spanish and English).

One of the most comprehensive non-commercial websites about the city and province of Málaga is **viajerosencortomalaga.com** 🔖 maintained by Francisco Jurado. It contains a wealth of information. (Spanish only)

facebook.com/muelleuno 🔖 is the best way to keep informed about the many seasonal events that take place on Muelle Uno, especially events for families and children and monthly craft markets (*zocos*).

guidetomalaga.com ⊕ is one of the most comprehensive — and certainly the best-known — websites about Málaga in English. The creation of Joanna Styles, a British travel writer living and working in Málaga, it is frequently updated with information about upcoming events and festivals.

genmalaga.com 🔖 is, alas, only in Spanish, but it maintains a very useful listing of current events and exhibitions.

visita.malaga.eu 🔖 ⊕ is the official tourist information website for Málaga. ⚠ Although most information is available in English, some of the 'news' and 'events' listings are only in Spanish.

malaga.es/en/laprovincia 🔖 ⊕ is the tourism section of the website of the *Diputación* (Provincial Government) and it has a wealth of information about patrimony, traditions, gastronomy, natural features, flora and fauna of the province (all available in English). This excellent website is well worth studying if you plan to explore beyond the city of Málaga.

visitcostadelsol.com 🔖 ⊕ This is another tourism website maintained by the Provincial Government (*Diputación*) of Málaga.

andalucia.com ⊕ Founded in 1996 by Chris Chaplow, few independent tourism information websites are so comprehensive or impressive. Despite the huge quantity of information, it manages to stay up-to-date thanks to its use of a team of contributors. There is also a lively forum.

malagafoto.com ⊕ A collection of lovely photos of Málaga taken by Christian Machowski.

📱 Apps

Arca

The Arca App is a project of the Municipal Archives of Málaga that links to dozens of historical photos via a GPS-enabled map (in English) enabling users to scan QR codes around the city:

  Android   iOS

Málaga in Your Pocket

A free and multilingual app (Spanish, English, French and German) developed by the Málaga *Diputación* (Provincial Government) covering 103 towns and villages in the Province of Málaga.

  Android   iOS

Málaga Destino

A new scheme (launched in 2023) to give tourists discounts in participating attractions and businesses. Sign-ups are limited, so if you're unable to register, try again later. You can also use the **Málaga In Your Pocket** app (above) to register for and use the scheme. **malagadestino.es**.

Callejero (City Street Map)

This is a web page rather than an app, but it works well on a smartphone (tip: if you lose the layers menu, swipe right from the left-hand side of the screen and select **GeoPortal**). **Callejero** is an official street map maintained by the *ayuntamiento* that you can use to find all sorts of amenities (🚰 only) from taxi ranks to drinking fountains to markets. It is especially useful if you are staying in an apartment because it shows the locations of communal refuse collection points. Under the '*Medio ambiente*' heading, select '*Envases*' (tins — yellow), '*Papel y cartón*' (paper & cardboard — blue), '*Residuos sólidos urbanos*' (general waste — brown), or '*Contenedores de vidrio*' (glass — green). 🌐 **sig.malaga.eu/territorio/callejero/?gp=o**

📅 Mondays in Málaga?

Throughout Spain, municipal museums and galleries are closed on Mondays, but there are so many places to visit in Málaga that one hardly notices. However, if your time is limited, especially over a long weekend, you will need to plan. The **Museum of Málaga**, **CAC** and **MUPAM** are all closed on Mondays, as is the **Carmen Thyssen**. The **Pompidou** is closed on Tuesdays. The **Cathedral** and both **Picasso museums** are open every day. However, although the **Alcazaba** is open to visit on Monday, the lift is not in operation.

🧴 Useful things to bring with you

💶 If you are going to be staying in an *hoſtal* or an apartment, have a look at the 'Money Saving Tips' in the chapter about accommodation.

💳 Using a euro-denominated debit card will save you money.

🩹 Over-the-counter medicines (like Aspirin or Paracetamol) are comparatively expensive in Spain (and can only be purchased from pharmacies, not supermarkets), so bring a supply.

➕ Nationals of EU member states should bring a current EHIC (European Health Insurance Card), and UK citizens should make sure they have an up-to-date 'GHIC', as well as health insurance.

🧳 If you normally travel with hand luggage only, consider whether it's worth checking in luggage for the return journey. There are no great bargains in the airport Duty-Free, but wine, spirits, olive oil, ham, charcuterie, cheese etc. are all cheaper in Spain than in the UK. You could bring back quite a hamper of delicacies.

🎧 Since the COVID pandemic, audio guides are now mostly free because they are accessed on your smartphone rather than requiring a handheld unit. Bring headphones or earbuds with you to enable you to use them.

Communication

This book uses Spanish words and phrases, especially relating to food and drink. A little facility with Spanish (also called *castellano*, or 'Castilian') is helpful when it comes to finding your way around (understanding signs), choosing what to eat and drink (decoding menus), making the most of bars and restaurants, and simply being polite and friendly.

💬 Transliteration

Many of the Spanish words and phrases that you might need have been transliterated in a simple way. I have used the small capitals **KH** to represent the **ch** of the Scots loch (IPA **χ**). I've also used **RR** in some words as a reminder that although the Spanish **/r/** is almost always a flap/tap (slightly 'rolled'), in certain positions (*e.g.* in the initial position and before certain vowels) and when doubled, it is stressed with considerable 'rolling'.

Bold type is used to indicate stress (*e.g.* Málaga = **ma**-la-gah; café = ka-**fay**). Stress is crucial in Spanish as it can significantly change the meaning of words. It's the same in English, but we often fail to notice it — think of the difference between 'My elderly uncle is an **in**valid' and 'My passport is in**val**id'.

🔤 Simplified Pronunciation Key

Letter	IPA	Pronunciation (English approximation)
Aa	a	Like **a** in **a**pple
Bb	b	Like **b** in **b**ad
	β	Between vowels the lips should not be fully closed, similar to the **v** in **v**alue
Cc	θ (TH)	Before the vowels **e** and **i**, like **th** in **th**in
	k	Everywhere else, like **c** in **c**offee
	s	You might hear it pronounced like the **c** in **c**entre

Ch	**tʃ**	Like **ch** in **ch**urch
Dd	**d, ð**	Very similar to **d** in **d**ay. Between vowels and after a vowel at the end of a word, similar to the **th** in **th**en
Ee	**e**	Midway between the **e** in t**e**n and the **ay** in s**ay** (or like the **ai** in **ai**r)
Ff	**f**	Like **f** in **f**our
Gg	**g**	Like **g** in **g**et
	χ (KH)	Before the vowels **e** and **i**, like the **ch** in the Scots lo**ch**
Hh	**–**	Silent, except in some loanwords, but sometimes aspirated in Málaga
Ii	**i**	Like **e** in h**e**. Before other vowels, it's like the **y** in **y**ou (when unaccented)
Jj	**χ (KH)**	Like **ch** in the Scots lo**ch**, although it can sometimes sound like the English **h**
Kk	**k**	Like **k** in a**sk**, and only in loanwords — Spanish prefers **c** and **qu**
Ll	**l**	Similar to the **l** in **l**ine, but shorter, somewhat clipped
Ll ll	**ʎ, ʝ**	Similar to the **y** in **y**awn or the **ll** in mi**ll**ion, but in some accents closer to the **s** in plea**s**ure
Mm	**m**	Like **m** in **m**ore
Nn	**n, ŋ**	Like **n** in **n**o (or like the **ng** in si**ng** before **c** or **g**)
Ññ	**ɲ**	Like the **ny** in ca**ny**on
Oo	**o**	Like **o** in d**o**g
Pp	**p**	Like **p** in **p**ort
Qq	**k**	Like **k** in **k**in (for the **qu** sound of **qu**een, Spanish prefers **cu**)
Rr	**r**	When soft, like **tt** in the U.S. pronunciation of bu**tt**er
	r (RR)	When hard (initial position, or doubled) it is rolled as in Scots English
Ss	**s**	Like **s** in **s**ix — sometimes slightly more aspirated, but never like the **sh** in **sh**erry. Spaniards do not say 'Ssshh!' but 'Ssssss!'
Tt	**t**	Like **t** in **t**en, but dental not palatal
Uu	**w**	Before another vowel (especially after **c**) like **w** in t**w**ig.
	u	Everywhere else like **oo** in p**oo**l, but a bit shorter
Vv	**b, β**	Identical to Spanish **b** in almost all cases

7

Ww	**g, w**	Used only in words of foreign origin (Spanish prefers **u**). Pronunciation varies from word to word.
Xx	**ks**	Like the **x** in extra. In some cases it may be pronounced like **gs** or **s**
Yy	**i**	Like the vowel **i** when a word on its own (*i.e. y* = 'and') or at the end of a word
	j	Between the **y** in yellow and the **s** in pleasure when in any other position.
Zz	**θ, s**	Always the same sound in standard Spanish — like the **th** in thin (but often like **s** in sale in Andalucía)

⏰ Telling the Time

Not the time, exactly, but the time of day and the days of the week. If you spot a bar or restaurant you fancy trying later, or another day, it's helpful to be able to understand the opening times displayed:

lunes	**Monday**
martes	**Tuesday**
miércoles	**Wednesday**
jueves	**Thursday**
viernes	**Friday**
sábado(s)	**Saturday(s)**
domingo(s)	**Sunday(s)**
festivos	**feast days (or holidays)**
fin de semana	**weekend**
laborales	**weekdays**
cerrado	**closed**
hoy	**today**
mañana	**tomorrow**
mañana(s)	**morning(s)**
tarde(s)	**afternoon(s)/evening(s)**
noche(s)	**late evening(s)/night(s)**

🄰🄱🄲 Learning the Basics

If you just want to learn 'just enough' of the basics to feel that you belong in the 'traveller' (not 'tourist') category then one quick and basic Spanish course that I can recommend is:

Quickstart Spanish (by Nuria Hervás — BBC Active) First published in 2003 and revised in 2008, this remains — in my opinion — the best short audio course to learn the basics of the language that will actually be useful to travellers. The teaching is done in the form of a number of slightly cheesy but sweetly entertaining dialogues covering all of the basics (greetings, directions, eating, drinking, etc.) in 2 hours and 20 minutes.

Phrase Books are probably relics of a bygone age, though two good ones are published by the **BBC (by Carol Stanley and Phillippa Goodrich, 2005)** and by **DK Eyewitness (2017)**. A better plan is to try to master the pronunciation of Spanish using a quick audio course, and then rely on your smartphone's Google Translate app.

📶 Wifi & 🖂 Postage

Even very basic *hostales* now offer free Wifi, and you should be able to connect to free Wifi while out and about, which is good news if you don't have a cheap data roaming plan. The *ayuntamiento* (city council) offers free public Wifi, but the access points are mainly located in or near municipal buildings (*e.g.* the tourist information office, museums, the town hall, etc.) so the signal is strongest near these locations and can be pretty weak in other parts of the *centro histórico* (the Callejero GeoPortal street map shows the locations). There are also plenty of apps (*e.g.* **wifimap.io**) that can help you to find other public Wifi hotspots. Most of the trendier coffee shops have customer Wifi, as do chains like McDonald's, Starbucks, VIPs, etc. Other establishments are increasingly likely to have Wifi available. You may need to ask the staff for the password — '*la clave del wifi*' (lah **kla**-bay del **wee**-fee).

Free Wifi is also available in shopping centres (*e.g.* **Centro Comercial Larios Centro**), **El Corte Inglés**, the **María Zambrano** railway station, on an increasing number of urban buses, almost all intercity buses and on AVE trains. If your plan makes data roaming prohibitively expensive but you'd rather not bother with constantly connecting to new free networks, then another option is to buy a prepaid ('*prepago*') data SIM (Movistar, Vodafone, Orange and Yoigo are the main Spanish operators) or use an 'eSIM' service like **airalo.com**.

 If you want to send a postcard (*postal* — poh-**stal**), you can buy a stamp (*sello* — **seh**-lyo) from a post office (*correos*), but it is quicker and easier to visit an *estanco* (tobacconist). To post the postcard you just need to find a yellow postbox (*buzón* — scan the QR code to visit the official 'postbox finder').

Why should you visit?
⏳ Importance and History

Málaga is a relatively large city (in Spanish terms), and an old city. With a population of just over half a million people (about the same as Sheffield in the UK), it is the second most populous city in Andalucía (after Sevilla), and the sixth largest in Spain. When it comes to economic activity, Málaga ranks fourth in Spain. The port, crucial to the *malagueña* economy for millennia, has ten wharves and is one of the largest in the Mediterranean, handling almost half a million containers and 40,000 vehicles annually. Between four and five cruise ships dock in Málaga each week, carrying almost half a million passengers, and two ferries per day link Málaga to Melilla, one of Spain's two North African autonomous cities.

Málaga is a spring chicken compared to Cádiz (founded 1100 BC), but it was still founded a decade or so before Rome, which makes it impressively old. When the Phoenicians established a trading post at 'Malaka' around the year 770 BC, they discovered a settlement of Ancient Iberians slightly to the west of modern Málaga (near what is now the airport). After the Phoenicians, Málaga was perhaps controlled by the Greeks (briefly), the Carthaginians, and the Romans. After falling to the Visigoths, the Byzantine emperor Justinian I recaptured the city for the Empire.

The territory passed back and forth between the Byzantines and the Visigoths until the city fell to the Moors in 743 AD, after a hundred years of skirmishes and incursions. For the next 744 years, it was a Moorish city and for a while the capital of a *taifa* (a semi-independent principality). In 1487, Málaga was reconquered by *los Reyes Católicos* (the Catholic Monarchs) Fernando and Isabel after a long, arduous and bloody siege. Being the last significant seaport under Moorish control, its fall was the final nail in the coffin of the Nasrid Kingdom of Granada, which would come only three years later in 1492 — a big year for Spanish history.

Málaga's status as an important port on the southern seaboard of Spain meant that its history has been marked by upheaval. After a period of reconstruction in the centuries following the *reconquista* there came a series of 17th and 18th-century disasters, including earthquakes and industrial explosions. And yet Málaga, like Bilbao in the north, became a centre of economic free trade doctrine and political liberalism.

☀ Climate

We tend to think of Spain as a warm and sunny country, and this perception is borne out by Málaga, which enjoys 320 days of sunshine a year and fewer than 40 days of rain. Winters are mild, while summers are warm and dry. Between June and August, the average temperature is 25° C (77° F) with an average maximum of 30° C (86° F). This means that it is warm enough to sit outside a café at midnight, but not (usually) so unbearably hot during that day that you have to seek refuge in your air-conditioned hotel room until dusk.

♨ Food and Drink

'This is sweet Málaga, known as the beautiful, from whence hail the famous raisins, the famous women, and the wine preferred for Communion'
(Nicaraguan poet and diplomat Rubén Darío, in La Nación, *c.1904)*

The bread and potatoes stodge of northern Europe does not suit the climate of Spain (although Spaniards love stews and pulses) and unlike in the French classical tradition, there is little reliance upon rich or clever sauces. In Spain, the quality and freshness of the ingredients take centre stage. A simple salad of tomatoes, mottled green and red, is a revelation — nothing more than oil, coarse salt and pepper is necessary because the tomatoes themselves are so intensely flavoured. Enjoying a tasting menu at one of Málaga's best restaurants, one of the courses consisted of a single 'Fea de Tudela' tomato with Ibiza salt and a dressing made with bright green olive oil from Jaén and sweet Málaga wine vinegar; just four ingredients. And it was phenomenal. The bar food staple of *huevos rotos* ('broken eggs') — fried chunks of potato with slivers of *jamón* topped with a runny-yolked fried egg — takes ham, egg and chips to a new level of deliciousness.

Just as appealing as the quality of food is the manner of its eating. Service *à la russe* (starter, main course, and dessert served sequentially) is the norm at lunchtime and in more expensive restaurants, but in the evening, the unfailingly sociable Spaniards prefer to share a selection of dishes (called *raciones*) — perhaps some fried peppers, a plate of anchovies, a platter of prawns, squid or lamb cutlets, maybe a salad, or some slices of barnyardy sheep's cheese.

As well as these heartier *raciones* (full, or sharing, portions), are *tapas*. A *tapa* is a small serving of food to accompany a drink, because you will rarely see a Spaniard drinking without eating. The *tapa* might be very modest and handed over for free when you order a drink — a couple of *escabeche* mussels, a triangular slice of slightly crystalline *manchego* cheese, a saucer of fat, green olives or just a handful of potato crisps. A small dish of crisps, by the way, is not quite as dull as it sounds. These crisps are not Walkers (or Lay's, as Walkers is known outside the UK). They will most probably have been fried that day, in local olive oil, at a nearby *freiduría* and delivered to the bar in huge paper sacks.

Tapas menus (or *cartas* in Spanish — *menú* refers to a prix fixe set menu) offer richer fare — crisp *croquetas* with an interior of molten *béchamel*, sliced *chorizo* braised in red wine, sizzling garlic prawns, chickpea and spinach stew, fried potato with gently piquant *brava* sauce, or a medallion of pork tenderloin flambéed in whisky. Some bars specialize in 'gourmet *tapas*', marrying the venerable staples of Spain with the culinary wizardry of Ferran Adrià or the flavours of Southeast Asia. For the visitor, the great advantage of this mode of eating (*tapas* and *raciones*) is that it's possible to sample an enormous variety of dishes. There's no need to feel torn between the meat and the fish: ordering *tapas* and small plates means that you can have both (and more besides) without feeling like a glutton.

In Málaga, you will find all the familiar Spanish favourites as well as quite a few local specialities. Fish and seafood are an obsession even in Madrid, which is as far from the sea as it's possible to be in Spain. On the coast — and Málaga is no exception — the bounty of the sea is front and centre. Many local dishes, especially those involving dried fruit, aubergines and molasses, have their origins in Moorish times and many have links to Sephardic (Jewish) cuisine. The province to the east, Almería, is the centre of Spanish market horticulture, and Málaga is famed for its subtropical fruit, which means that the salad vegetables and fruit available in Málaga are of exceptional quality and freshness. Andalucía is the largest olive-growing region on earth, accounting for 40% of all olive oil produced worldwide. Even if you only ever purchase 'Italian' olive oil, some proportion of what you buy will almost certainly have originated in Andalucía.

As well as olives, the Province of Málaga is known for almonds and grapes. Málaga is the only region of Spain to have a separate *Denominación de Origen* for its grapes in their dried form as well as in their fermented liquid form. The Province of Málaga produces excellent wine, both table wine and fortified wine in 'sherry' and dessert styles. Shakespeare's bon viveur Sir John Falstaff was fond of 'Sherris Sack' — the fortified wines now known as 'Sherry' (*i.e.* Jerez) — but some 70 years after *Henry IV Part 1* was performed, Samuel Pepys would write in his diary that, 'Malago Sack... [is] excellent wine, like a spirit rather than wine.'

It is for sweet white wines made from Moscatel (Muscat) grapes that Málaga is most famous, but nowadays the region's red, rosé and dry white wines are becoming much better-known. As well as wine, Málaga is also home to a variety of spirits. Most famous is probably Resoli — a rich anisette embellished with coffee, cinnamon and cloves. There is also a local premium brandy (1886 Gran Reserva), and rum (a spirit first exported from Andalucía to the Caribbean, rather than vice versa). The undisputed king of *malagueño* spirits, however, is gin. It comes as a surprise to many to learn that Spain is the third largest consumer of gin in the world (after The Philippines and the USA). When it comes to per capita consumption, Spain outdrinks everywhere else at a fraction under 70 centilitres (*i.e.* a bottle) per person annually, with the UK (48 cl) and even the largest gin market of The Philippines (39 cl) trailing considerably behind. Much of that gin is produced by Larios, a distillery founded in Málaga (though now located in Madrid). Like Cadbury in Birmingham, the name Larios is intertwined with the history and geography of its home city.

Gin is produced in several areas of Málaga province. In the eastern region of Axarquía, they produce Gin Ballix flavoured with local variety 'Osteen' mangoes. The Vélez-Málaga neighbourhood is home to Alborán Gin. The village of Cuevas Bajas is famous for its purple carrots, and since 2016 the taste of this unique carrot is also found in the gin Simbuya, produced by Esalui. Oxén Spiritus is produced in Ojén just outside Marbella. And Málaga's oldest functioning distillery, El Tajo, in Ronda, launched its gin onto the market in 1895 (which is also the name of the gin). As for Málaga City, in 2015, the gin connoisseur and manager of the 'Gin Tonic' bar,

Carlos Villanueva, launched two gins. He named both gins after Málaga: Malaka London Dry contains classic botanicals, whilst Malaka Premium has a Mediterranean profile with a faint note of jasmine.

🚶 Culture

Málaga is neither the capital of Spain nor of Andalucía, but of the Province of Málaga. It is, then, 'provincial' by definition, and for many years was regarded as the less sophisticated sibling of Sevilla, once the wealthiest and grandest city in all of Europe. Partly thanks to Washington Irving, the Dan Brown of his day, millions flock to the Moorish Alhambra of Granada, and rightly so (though in my opinion, the Alcázar of Sevilla is in some ways even more impressive). What few people know is that Málaga has a Moorish citadel (Alcazaba) of its own. Though rather less grand than the Alhambra and not a royal residence like the palace in Sevilla, it is older than either. Many architectural historians agree that only the Krak des Chevaliers in Syria is better preserved.

The Alcazaba was built on a hill to protect the strategic port of Málaga, and in due course, a second Moorish fortification — the Castillo de Gibralfaro — was constructed on the summit of a slightly higher hill to protect the Alcazaba. Hard against the walls of the Alcazaba is a Roman theatre built in the first century BC. Although quarried by the Moors when building the Alcazaba, much of the *cavea* remains. It was only rediscovered in 1951, ironically enough beneath Málaga's Cultural Centre. Restoration was completed in 2011 and it is now open to visitors and used for open-air concerts.

After the *reconquista*, churches were built upon the sites of mosques (that had themselves displaced far older Visigothic churches that had probably displaced Roman temples that had displaced Celtiberian worship sites) including a fine, though unusual, Renaissance cathedral. Patches of the medieval footprint of Málaga's old city remain, as do many buildings, but successive wars, sieges, revolutions and even earthquakes have also left their mark. Much of central Málaga was renewed in the 19th century during the period of confidence that followed the Napoleonic wars, and many of Málaga's most beautiful streets are pure *Belle Époque* (albeit in the markedly Spanish style of Eduardo Strachan Viana-Cárdenas). Yet more devastation came with the Civil War and a period of deep economic decline, but visiting Málaga today, one would hardly know.

The centre is largely and mercifully free of the sort of monstrosities that filled the lacunae of many other European cities. A few high-rise blocks were built in the 1960s and 1970s near the Malagueta Beach, but are contained within the space of a few streets. Across the river in the other direction, towards the railway station, the no doubt picturesque hovels of Roma and working-class *barrios* have been demolished and replaced with decidedly unpicturesque tenements. But whilst nineteenth-century slums might be 'colourful' for tourists to explore, they were not as much fun for the people who had to live in them.

The biggest change, though, has come about in the last couple of decades. Residential, commercial and ecclesiastical buildings have been restored and cleaned. Sixteenth-century urban palaces have been tastefully converted into galleries, museums and boutique hotels. The scruffy port area of El Ensanche ('the expansion'), once home to dosshouses, brothels and sex shops, has been transformed into Málaga's most vivacious, arty district.

Málaga has always had a 'respectable' and sophisticated side that has charmed visitors, but in the past, there was a louche underbelly — the seedy Mr Hyde emerging at night to eclipse Dr Jekyll. Nicholas Luard wrote in the 1960s of Málaga's 'stately old-fashioned feel,' describing how '[h]orse-drawn carriages clop slowly in the shadow along the broad leafy boulevardes, and jacarandas blossom violet against crumbling façades with windows covered by ornate wrought-iron grilles.' At night, however, the city 'changes and becomes a sailors' town. Prostitutes patrol the streets, and the bars, together with the little satellite businesses that circle round them, the boot-blacks, lottery tickets sellers, cigarette ladies and pinchito stalls, stay open until the early hours.'

Nothing symbolizes the transformation of Málaga from faded port to buzzing city destination quite so much as the recent proliferation of new museums and galleries. Claims vary regarding the number of museums and galleries in Málaga, but 'around 40' is a phrase one often hears. It's true that some of these museums are very small and somewhat niche, but for a city of its size, it's an impressive number. My favourite example of the niche is the Wine Museum, which regularly receives excoriating one-star reviews on TripAdvisor. Admittedly there is very little on display apart from infographic displays (in Spanish) and a lot of wine labels. On the other hand, the ticket price also includes a tasting of two local wines meaning that you 'get back' most of the admission charge.

The building the museum occupies is, in fact, the headquarters of the *Consejo Regulador* (regulatory authority) for the two Málaga wine regions (Málaga, and Sierras de Málaga) as well as for Málaga Raisins. The museum is meant to showcase and explain their work. It is lovingly curated, the staff are kind, enthusiastic, knowledgeable and friendly (they faithfully respond to all their TripAdvisor reviews, thanking patrons for their visit — always a good sign of a well-run attraction), and if you make use of the free audio guide you will learn quite a lot about winemaking in the Málaga region. Sure, it might be far more interesting to visit a vineyard in the hills, but one can't do that in an hour and a half on a (rare) rainy day.

Many of the city's museums are fairly recent foundations. Even the Picasso Museum, devoted to Málaga's most famous son, only opened its doors in 2003. Málaga is home to the first branch of the Centre Georges Pompidou outside France. Another accolade for the city was winning the competition to host the first museum outside Madrid to exhibit works from the collection of Doña Carmen Thyssen-Bornemisza. A number of cities vied for the honour and Málaga won, much to the chagrin of her native Barcelona. The third big jewel in the crown was another satellite — that of the Russian State Museum (though the invasion of Ukraine in 2022 has strained the cultural relationship between Málaga and St Petersburg, to say the least).

👥 *La Gente*

La Gente — the people — are of course an important element of any city and perhaps the most significant factor in determining the *ambiente* of a place. A huge part of the enjoyment we derive from staying in a lovely hotel or eating and drinking in a gourmet restaurant or a buzzing bar, is due to the people we encounter in those places, both members of staff and fellow patrons and guests.

In the 1960s, the Ministry of Information and Tourism under the Franco regime came up with the slogan 'Spain is Different'. For those early British tourists, Spain must have seemed very different indeed, not just in terms of heat and sun, but in its enjoyment of wine, garlic and olive oil. However, being different to the UK is not the same thing as homogeneity. I suspect that if one asked the man on the Clapham Omnibus what 'Spain' suggested to him, he might mention garlic, flamenco, bullfighting, beaches, and *paella*, among other things. Yet bullfighting is popular in some regions of Spain and proscribed in others, *paella* is jealously guarded by the people of Valencia and flamenco is seen as an *andaluz*, rather than simply a Spanish, art form. Spain is as 'different' from region to region and city to city as anywhere else in the world.

Spaniards from Galicia to Valencia, Barcelona to Huelva, do tend to share a number of traits. The first thing one notices is their sociability; a *joie de vivre* enriched by the fellowship of others. They tend to be stylish and smart, taking pride in their appearance. They relish good food and love to drink, but disapprove of gluttony or drunkenness. The passionate 'Latin temperament' is no myth — their enjoyment of flamenco, folk songs, dancing, religious processions and, for many, bullfighting, is visceral. And they love to party. Every city, town and village has at least one major annual *feria* (fair) and usually a couple of minor ones, and these are celebrated at full throttle by young and old. Everyday life is put on hold for a weekend (or for an entire week) and everything is about the party.

Malagueños — the people of Málaga — exhibit all these attractive qualities. They even have their own word to describe themselves — '*malaguita*'. Simply being from Málaga is not the same as being *malaguita*. Anyone born in Málaga is a *malagueño* or a *malagueña*, but only those who are passionate about all the typical traditions of the city — Holy Week, carnival, the *feria*, Málaga Football Club, anchovies, clams with lemon and black pepper, Moscatel wine — will be *malaguitas*

This fierce pride in, and identification with, their city manifests itself in the language they use. Málaga is Spanish speaking, but they speak it in a *malaguita* way. In Sevilla, a sandwich roll and a coffee with milk is a *bocadillo* and a *café con leche*, just as it is in the rest of Spain. In Málaga, though, it is a *pitufo* and a *mitad*. In the rest of Spain, during Holy Week, large floats called *pasos* (often mistranslated as 'steps', but derived from the Latin *passus* meaning 'having suffered') are carried through the streets, but in Málaga they are called *tronos* (thrones). Málaga prides itself in being different, and yet the wonderful thing is that this sense of pride and distinctiveness does not make the locals aloof or unwelcoming in the slightest. If anything, the opposite is true.

One of the things that strikes the first-time visitor to Málaga is the kindness and hospitality of its denizens. This can be seen very clearly at the annual *feria* held in August. Perhaps the most famous, and probably the most impressive, *feria* in Spain is the April Fair in Seville, a week-long party involving music, dancing and drinking. The fairground is composed of *casetas* (hospitality tents) filled with the great and the good of *sevillana* society. However, apart from a handful of *casetas* hosted by the municipality, a couple of trades unions, and the Communist Party, they are all private and you need an invitation to gain entry. At the Málaga *feria*, however, all the *casetas* are open to the public and free.

Malagueña hospitality extends to visitors and tourists. Large-scale tourism is a fairly recent phenomenon for the city, and despite occasional grumbles in the letters pages of the newspapers about new hotels and the number of apartments being offered as holiday rents, most *malagueños* seem to think that growth in the tourist sector has been positive overall for the city. Local politicians will have to keep an eye on the situation, however, if Málaga is not to go the same way as Sevilla and Barcelona, where one frequently sees graffiti urging tourists to 'Go Home!'

The *Ayuntamiento* (Town Hall) promoted the motto, '*Málaga: Ciudad Genial*' to market the city, and it is an apt moniker. In Spanish, '*genial*' nowadays tends to mean 'great' or 'cool', but its more literary meaning is closer to the English word, *viz.* 'friendly; causing delight or happiness'. Any city may evoke delight or happiness through its appearance, but only its people can make it actually 'friendly'. Málaga is justly proud of its beautiful buildings, fine museums and delicious food and drink, but its greatest treasure is its people.

🛡 Safety

Spain is a pretty safe country to visit. Police-recorded assaults in Spain as a whole average around 60 per 100,000. By way of comparison, Italy and Germany record around twice as many, France five times as many, and England and Wales a staggering 12 times as many (though this may, of course, simply reflect greater efficiency with paperwork in the UK).

There are certainly areas in some Spanish cities with the same sorts of crime problems as in the UK (drugs, gangs, theft, illegal prostitution, etc.) and Málaga is no exception. However, city centres are pretty safe at any time of the day or night for a number of reasons. One is that Spaniards are very keen on 'public space' and they like to occupy it — parks, streets, pavements, squares, etc. — and therefore nowhere in any city centre is ever really 'deserted. Spaniards rarely sit down for dinner before 9 pm, very few bars close before midnight, and many stay open until 2 or 3 am. Another reason is that Spaniards don't really understand 'personal space', at least not in the public sphere. It would be unkind to say that they are 'nosey', but they certainly take an interest in what is going on around them. That means keeping a look out for thieves and pickpockets. You might find that a man peddling novelty key rings is angrily chased from a bar by its owner, while the guy selling other trinkets is unmolested. This is probably because the former is a known swindler or thief whilst the latter is trusted.

Even so, the usual advice holds true. Use the safe in your room (or, in smaller guest houses, in reception) and do not carry all your cash and cards with you. The easiest way to spend euros in Spain is by using a prepaid currency card (**bit.ly/WhichCurrencyCards**) which can be topped up online or via a smartphone app. You tend to get a better exchange rate and will not be at the mercy of the often eccentric conversion charges levied on non-euro card transactions. It may also be used for withdrawing cash from ATMs. Keep the currency card on your person, and your main bank card back at your accommodation; then, in the unlikely event of your pocket being picked, you will be able to cancel the currency card and still have a means of accessing money and making purchases.

Try to keep money and valuables in a zipped or buttoned pocket, and better still, separate pockets. Women can use a small handbag which they should keep to the front, rather than slinging behind (with three branches in Málaga, the Spanish chain Misako sells quite stylish small handbags and bum bags at bargain prices). Some men might feel confident enough to use a 'man bag' too, of course. Never hook handbags or jackets over chair backs in bars or restaurants. Know where your phone is, and never place it on the table. Be alert when you use an ATM.

Make sure you have a made note of your credit card numbers and relevant emergency phone numbers. Also, keep a note of your phone's model name and IMEI number, serial number, etc. If your phone is stolen, the police will ask for this information when you report the theft.

It is a **legal requirement** to carry ID in Spain. For UK citizens, that means a passport. In practice, however, most tourists are unaware of this law, and the police probably realize this. Even those who do know of the existence of Article 4 of *La Ley Orgánica 4/2000* do not usually cart their passports around with them, understanding the nightmare that a lost passport would initiate. Anecdotally, the only people I have heard of falling foul of this law are tourists who make trouble in other ways (drunken stag weekenders, for example).

On the other hand, a number of museums and galleries are free for EU citizens, so if you have an EU passport, there will be occasions when you will need to have it with you. Increasingly, ID is required for entry to pre-booked attractions and for train and long-distance bus travel. My advice, in accordance with Spanish law, must therefore be to keep your passport with you at all times. I merely observe that many foreign visitors to Spain keep about their person either a photocopy of their passport, or a colour photo of it on their smartphones.

♿ Accessibility

Málaga is a pretty easy city to visit because it is a very compact city. Most of the main sights are in the *centro histórico* (historic city centre) and around the port redevelopment, an area of less than a square mile. This area is almost completely pedestrianized, making it relatively easy for visitors with disabilities or limited mobility to access.

The daily *paseo* (stroll), though enjoyed by families and people of all ages, is *par excellence* the preserve of elderly *malagueños*, strolling through the park or along the quay. Older people are valued and respected in Spanish society and deference is shown them. Wherever older people go for the *paseo* (the quayside, the park, the Alameda, etc.) one tends to find abundant benches upon which to rest weary bones. Málaga, then, is generally an elderly-friendly city, which means that it takes accessibility seriously too.

Only two of the main attractions might be challenging or unsuitable for people with mobility problems — the Gibralfaro Castle (but you can still take the bus and admire the unequalled view of Málaga), and the Alcazaba. However, in the case of the latter, there is a lift on the Calle Guillén Sotelo to enable visitors to at least visit the main Nasrid buildings in the heart of the complex, though not the rest of the citadel which has some steep paths and steps — look for 'Ascensor a la Alcazaba' on the companion Google map.

According to the website of the Málaga City Council, all of the main museums are adapted for the disabled, as is the Cathedral (though not the '*cubiertas*' or roof). Even the Botanical Gardens, a short bus ride from the city centre, has an extensive 'wheelchair route' which could equally be used by anyone wishing to avoid uneven paths.

All hotels, of any star rating, must have a lift, and most of the larger ones will have some suitably adapted rooms. *Hostales* and apartments are not legally required to have lift access, so always check when booking. Bars and restaurants have been encouraged to provide disabled access through the city council's 'Accessible Málaga' campaign but, to be honest, the picture is mixed. The new establishments on the quayside and in 'Soho' tend to have very good accessibility and facilities, whilst some of the older establishments in the centre are somewhat limited when it comes to space. Many bars and cafés in the centre have easily accessible outdoor terraces ('*terrazas*'), but you should ask about lavatory facilities if you have difficulty with steps.

Lavatories are a problem for many older and smaller venues. Many of the more ancient bars are very small, with loos up or down a flight of stairs. Not that it is any comfort, but the provision of public lavatories is a challenge for most visitors to Spain. If you have mobility issues, then my advice is broadly the same as in the 'Lavatories' section — basically, use the loo whenever you encounter one, whether you need to or not! Museums all have accessible toilets, as do El Corte Inglés, the Larios Shopping Centre and the railway station. All new buildings and new reforms of buildings must include accessible lavatories. Some facilities are out of date, while others are way ahead of the game. For example, the accessible facilities on Muelle Uno have recently been adapted to the needs of people who are ostomized.

Málaga Airport offers assistance to adult travellers (and accompanied children) with disabilities and/or limited mobility. Information about these services, with links to smartphone apps can be found here: **bit.ly/AGPAirportAccessibility** (QR code left).

The Spanish National Rail operator, RENFE, offers similar assistance, also with smartphone apps: **bit.ly/MalagaRailAssistance** (QR code right). All stations on the local Ⓢ *Cercanías* train network are fully accessible, with lifts and escalators when the station is underground.

The ⋀⋀ Málaga Metro is fully adapted, not only for those who use wheelchairs or have limited mobility but also for those with sensory impairment. If you want to head out of the city centre, the Málaga bus network ('EMT') has reserved seats for the elderly and disabled, and the main routes are served by vehicles that have been fully adapted with wheelchair ramps (*e.g.* 🚌 19 serving the airport, as well as 🚌 1, 3, 4, 10, 11, 16, 24, 33, 34, 35 and C2). You can book a specially adapted taxi by calling: 📞+34 952 333 333, 📞+34 952 320 000, or 📞+34 952 040 805.

Remember, too, that although the centre of Málaga is largely pedestrianized, taxis have access to all but a few streets, so wherever you want to go, you will be able to take a taxi almost to the door for a few euros.

 As part of the *Málaga Ciudad Accesible* (Accessible City Málaga) initiative, the Town Hall offers guided visits, tailored to the needs of visitors. Booking is essential, at least three days ahead. More information (in Spanish) here: **bit.ly/AccessMalaga** (QR code left). You could also ask at the *turismo* (*oficina de turismo* or tourist information office).

Another project of the city council is *Disfruta La Playa* (Enjoy the Beach), a support service for people with disabilities and reduced mobility, to facilitate their enjoyment of the beach and help them access the sea through the use of amphibious chairs, flotation materials, etc. It is available from 23 June to 15 September (when the beaches are manned by lifeguards) and information and the phone numbers to book the services are to be found on the '*Málaga Ciudad Accesible*' web page above.

A Brief History

Phoenicians

The region around Málaga has been inhabited since ancient times. In the Nerja Caves, paintings of seals have been dated that could well be the first known work of art in the history of mankind, dating back 42,000 years. The Phoenicians arrived in the 9th century BC to trade with the Bastetani people (an ancient Iberian tribe). They first established an enclave at Cerro de Villar at the mouth of the Guadalhorce River (close to where the airport is now located). Gradually the centre of commercial activity moved towards the area of the city of Málaga as we now know it due to the natural harbour at the foot of Mount Gibralfaro and plentiful silver and copper deposits. The colony of Mlk (𐤌𐤋𐤊) or Malaka was founded, again by the Phoenicians, in the 8th century BC. The name is almost certainly derived from the Phoenician word for 'salt', probably because fish was salted near the harbour. The most significant economic activity was fish processing (salting and fermenting) and the production of Tyrian Purple, the enormously costly dye extracted from sea snails. A sign of the importance of Malaka was the existence of its own mint.

Romans

The Romans conquered the city, like other regions under the rule of Carthage, in the year 218 BC after the Punic wars. Unlike the Phoenicians, who were primarily interested in trade, the Romans unified the people of the coast and the interior under a common power. Malaka was integrated into the Roman Republic as part of Hispania Ulterior. The *municipium Malacitanum* was a transit point on the Via Herculea, revitalizing the city by connecting it with Hispania Interior (Spain) and with the other ports of the Mare Nostrum (the Mediterranean). Like the Phoenicians before them, the Romans continued to prize Málaga as a source of Imperial Purple dye and of salted and fermented fish (garum).

Towards the end of the period of Roman rule, Malaca emerged as a centre of Christian belief, something we know about partly due to the wave of persecution that took place under the emperor Diocletian. The first known bishop of Malaca, San Patricio (Patrick) attended the Council of Elvira in c. 305, one of 19 bishops from the province of Baetica. Under the Hispano-Roman Emperor Theodosius (379–395 AD), Christianity became the official creed of the Empire.

Vandals, Goths, Byzantines, and Goths again

The Western Roman Empire, mired in decadence, gave way to the dominance of the Vandals, who around the year 411 AD devastated the coast of Malaca. After the division of the Roman Empire the fractured remnants of the Western Empire were consumed by ill-considered land grabs and infighting between various Germanic tribes. In 552 AD the Byzantine Emperor Justinian I conquered Malaca with the intention of rebuilding the Roman Empire (the '*Recuperatio Imperii*').

The city was sacked and conquered again for the Visigoths by King Sisebut in the year 615 AD, but it would be in 624 AD, during the reigns of the Visigoth Suintila and the Emperor Heraclius, when the Byzantines definitively abandoned their hold on cities in the area of the strait and the Visigothic king Sisebut razed a large part of the city. Such was the devastation that the first Islamic invaders of the old Visigothic county of Malacitano initially located their capital inland, in Archidona.

Conquista

The beginning of the 8th century AD saw the collapse of the Gothic monarchy and the penetration of Islam into the Iberian Peninsula from North Africa (though directed by the Caliphate in Damascus). The Umayyad invasion represented an imperial expansion, but it was also a colonial adventure bringing large numbers of Arab and Berber settlers. After the Arab conquest, the city became part of the Muslim polity of al-Andalus and was known as Mālaqa (مالقة). In 743 Mālaqa definitively entered the area of Arab influence, after years of uprisings by its Hispano-Gothic inhabitants. By 750, the Umayyads were overthrown in Damascus by the Abbasids and moved the seat of the caliphate to Córdoba.

Mālaqa became a city surrounded by walls with five large gates and a number of suburbs and neighbourhoods (also walled), dotted with orchards on the banks of the Guadalmedina. Next to the Muslim medina were neighbourhoods of Genoese merchants, Jews, and 'Mozarabs' (indigenous Christians).

The Arabs brought with them fresh ideas about town planning and administration and advanced agricultural technology, particularly irrigation. In the 11th century, in the Jewish quarter of the medina of Mālaqa, the Hebrew philosopher and poet Solomon ibn Gabirol rhapsodized his natal town as the 'City of Paradise'. In this long period, Mālaqa grew to a population of more than 20,000 inhabitants and became one of the most densely populated cities in the entire Iberian Peninsula.

A simplified time-line of Málaga under Muslim rule may be useful at this point:

- Muslim conquest (711–732)
- (Umayyad) Emirate (later Caliphate) of Córdoba (756–1031)
- First Taifa period (1009–1110)
- Almoravid rule (1085–1145)
- Second Taifa period (1140–1203)
- Almohad rule (1147–1238)
- Third Taifa period (1232–1287)
- (Nasrid) Emirate of Granada (1238–1492)
- *Reconquista* by the forces of Fernando and Isabel (1492)

On the death of Ibn Zannun, the last king of the *Taifa* of Mālaqa, in 1238, the city became part of the Nasrid Kingdom of Granada, remaining under the rule of this dynasty until the reconquest by the Catholic Monarchs. The traveller Ibn Battuta, who passed through around 1325, described Mālaqa as 'one of the largest and most beautiful towns of al-Andalus [uniting] the conveniences of both sea and land, and abundantly supplied with foodstuffs and fruits'. He praised its grapes, figs, and almonds; and claimed that 'its ruby-coloured Murcia pomegranates have no equal in the world.'

Reconquista

The *reconquiſta* of Andalucía by the Spanish Crown began with the capture of the rather insignificant town of Alhama de Granada in February 1482. A few months later, the former Emir of Granada Abu'l-Hasan Ali ibn Sa'd took refuge in Mālaqa after being overthrown by his son Muhammad XII (Boabdil). Following this loss, the Arabs built a large number of defensive towers for the city, including Torre Molinos to the west..

The conquest of the city of Málaga by the *Reyes Católicos* in August 1487 was a bloody and drawn-out episode lasting six months. A powerful Castilian army made up of 12,000 cavalrymen, 25,000 infantry and 8,000 more soldiers in support advanced on a city defended by 15,000 Nasrid soldiers and Ghomara Berbers. The city fell on 13 August 1487 and the *Reyes Católicos* entered the medina on 19 August.

The reconquest of the city was a harsh and definitive blow to the Nasrid kingdom of Granada, which had now lost its main seaport. Determined to make Málaga an example of the futility of resistance, Fernando granted only 25 families permission to remain, enslaving (or executing) thousands of the vanquished.

The Modern Age

New communities coalesced around the churches and convents built outside the walled enclosure of the old medina, giving rise to the formation of *barrios* outside the walls, such as La Trinidad and El Perchel, and the so-called '*Málaga conventual*' (Málaga of the Convents). From the 16th to the 18th century, the city underwent periods of instability due to frequent and devastating epidemics, floods caused by the Guadalmedina River (often in years of bad harvests), earthquakes, explosions of gunpowder mills, Berber slaving raids and relentless military conscription campaigns. Despite all these challenges, the population increased from 3,616 to 4,296 families within 100 years of the *reconquista*.

In 1588, the Port was extended both west and east. In the 17th century, wine and raisins were the backbone of Málaga's exports and constituted the main source of income. In the textile field, silk stood out (an inheritance from the Moors). Málaga attracted a significant influx of foreign merchants largely from Flanders, England, and France. During the second half of the 18th century, the chronic water supply problems suffered by Málaga were solved with the completion of one of the most important engineering projects yet carried out in Spain: the San Telmo Aqueduct. The *malagueño* bourgeoisie was already beginning to germinate and would lay the foundations for the economic boom of the 19th century.

19th Century

In many ways, events of the 19th and early 20th centuries militated against what should have been a Golden Age. Málaga has always thrived when she has traded. Industrialization brought new opportunities for Málaga but the French invasion, the ignominious abdication of the Spanish Royal House, the Spanish War of Independence and the continual tug of war between the forces of autocracy and liberalism that all conspired to hold Málaga back in comparison with other European cities.

Málaga was a pioneer at the beginning of the Industrial Revolution, becoming the first genuinely industrial city in Spain and holding second place after Barcelona for much of the 19th century. Due to its enterprising bourgeoisie and its strong desire for modernity, Málaga was one of the most rebellious cities in Spain during the nineteenth century and the scene of various uprisings. This revolutionary activity earned the city the title 'Always intrepid' and the motto 'The first when freedom is endangered' from Isabel II.

Industry

In the 19th century, Málaga had two well-defined sectors, both located outside the historic centre. To the west, the urban landscape began to industrialize, while to the east, villas and hotels appeared. In 1834, the foundry of Manuel Agustín Heredia — 'La Constancia' — opened. Between 1860 and 1865, communications received a significant boost with the construction of the Málaga–Álora, Málaga–Cártama and, most importantly, Málaga–Córdoba railway lines, linking the city with the rest of Spain. Towards the end of the 19th century, the tram transformed travel within the city. From the 1860s, working-class *barrios* like El Bulto and Huelin were created to house workers employed by nearby factories.

The end of this century of prosperity was visible over the horizon in the 1880s due to high import tariffs on British coal and the lack of competitiveness that this generated in the Málaga steel industry. Arguably more catastrophic was the phylloxera blight that all but annihilated Málaga's vineyards and thus wine production.

These serious crises and their aftermath, the loss of employment, the collapse of companies, the rise in poverty and a general decline in economic activities, led many people from Málaga to seek other sources of wealth to replace what had been lost, founding in 1897, for example, the *Sociedad Propagandística del Clima y el Embellecimiento de Málaga* (Society for the Promotion of the Beautification of Málaga), an initiative aimed at promoting tourism and a distant antecedent of the tourist boom that arrived in earnest in the 1950s.

20th Century

In May 1931, after the proclamation of the Second Republic, convents, churches and religious buildings were burned in Málaga, destroying a large part of the historic, artistic and architectural heritage of the city. Agitators took to the streets at dawn on 11 May 1931, damaging or destroying over 40 religious buildings in what became known as the *Quema de conventos* (Burning of the Convents). In 1933, the first deputy of the Spanish Communist Party, Cayetano Bolívar, was elected for Málaga. Due to its association with anticlerical, republican, radical and socialist politics for many years, the city was known as '*Málaga la roja*' (Red Málaga), even though Catholic, liberal and conservative interests have always had important representation and are well-rooted in the city.

In 1936, at the outbreak of the Spanish Civil War, the military *coup d'état* was put down in Málaga thanks to the intervention of (mainly anarchist) workers' militias. However, the province was soon practically isolated from the rest of the region loyal to the Republic, being connected only by the Almería highway. On 7 February 1937, the Francoist army, in collaboration with soldiers from the Italian *Corpo Truppe Volontarie*, launched an offensive against the city that was met with little resistance.

The occupation of Málaga led to an exodus of civilians and soldiers along the Almería highway, where they were subjected to air and sea bombardment causing multiple deaths. This episode is known as The Crime of the Málaga–Almería Highway. In Málaga, the repression of the Francoist military dictatorship was one of the harshest of the war, with an estimated 20,000 shot and buried in common graves.

El Caudillo

After the Civil War, recovery was slow. A trickle of foreign visitors wrote about the grinding poverty they encountered. At Almuñecar — just along the coast from Nerja — Laurie Lee related the sad spectacle of malnourished villagers struggling to land a net containing 'a pink mass of glutinous jellyfish and … quivering sardines,' a haul too meagre to go for auction, being shared out instead, after which 'the children and the workless poor were left to scratch in the sand for the small fry which had passed unnoticed, and these they ate raw on the spot'.

Spain was a basket case, impoverished by years of unrest, revolution and then Civil War, yet with an authoritarian government that presided over an unproductive, centralized economy. Even now one still sees the occasional example of what used to be a very common sight in Spain — an elderly Spaniard, a child of the Civil War years, short in stature and bow-legged — not the effects of old age so much as childhood malnutrition and rickets.

Málaga moderna

For all that writers like Laurie Lee and Gerald Brenan wrote movingly about the grinding poverty of Spain in the first half of the 20th century, it was clearly part of Spain's appeal for them, at least early in their writing careers. In his 1949 preface to *The Face of Spain*, Brenan is keen to encourage his countrymen to visit 'one of the most beautiful countries in the world … unlike any other'.

The Province of Málaga experienced the demographic and economic expansion and upheaval caused by the boom in the tourism sector on the Costa del Sol, and while many Spaniards flocked to the area looking for work, almost an equal number left for other parts of Spain. The *Cercanías* local train network was inaugurated in 1968 and in 1972 the University of

Málaga was founded.

Málaga looked on as her neighbours on the Costa del Sol attracted huge amounts of foreign income through tourism, while at the same time observing how these former coastal villages were transformed into seas of concrete. At the beginning of the 21st century, the *Ayuntamiento* set out to develop the city as a whole, not as a typical tourist 'resort' but as a lively, attractive, culturally rich destination that people will not only want to visit but also move to. They also worked hard to attract business. The Andalucía Technology Park, in the west of the city, is home to 646 companies employing almost 20,000 workers. In November 2022, Google's announcement that it would be setting up its main cybersecurity hub in the city was a symbolic boost, bringing with it an investment of $650 million.

I hesitate to engage in crystal ball gazing, but it is clear to any observer that there are both opportunities and dangers as Málaga looks to the future. The growth of tourism has been a success insofar as tourism has grown (faster than anywhere else in Spain, in fact). The government of Málaga will need to find the 'Goldilocks Zone' for tourism, *viz.* neither too little nor too much. The difficulty lies in agreeing on what level is 'just right'.

Symbols of Málaga

The coat of arms of the city was created by a Royal Decree of the Catholic Monarchs on 30 August 1494. The motto reads, in my translation: 'The First When Freedom is in Danger, the Very Noble, Very Loyal, Very Hospitable, Very Beneficent, Very Illustrious and Always Daring, the City of Málaga'. In the documents of the Catholic Monarchs, Málaga had already been given the title of 'Very Noble'. Felipe IV, in 1640, granted the city the title of 'Very Loyal' for the services provided by the city, especially the large amounts of money contributed to the Crown.

The title of 'Very Illustrious' was granted in 1710 by Felipe V for the services rendered to the Crown by the city during the War of Succession. 'Always Daring' and 'The First When Freedom is in Danger' were granted by Queen Isabel II in a Royal

Decree of 21 August 1843, in thanks for the struggles that caused the fall of General Espartero (Regent of Spain during the minority of Queen Isabel II). The title of 'Very Hospitable' was granted by King Alfonso XIII in a Royal Decree of 1 January 1901 for the noble and selfless conduct of the people of Málaga on the occasion of the sinking of the German war frigate Gneisenau. And in 1922 and as proof of Royal appreciation for the city, recognizing the charitable help given to the soldiers of the Army of Africa and support of a hospital for them, Málaga was awarded the title of 'Very Beneficial'. The motto '*Tanto Monta*' is a quotation of the motto of the Catholic Monarchs, '*Tanto monta, monta tanto*' ('They amount to the same, the same they amount to').

The principal patrons of Málaga are the martyrs Ciriaco and Paula, and the Virgin (Mary) of Victory. The first were two young people who lived at the end of the 3rd century and who, on the occasion of the tenth persecution decreed by the Emperor Diocletian against the Christians, were arrested and required to offer sacrifices to the Roman divinities. Ciriaco and Paula refused to engage in pagan worship and they were therefore sentenced to death by stoning on 18 June 303 AD on the bank of the Guadalmedina in a place today called Martiricos (near the football stadium). After the *reconquista*, King Fernando gifted Málaga the image of the *Virgen de la Victoria*, a sculpture of German origin given to the monarchs by Emperor Maximilian I, and she has been patron of the city ever since. In the place where the camp of *los Reyes Católicos* was located, the church of *Nuestra Señora de la Victoria* was founded and the image is enthroned here. Her feast day is 8 September (The Nativity of Mary), a local holiday.

One of the most popular emblems of Málaga is the statue of El Cenachero (the fish seller) made by the sculptor Jaime Fernández Pimentel in 1968 and located in the Plaza de la Marina. The flower that symbolizes Málaga is the *biznaga*, a jasmine flower corsage. The *biznaguero* (*biznaga* seller) is another iconic character immortalized in a statue in the Pedro Luis Alonso Gardens. The other popular symbol is the *boquerón* (anchovy) — the favourite fish of the city and the nickname of both the local football team and of *malagueños* in general. Another symbol is La Farola — the lighthouse. There are many more unofficial and more recent symbols like the perspiring, red-faced German beer drinker of the Victoria beer advert and the sweet Moscatel 'Cartojal' wine drunk during the *feria*. Málaga also has its own favoured Holy Week images of Jesus and Mary. The *Cristo Cautivo* from the La Trinidad neighbourhood and the *Esperanza* (*María Santísima de la Esperanza Coronada*) from neighbouring El Perchel are known as the 'Lords of Málaga'.

When to visit?

Unlike Madrid or Sevilla, which can both be uncomfortably hot in high summer, and unlike cities in central Spain like Burgos and Albacete which can both get very cold, Málaga has a pretty pleasant climate all year round. It cannot be said to be hot all year round but even in winter, the mercury rarely dips below the mid-teens Celsius during the day.

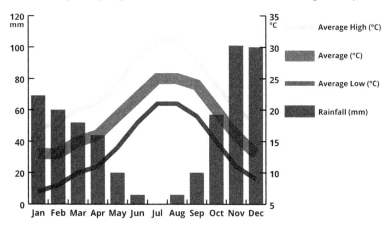

As the chart shows, average temperatures fall in the 'pleasant' and 'pleasantly warm/hot' zone between the mid-teens and high twenties. Apart from a handful of freak weather events, it is rare to experience sustained temperatures of much more than 30°C. And while the rainfall figures may look alarming in the Winter, the number of rainy **days** is low. Although almost 100 mm of rain on average falls in November, it does so over just five or six days, meaning that 24–25 days are a sunny 15°–20°C. So for any given day in November, the odds of its being dry are 5:1. Hans Christian Andersen wrote that Málaga's 'warm sunshine was a magic veil' and Málaga is a very sunny city: the second sunniest in Spain after Alicante, with just under 3,000 annual hours of sunshine. Even in dark December, which manages 'only' 160 hours of sunshine, Málaga still manages to be more than 100 hours sunnier than London or Paris.

While towns that roast in the summer can often be extremely cold in the winter due to their elevation or inland position, Málaga rarely feels truly cold. Indeed, Málaga is the warmest city in mainland Europe between December and February. Frosts are not unknown, and in the far northern suburbs there can be snow, but the last recorded snowfall in the *centro histórico* — in fact, the **only** recorded snowfall — was on 2 February 1954. Two days later came the lowest temperature ever recorded in Málaga: −3.8°C (25.2°F) on 4 February 1954.

Where to Stay?

This section contains no listings of recommended hotels partly because accommodation is a very personal choice. Hotels tend to be very effective when it comes to providing information online. Almost by definition, there are no 'hotels that only the locals know about'. Also, the hotel landscape in Málaga is changing **very quickly**. But although I give no specific recommendations, I hope that the information in this section will help you to choose overnight accommodation that is perfect for you.

For some people, what matters is the place (the town, city, or locality) visited and a hotel is just somewhere to shower and sleep. For others, the hotel is a major part of the experience. The buffet breakfast, the room service, spa treatments and the services of a concierge are all indispensable aspects of any holiday.

Unlike the beachfront developments of Torremolinos or Fuengirola, in Málaga, the primary attraction is the city — its museums, bars and restaurants. So think carefully about what you want from your accommodation. Do you enjoy staying somewhere sleek and modern, or do you prefer the appeal of a historic building? Do you like a little luxury to be part of the experience, or do you really only need somewhere to sleep? If the former, then you will want to book into a hotel with a 4 or 5-star rating or a 'boutique' hotel and, if the latter, then a modest hotel or an 'hostal' (not to be confused with a 'hostel' — see below!) may be a better choice. If you are looking for a measure of independence with the use of a fridge, microwave and washing machine, or if you want a more 'homely' vibe, then look for an Airbnb let or an apartment.

You'll no doubt have your preferred website through which to make accommodation bookings (I have mainly, though not exclusively, used **booking.com** quite happily for well over a decade) so I make no specific recommendations. Websites can rise and fall with alarming speed. A decade ago, **venere.com** was a market leader, but now it no longer exists. **TripAdvisor**, **Google** and **Skyscanner** have all entered the hotel aggregator (websites offering services from multiple providers) market in recent years, so the situation will no doubt continue to change, year by year. But here follow some general tips, regardless of which booking website you choose to use.

Make a flexible booking if you can

If you absolutely **must** stay in a 5-Star hotel within 200 metres of the Cathedral, or in an apartment with a roof terrace in Soho, then **book early**. If you are more flexible, then booking three months ahead will still give you plenty of choice. But even in this case, I strongly recommend using a 'book now pay later' option. You will pay a modest premium — usually a few euros per room/property per night — but you can cancel if you find a better deal later on.

Don't Ignore the Suburbs

When deciding where to stay, somewhere in the centre of the old city (*centro histórico*) might seem like the best option, but bear in mind that you will pay a premium for the location. The tourist centre of Málaga is made up of the *barrios* of *centro histórico* and 'Soho'. But accommodation in the *barrios* of El Perchel, Mármoles, La Goleta, La Merced and parts of La Trinidad near the river is unlikely to be more than a 10–20 minute (up to one kilometre) walk from the centre, or a short bus ride costing less than a euro. It is also likely to be considerably cheaper.

Hosteles

There are quite a few hostels in Málaga, catering mainly for backpackers, young people, and (*horribile dictu*) stag and hen parties. They can be extremely cheap — less than €20 per night — but you will have to share a (same-sex) dormitory and you won't have your own bathroom (which means jostling for position in the morning queue). Out-of-term, rooms in university halls of residence are often available for rent — often very comfortable.

Apartamentos

Apartments (and even entire houses) can be rented through Airbnb and most aggregator sites: some are owned and operated by private landlords, others are managed by property agents. They range from the rather small and basic all the way up to luxurious penthouse apartments with Scandinavian mattresses, hot tubs, roof terraces and an option to pay extra to have staff clean your rooms and make your beds each day.

If you are travelling in a couple or as a family or group, an apartment is almost always a far more cost-effective option than a hotel. Read the reviews carefully, of course, but in my experience, the standard of apartments available in Málaga for holiday rent is pretty high.

There are still a few things to bear in mind. First, apartment bookings usually require a deposit against damage, which is charged to your debit or credit card upon arrival, and returned after check out. This means that a fair chunk of money (either from your bank account or towards your monthly credit card limit) is not going to be available to you during your stay.

Second, although apartments are always furnished with what you will need during your stay (most have a washing machine, iron, coffee maker, etc.), don't expect an especially well-equipped kitchen. Utensils are often basic and most lets do not have any larder of ingredients, not even basics like salt and pepper. However, the ability to prepare breakfast, snacks and light lunches is a real advantage. Remember, though, the knives are usually so blunt that they might as well be made of jelly. **Tip:** buy a matchbox-size knife sharpener from (e.g.) ebay and take it with you.

Third, unlike hotels and most *hoſtales*, which have 24-hour front desks, apartments may add a surcharge if you arrive late at night. Last, unlike hotels, they will not have facilities to look after your luggage after you check out, so you will need to make other arrangements (though this is easily done: visit **bit.ly/LuggageMLG** or scan the QR link).

Hoteles

These are regular hotels with a front desk, foyer, usually a bar and/or dining room (even if only for breakfast), and rooms with *en suite* bathrooms. Hotel star ratings in Spain are partly determined by hotel facilities as in the UK but also by room size and features; so a four-star hotel might be rather faded and tatty, while a two or three-star hotel might be chic and luxurious with hydromassage showers and original art on the walls. All hotels, of any star rating, must have private bathrooms, central heating and a lift.

In 2020, the Government of Andalucía introduced new norms for awarding star ratings, partly based on minimum requirements and partly based on the accumulation of points. These new regulations come fully into force in 2025, so the picture remains mixed at the time of publication.

In summary, while star ratings are a reasonable guide to the level of comfort, service and luxury, it is far more useful to read recent reviews.

Hostales

An *hoſtal* (pronounced **oss-tal**), is NOT a hostel! Although '*hoſtal*' is the most common term, an *hoſtal* might also be called a *pensión*, *posada*, *casa* *de huéspedes* or *albergue*. *Hostales* are (usually) family-run and are simi-lar to *pensions/pensioni* found in France and Italy. Some of the more basic *hostales* are not too far from (British) bed and breakfasts, but nowadays many are closer to small hotels in quality. Many are even rather luxuri-ous, but cannot call themselves hotels because they have rooms of dif-ferent sizes and lack dining facilities and/or a ground-floor reception. From 2025, *hostales* will be star rated according to the same points-based system as hotels and will be categorized as 1 or 2 stars. Once again, look at the reviews!

Pros and Cons of *Hostales*

The cons are few. As most *hostales* are converted apartments, many of the rooms can be quite dark. Some will be street-facing, even with balconies, but many will be 'interior', arranged around a central patio or courtyard (sometimes little more than a ventilation shaft). This is no bad thing in the heat of summer as it means that your room stays relatively cool. It will also be quieter at night because it's not overlooking a noisy bar.

Some of the very cheapest rooms do not have private bathrooms (a re-quirement for a hotel, but not an *hostal*); so you always need to look care-fully at the room description. One-star *hostales* are not required to have a lift, so if mobility is an issue, please check. Some *hostales* offer simple breakfasts or have a deal with a nearby bar, and many have vending ma-chines in reception with hot drinks, chilled soft drinks and snacks, but there may be no food or drink at all. Larger *hostales* have 24-hour recep-tion, but an increasing number are completely unstaffed, with check-in conducted entirely online and entry controlled by keypads.

On the other hand, *hostales* are usually family-run and so even the most old-fashioned *hostales* are likely to be spotless. In many decades of stay-ing in some very low-cost accommodation, I have never stayed in an *hos-tal* that was even mildly grubby — a bit frayed around the edges, perhaps, but never dirty.

Hostales do not (usually) have bars or restaurants, but in Spain, this hard-ly matters as there will always be about a dozen bars (probably more) within a hundred metres. If you want a massive buffet breakfast, that means staying in a 3 to 5-star hotel and paying upwards of €15 per day for the privilege. You can buy a lot of food and drink for €15 in a bar! The biggest 'pro', however, is that an *hostal* is likely to be around half the price of a 3-star hotel.

Being Review–Savvy

Interpreting hotel and *hostal* reviews is an art in itself. A lot of small ho-tels will offer a typical Spanish breakfast: tomato bread, olive oil toast (*tostada*), pastries, juice, coffee, etc. Spanish guests might judge such provision as 'excellent' whereas British (and especially US) guests will describe it as 'disappointing' because it lacks the huge variety of UK/US breakfast buffet troughs. Other common complaints from British/American guests often concern the fact that staff 'do not speak English' and 'noise' from the street.

The 'noisy' complaint is my personal favourite. After raving about how such-and-such a hotel is 'right in the centre of the city', the reviewer then complains about noise, as if the centre of a city packed with bars, restaurants and clubs should be expected to be deathly quiet after a British person's 'bedtime' (a time at which many Spaniards are just sitting down to dinner).

What I mainly look for are comments about cleanliness, location, staff helpfulness and the quality of the Wifi signal. Most smaller establishments don't have websites, so check the Google reviews. As a rule of thumb, if an owner takes the time to thank guests for positive reviews (and politely engage with negative ones), that's usually a sign that they take good service seriously.

Tips for aggregator booking sites

First, open an 'incognito' or 'private' browser window. A booking site will use your IP address and cookies to record the fact that you are looking for accommodation in a particular location on particular dates. It is then possible for the algorithm to increase the quoted prices for that place and time. So, browse in private until you are ready to log in and book.

Search for your location and dates, number of people and number of rooms. The top results will be the 'top picks' or 'recommendations'. These may be the most popular places, or they may be those that have paid a fee to be placed higher in the results. If money is no object and your aim is luxury, then you might want to rank the results according to review score (generally more instructive than the star rating). However, if you are looking to find the best value 'bang for buck' accommodation, then use the filters to exclude shared accommodation, stipulate private bathrooms (if you like) and display in price order.

When it comes to 'room type' look out for 'balcony' if you want an outside/street-facing room. A 'balcony', by the way, doesn't mean a balcony you can sit out on; it just means a window opening onto the street. To see what kind of balcony it is, you'll need to peruse the photos. When given the list of accommodation options, start clicking on properties and look first at the location (most sites have a map feature). Study the room and hotel/*hostal* facilities.

To keep track of your expenditure and limit transaction fees, pay for accommodation using a euro-denominated payment card. Known as 'Forex' or 'FX' cards, these are prepaid travel cards that you can load using your regular credit or debit card, converting it to the foreign currency of your choice. You can use a Forex card just like a debit card to pay for your expenses in a local currency. You can also withdraw local cash from ATMs (though some charge a fee, so you may need to try a few to find one that doesn't). The advantage of using a Forex card is that when paying for goods and services in euros, the conversion to euros has already been done so you won't need to pay the often considerable conversion fees on individual transactions. In the UK, the main euro prepaid cards are from CaxtonFX, FairFX and The Post Office. There is also Currensea, which is not prepaid but linked to your bank account. Have a look at comparison sites (*e.g.* **bit.ly/WhichCurrencyCards**) to see which one would work best for you. You can also use your prepaid card for other online transactions ahead of your trip, such as ticket purchases and train and bus journeys.

💶 Money Saving Tips When Staying in *Hostales*

If you are going to be staying in a top-end hotel then this section is not for you, but if you are staying in a basic hotel or in an *hostal* and want to make your holiday budget go a little further, then read on!

If you are flying with a budget airline, the easiest way to save money if by travelling with hand luggage only.

Unless you have very particular requirements when it comes to the shower gel and hair products you use, then buy these in Málaga, especially if you are spending more than a couple of nights. Those 100 ml 'travel miniatures' on sale in the UK are very poor value for money. Even the cheapest *hostales* provide complimentary shower gel and shampoo, but unless you are going to arrive late at night, or on a Sunday or public holiday, the best plan is to buy your toiletries when you arrive. There is a well-stocked branch of the Mercadona supermarket at the main railway station (María Zambrano). Here you'll be able to buy shower gel, shampoo, conditioner, deodorant, toothpaste etc. in full sizes for less than the cost of the travel-size equivalent purchased in the UK. There are also several branches of Lidl, Aldi and other supermarkets dotted around the city.

Unless you are renting an apartment, bring with you:

A corkscrew — almost all Spanish wine is sealed with corks, rather than screw tops. With excellent wine on sale in supermarkets at considerably under €5, it's useful to be able to open it. If you are travelling with hand luggage only (which makes a corkscrew a potentially offensive weapon), the Eroski supermarket in the Larios Shopping Centre near the bus station sells decent quality corkscrews for €1 (in an aisle containing 'bargain' goods on sale for €1–€2). The word in *castellano* is '*sacacorchos*' (**sakka-kor**-choss).

A knife, fork and spoon — supermarkets and shops selling *comida casera* (home made food) sell prepared salads, pastries, snacks, yoghurts, desserts, etc. Having basic cutlery will enable you to enjoy some cheap snacks and make up a picnic if the mood takes you. If you are travelling with hand luggage only, you can buy cutlery cheaply in Eroski, or else bring plastic picnic cutlery with you — available from IKEA or eBay.

Travel Wash — Dr Beckmann, Stergene and Dylon are the well-known brands and are packaged in travel-friendly 100 ml sizes. This is a handy product to have with you in case you stain an article of clothing, or need to wash some underwear or a T-shirt. You can also buy laundry detergent sheets online. Be aware that your bathroom may not have a sink plug, so you will need to be creative if you want to soak any articles of clothing. Seasoned travellers will bring their own one-size-fits-all travel plug — 'Trekmates' produce a very effective silicone travel plug: **bit.ly/TMTravelPlug**. There are also a few self-service laundrettes in the centre of Málaga — search for '*lavandería*' on Google Maps: **bit.ly/MLGLaunderettes**

If you are travelling with hand luggage only but want to bring back wine, spirits, olive oil, vinegar or other liquid goods from Málaga, then you could check in luggage for the return flight only. Make room in your case by packing your 'small cabin bag' as tightly as possible with heavier non-liquid items. The choice of wines, spirits and foodstuffs available at the post-security 'Duty-Free' section at Málaga airport is fairly limited and relatively expensive so it's far cheaper to buy these items from a supermarket or *ultramarinos* and put them in your checked-in luggage if you can. As late as 2023, there were no restrictions upon bringing food (*e.g. charcuterie*, cheese, etc.) from an EU country into the UK (though not vice versa).

Whether you are staying in a grand hotel or a humble *hostal* (but not in an apartment), you will always be able to leave your luggage at reception if you arrive before check in, or need to check out before heading for the airport. Ask, '*¿Puedo dejar mi equipaje?*' (**pway**-do day-**khar** mee ayk-ee-**pakh**-ay).

🍶 Forgotten Something?

It's easily done. You arrive in Málaga, eager to head out for some *tapas* and a glass of wine and, as you unpack, you realize that you have forgotten to bring something quite important. Top of your packing checklist should be: passport, credit/debit cards, smartphone (and other devices if you need them), AC plug adapter(s), charging cables, and essential medication. If you've forgotten to bring any items of clothing, then Primark (in the Larios Shopping Centre) is the cheapest place to buy emergency replacements. They also sell charging cables, hats and inexpensive sunglasses. If you have forgotten to bring an AC plug adaptor, try Media-Markt (in the main railway station), FNAC or Eroski (in the Larios Shopping Centre) or El Corte Inglés.

If you forget your medication, then visit a pharmacy ('*farmacia*' — supermarkets do not sell medicines, even aspirin). They will either be able to provide you with what you need or tell you if you need to visit a doctor (and help you find one). It's a good idea to take photos of your medicine bottles and packets, and your prescription(s), and keep them on the camera roll of your smartphone. Many drugs are available '*sin receta*' (without a prescription) in Spain. However, some very basic medications, such as paracetamol and antihistamines, are far more expensive than in the UK and can only be purchased from pharmacies.

🛍Tourist Taxes?

At the time of publication, there were rumours of an imposition of a *tasa turística* (tourist tax). The mayor, Paco de la Torre, had a well-publicized discussion with his opposite number in Sevilla about it in 2022 and the main left-wing parties have also made it a manifesto commitment. Málaga has certainly been enriched economically as its popularity as a tourist destination has grown over the last decade, but not all have felt the benefit. The benefits for a city centre bar owner may be obvious, but people in jobs apparently unconnected with hospitality feel that they have missed out. Many protest that the *ayuntamiento* has lavished funds upon the *centro histórico* to the neglect of the *afueras* (suburbs).

My guess is that Málaga will have imposed a (modest) tourist tax by 2024 or 2025. It is unlikely to reach the levels seen in Barcelona, where tourists staying in top-end hotels pay up to €5 per night, and is more likely to be around €1 for cruise passengers and those staying overnight, and possibly a little more for those staying in 4 and 5-star hotels. It would also help to calm the complaints of local ratepayers. As with so many issues, the economic benefits may be meagre, but the political case is strong.

The Basics

City:	**Málaga**
Province:	**Málaga**
Autonomous Community:	**Andalucía**
City rank (Spain):	**6th**
City rank (Andalucía):	**2nd**
Airport rank (Spain):	**4th**
Airport rank (Andalucía):	**1st**
Port rank (Spain):	**13th**
Port rank (Andalucía):	**3rd**
Foundation:	**Phoenician, c.770 BC**
Population (City):	**579,076**
Population (Municipality):	**987,813**
Population (Province):	**1,717,504**
Highest point (Municipality):	**Cresta de la Reina (1,032 m)**
Highest point (Province):	**La Maroma (2,066 m)**
Government:	***Ayuntamiento* (City)**
	***Diputación* (Province)**
Head of Government:	***Ayuntamiento:* Mayor**
	Diputación: Presidente
Budget (2023):	**€976 million *(Ayuntamiento)***
	€374 million *(Diputación)*
GDP growth (Province)	**2.2% (2023) 7.7% (2022)**
Diocese (Catholic)	**Málaga (1st c. AD, re-founded 1486)**
Demonyms:	***malagueño, -a	malacitano, -a***
Primary Patron:	**Our Lady of Victory**
Patrons:	**Holy Christ of Health (*Santo Cristo de la Salud*)**
	Saints Ciriaco and Paula

Directory
ℹ️ *Oficinas de turismo*
(Tourist Information)

The main office is located at **Plaza de la Marina 11**, but there is also a small kiosk near the **Alcazaba**, and a useful information point on the main concourse of the **María Zambrano railway station** (where, for example, you can purchase a bus pass ('*bonobús*').

British Consulate Málaga:
📍 Calle Mauricio Moro Pareto 2
(opposite the bus station)
☎️ +34 952 352 300

Pharmacy (24 hours):
Farmacia Caffarena
📍 Alameda Principal 2

Emergency Services: ☎️ 112

Health Emergency: ☎️ 061

Police Emergency: ☎️ 092

Fire Brigade: ☎️ 080

Emergency tourist assistance
(S.A.T.E.): ☎️ **+34 951 92 61 61**

Defibrillators:
🌐 **bit.ly/DefibMLG**

Taxis:
☎️ **+34 952 333 333**
☎️ **+34 952 040 804**
☎️ **+34 952 040 090**
📱 **pidetaxi.es**

Responsible Tourism

The pro-tourism policies of the Málaga *Ayuntamiento* are not without their critics. Tourism contributed around €7.4 million to the local economy in 2022 (a figure set to rise considerably judging by current growth), but while it is undoubtedly good for hotels, bars and museums, many ordinary residents feel that it does little to improve their lives. Indeed, some claim that the growing number of tourists impinges upon them negatively. Unsurprisingly, the authorities have been at pains to point out that their tourism strategy is targeted at 'responsible tourists' — the sort attracted by art galleries, Renaissance churches and fine dining, rather than bottomless brunches, cut-price cocktails and the club scene.

The antics of British stag weekenders, hen party-goers and the like are well-known to the residents of Torremolinos and even Marbella, but in recent years the denizens of Málaga have taken to social media to post photos of revellers and to express their utter confusion regarding their behaviour. In 2022, new by-laws were passed to impose fines for the possession of 'novelty' inflatable dolls, headbands featuring genitalia or megaphones, among other nuisances. The *ayuntamiento* also launched a campaign in collaboration with the main hoteliers setting out the sort of behaviour they expected of visitors (**bit.ly/ImproveYourStay**).

It's not just boozed-up young people who behave badly, however. I am often shocked by how casually many British visitors drop litter, despite the excellent provision of bins. Northern European tourists probably do not quite grasp how precious a resource water is in southern Spain (more rubbish on the streets requires more water for cleaning). In July 2023 one of the reservoirs supplying the east of the Province was at only 7% of its usual capacity. I will add, if I may, three other suggestions for being a better tourist:

- If you visit a municipal market (and you definitely should), please buy something!
- Traditional grocers ('*ultramarinos*') are great treasures and your custom will help to keep them in business. They are usually excellent places to buy snacks and sandwiches.
- Venture outside the *centro histórico* to have a drink, some *tapas* or even a meal in a local bar, café or restaurant. It's far too easy to stick to the same city centre streets and go back to the same haunts. Explore a little!

Arriving

✈ By Air

It's easy and cheap to get from the airport to the city centre. In 2023, a taxi from the airport to the centre of Málaga cost around €28, while taking a train and a bus cost less than €4. Even if you take a taxi to your hotel or apartment, you will lose little time and save up to €20 by first catching the ⊘ 'Cercanías' train into town and picking up a taxi at the railway station.

Leaving the airport terminal through the main exit, turn to your left. Follow the building until you come to a zebra crossing (*cruce peatonal*). Cross and walk straight ahead. The distance between the airport and the train station is no more than 250 metres.

You can pay at the barrier with a contactless payment card, 'touching out' at the end of your journey. You can also buy a ticket if you prefer (or want to use cash). The ticket machines are on your right as you enter the station and are touch-screen controlled, offering a choice of languages. Your destination will be **Málaga–María Zambrano** (main rail station) if you want to pick up a taxi, or **Málaga–Centro–Alameda** if you want to walk across the river into the city centre. To buy more than one ticket, press the **+** sign to select the quantity you require. Use your ticket to go through the barriers and go down the escalator on your left for trains to the city centre (or right if you are heading to Torremolinos and points west). You'll need to adapt these instructions if you are not staying in the centre of Málaga.

Trains are every 20 minutes at 14', 34' and 54'. The journey to María Zambrano takes 8 minutes (3 stops). In front of María Zambrano station there will be dozens of taxis to take you on the rest of your journey or you could take a bus. Alternatively, you could switch to the Metro (follow signs inside the railway station to **Perchel** metro station) and catch the subway to **Atarazanas**.

Alternatively, you can take the bus (🚌**A at 00' and 30'**) all the way to the city centre.

Returning to the airport is just as easy. From the centre of Málaga, travel to María Zambrano station from whence trains to the airport leave at similar times past the hour: 13', 33', 53'. Local trains leave from the Málaga–Centro-Alameda station (entrances on the Soho and El Perchel sides of the river) a few minutes earlier.

Málaga–Costa del Sol is a small but very busy airport, so allow yourself enough time, especially if you need to check in yourself and/or your luggage. Experience has taught me that the later in the day your return flight is, the higher the likelihood of its being delayed.

🚢 By Cruise Liner

There are four passenger terminals in the Port of Málaga. Muelle 3 is the berth for Trasmediterranea and Balearia ferries to and from Melilla (Spain's autonomous exclave in North Africa) and it is a short walk from the *centro histórico*. The cruise liner terminals are not operated by the Port Authority but by a company called 'Cruceros Málaga' (**malaga.globalportsholding.com**). Terminal Palmeral is on Muelle Dos and is used by smaller and luxury craft. If you dock here then you will probably have concierges and personal shoppers at your disposal.

Large cruise liners dock at Terminals A and B (located on the Muelle de Zona de Levante). There is a shuttle bus (every 15 minutes or so) operated by Cruceros Málaga which costs a few euros and there are usually plenty of taxis waiting. An alternative is to walk to the Farola lighthouse and take the Bus (🚌14) from the Paseo de la Farola (Ⓑ1301). In the city centre, there are stops on the Paseo del Parque (near the Cathedral) and on the Alameda Principal (near the Atarazanas Market).

🚆 By Train

One of the great advantages of Málaga is that because its airport serves the entire Costa del Sol, it is very easy to fly to, quite cheaply, from practically every airport in Europe. However, it is also possible to reach by train or even intercity coach. If your local airport has flights to Sevilla or Granada, you can easily travel to or from Málaga by coach or train.

If you love trains or fear flying, then it is certainly possible to travel to Málaga from pretty much anywhere in Europe, including the UK. For up-to-date information about how to do so, consult the European rail guru par excellence, 'The Man in Seat 61' **bit.ly/MalagaSeat61**.

🚗 By Car

How you arrive by car depends upon where you are travelling from, of course. As long as your satnav has the latest data downloaded you should be directed along suitable roads (remembering that there are a lot of toll roads in Spain, so make sure that you decide whether to include this option or not). For more detailed route planning, involving meal, fuel or charging stops, give **abetterrouteplanner.com** a try.

Most hotels (and all 4 and 5-star hotels) offer parking and most *hostales* and apartments can arrange it for you. There is a certain amount of free on-street parking in Málaga (outside the historic centre, mainly on the western side of the river). You may have to spend quite a long time searching for it. In general, yellow lines always mean no parking, green means residents' parking, blue means paid-for parking (look for a ticket machine nearby) and white boxes mean free parking spaces (though there may be a time restriction). Although Málaga has a number of underground car parks totalling over 5,000 spaces (**smassa.eu**), they are only affordable for short stays (but some hotels have '*abono*' permits for the use of guests). The cheapest long-term parking option in central Málaga is the María Zambrano railway station. Search online for a provider and compare deals, which can be competitive: **bit.ly/LTParkingMalaga**.

🚲 By Bicycle

If you are on a bicycle touring holiday, one challenge will be storing your bicycle. May sure you have insurance that covers Europe (**eta.co.uk** is excellent). Even with insurance, there will be a time limit for on-street bicycle storage. A lot of cyclists opt for apartments with balconies on which they can store their bikes. For other types of accommodation, enquire with the hotel or property. Even small *hostales*, for example, may have access to a private '*patio interior*'. Málaga's very modest, but slowly growing, network of cycle paths (*carriles bici*) can be seen here: **bit.ly/MalagaBici**. The open cycle map is also useful: **cyclosm.org**.

Finding Your Bearings

The outline map below shows the extent of the Málaga municipality, an area of approximately 22 km by 15 km, divided into eleven districts (*distritos*). The urban area of Málaga, extends north to the Autovía del Mediterráneo, a 1,300-kilometre-long non-toll motorway that runs from the French border all the way down the Mediterranean coast before sweeping west as far as Algeciras in the Bay of Gibraltar. The airport is only 5 miles south-west of the city centre, a journey of less than 10 minutes by train. Between the Airport and Málaga proper is the Guadalhorce River and its estuary (now a beautiful, if somewhat wild, nature reserve). This is where Phoenicians first encountered Ancient Iberians, later moving the embryonic port north-east to a more sheltered position in the bay that forms a natural harbour.

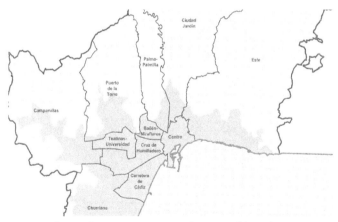

Almost everything that a visitor to Málaga would wish to see is to be found in the centre ('*Distrito Centro*' — see opposite for more detail). The Gibralfaro Castle and Alcazaba, the Cathedral and *Teatro Romano*, the historic centre and Market, the trendy 'Soho' *barrio*, the quayside development and most of the galleries and museums are all found here and the rail and coach stations are just a few metres outside it. Outside this couple of square miles are the suburbs — old residential districts to the south-west, north, and east; newer settlements, including the university, to the north-west.

The map below zooms in on part of a single municipal district — 'Centro' — which is made up of 35 barrios (wards), some amounting to no more than a few streets, and in the following pages I describe those of most interest to visitors. 'Centro' is approximately 3 km by 3 km, meaning that almost any point on the map is less than 1.5 km from the centre point (the Plaza de la Constitución). To simplify matters, I have further divided some areas likely to be of interest to visitors and combined some of the more far-flung barrios. For example, I have combined Perchel Norte, Perchel Sur and Plaza de Toros Vieja under the single designation 'El Perchel', and I have separated 'Alameda' from 'El Ensanche' (aka 'Soho').

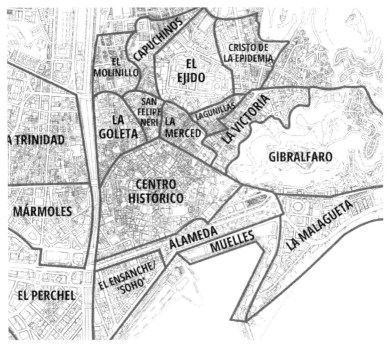

What counts as a barrio is a matter of some debate, as it is the world over. Places disappear but names remain. The picturesque but insanitary barrio of La Coracha was demolished in 1990, and the fishermen's hovels of El Bulto were razed ten years, yet both names survive. The convent of La Merced was confiscated in the 1830s and the church of the same name demolished in 1963, but the name of the barrio, market and square survives.

Centro Histórico

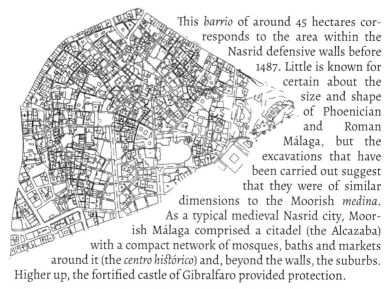

This *barrio* of around 45 hectares corresponds to the area within the Nasrid defensive walls before 1487. Little is known for certain about the size and shape of Phoenician and Roman Málaga, but the excavations that have been carried out suggest that they were of similar dimensions to the Moorish *medina*. As a typical medieval Nasrid city, Moorish Málaga comprised a citadel (the Alcazaba) with a compact network of mosques, baths and markets around it (the *centro histórico*) and, beyond the walls, the suburbs. Higher up, the fortified castle of Gibralfaro provided protection.

After the *reconquista*, the *medina* was Christianized, with mosques converted into churches and bath houses closed. Málaga's oldest churches (*i.e.* those founded by Fernando and Isabel) are found within the *centro histórico*. The most important of these is the Cathedral of Our Lady of the Incarnation, built on the plot of land formerly occupied by the principal mosque of the city (which had itself probably supplanted a far earlier Visigothic church). Work on the Cathedral finally began in 1528, 41 years after Málaga was reconquered. It was consecrated in 1588 and completed in 1782 after a succession of vicissitudes and interruptions. Or rather, it was not completed. The first thing anyone notices about Málaga's Cathedral is its lop-sided appearance. The south tower of a façade is unfinished and has an odd, stunted appearance. It is not simply that the tower is missing, but that the building is visibly incomplete; as if the stonemasons clocked off on a Friday afternoon in 1782 and simply forgot to return. As a result, the Cathedral is known locally as *La Manquita* or 'the maimed woman'.

The *centro histórico* is divided into four parishes established by command of *los Reyes Católicos*. Of these, the church of Our Lady of the Sacristy (*Santa María del Sagrario*) is the oldest, having been constructed at the base of the minaret of the old mosque in 1498. It now forms part of the Cathedral complex, occupying part of the orange tree patio once used for ritual ablutions.

Málaga's antiquity is evident in its street layout. However, cutting through the medieval labyrinth is the Calle Marqués de Larios It runs south from the old main square (*plaza mayor*) to the Alameda Principal. Though only 300 metres long and 15 metres wide, Calle Larios is the fifth most expensive street in Spain (in terms of rent), the top four streets being in Barcelona and Madrid.

The plan to give Málaga a grand thoroughfare first took shape in the 1870s and was the brainchild of the renowned civil engineer José María de Sancha. The *ayuntamiento* lent their support to the project in 1880, creating a public company to oversee the work and selling one million pesetas' worth of shares (over €28 million today). Ninety per cent of the shares were purchased by the Second Marqués de Larios & Larios, giving him effective control of the project. Larios appointed the 32-year-old architect Eduardo Strachan Viana-Cárdenas to oversee the design and construction. The first change was to the trajectory of the street, which had originally been intended to run south-east past the Cathedral. In Strachan's design, the street runs due south from the square to the Alameda.

Unsurprisingly, because Calle Larios was the creation of a confident bourgeoisie, its official inauguration in 1891 raised the hackles of the many unemployed working class in Málaga. An ill-judged attempt at largesse — throwing sugared almonds to the crowds — spectacularly misfired when the donors were pelted by the sweets being lobbed back.

The Calle Larios was once known as '*el salón de baille*' (the ballroom) because it had pavements of wooden parquet. The *ayuntamiento* banned pet dogs from the street in an attempt to preserve the wooden 'paving' from the effects of their ordure, but in the end, it was the flood of 1907 that put an end to this slightly bizarre feature of urban design.

As the city's main thoroughfare, the Calle Larios forms part of the route for all of the *hermandades* and *cofradías* that take part in the processions of *Semana Santa* (Holy Week). Both *cofradía* and *hermandad* mean 'brotherhood' — the former formed more obviously from the Latin (*cf. confrere*), and the latter from the Spanish word for brother, *hermano*. The brotherhoods are examples of what the Catholic Church calls 'associations of the faithful' (as distinct from religious orders or institutes). Being a member of a brotherhood is a year-round commitment, undertaking works of charity and raising funds for social projects. Much of the restoration work in churches damaged before and during the Civil War has been organized and partly financed by the brotherhoods who have their 'canonical headquarters' in those churches. Some brotherhoods have particular apostolates with children, young people, the sick or elderly, and many are associated (at least historically) with hospitals and care homes.

Each brotherhood has its own *imágenes* ('images' or painted wooden sculptures); usually one of Jesus and one of the Virgin Mary. Some brotherhoods are custodians of an entire tableau of images, for example depicting Jesus before Pilate, or the Last Supper. These *imágenes* have particular names or dedications, so a statue of Jesus might be 'Jesus of the Great Power', 'Jesus of the Five Words', 'Jesus of Silence', etc. At a particular time on an appointed day, the *imagen*, placed on a bier and surrounded by flowers and candles, will leave the church of the brotherhood and make its stately way to the Cathedral. The processions begin on Palm Sunday and continue until Good Friday, long into the night and small hours.

Calle Larios is also the city centre location of the *feria* (Fair) of Málaga held in August. The nocturnal revels in Málaga take place in the *recinto* (fairground) out towards the airport, but there is also a 'daytime *feria*' and this takes place in and around Calle Larios.

Every September, Calle Larios also hosts Málaga Fashion Week (more accurately weekend — an event that attracts 30,000 people) when the street becomes a 350-metre-long couture catwalk. Since 1998, Málaga has hosted an annual film festival in Spring for (mainly) Spanish language cinema. The 'red carpet' is laid along the entire length of Calle Larios.

The *centro histórico* is much more than the Cathedral and Calle Larios, of course. Also, *malagueños* subdivide it into smaller *barrios*, largely reflecting the original division into parishes. The area northwest of the church of Los Mártires Ciriaco y Paula, for example, has quite a different feel in comparison to the streets to the south. Locals call this *barrio* Pozos Dulces ('Sweet Wells') and it is characterized by narrow, winding streets largely consisting of houses with a handful of bars and almost no other commercial enterprises. For a long time, it was assumed that the street layout was Moorish, but more recently historians have concluded that it dates from the early years following the *reconquista* and that in Moorish times there was an orchard here.

El Ensanche ('Soho')

Málaga's 'Soho' is south of the historic centre and was formerly an area known for, among other attractions, its brothels and sex shops. Sailors looking for ladies of the night have to venture further afield these days because the new Soho (like its London namesake) is rather cool and upmarket. Establishments that once promised 'XXX Movies' have given way to fusion restaurants, cocktail bars and boutique hotels.

This is not a district in which to find venerable bars unchanged by progress, or old-style restaurants serving the heavy Spanish stews of yesteryear. What you will find, however, is some seriously good food and cool, bijou accommodation. Soho is also home to Málaga's contemporary art museum (CAC) and a 'street exhibition' of urban art (MAUS — 'Málaga Arte Urbano en el Soho').

The *ensanche* was reclaimed from the sea in the 19th century, a time of relative prosperity for Málaga, and was part of the expansion of the port (which has been moving increasingly southwards ever since). The 'Soho' re-brand began to take shape in the early 2000s with the impetus coming from local residents and businesspeople (and this is why I ultimately support the name-change, my pedantic grumbles notwithstanding) who formed an association to bring about renewal. A logo was chosen by public competition and a plan proposed to the *ayuntamiento*. It's perhaps fair to say that 'El Ensanche' is a locality, while 'Soho' is a concept...

Alameda

This is the area of the city, par excellence, to witness the daily *paseo*. The main street running parallel to the port, the Alameda Principal is a wide boulevard shaded with 100-year-old fig trees. Travelling east, it becomes the Paseo del Parque. These thoroughfares follow the line of the southern city walls, which Carlos III allowed to be demolished in 1786, and are built on partly reclaimed land.

Throughout the 19th century, the Alameda Principal was **the** boulevard. Until the inauguration of the Calle Marqués de Larios in 1891, this broad thoroughfare was where the cream of *malagueña* society came for the *paseo*; to see and be seen. It was the location of the finest and most fashionable hotels where German Pilsners and French wines were served. The commercial bourgeoisie who congregated here even became known as '*la oligarquía de la Alameda*' ('the Alameda oligarchy'). Until 1925, it was closed to traffic, so was more like an urban park than the busy road it now is, and was lined with white poplars, hence its name ('*alameda*' means 'poplar grove').

When Hans Christian Andersen stayed in Málaga in 1862, his hotel overlooked the Alameda, and his description of it is vivid: 'There were bare-legged Bedouins in their white burnooses, African Jews in long embroidered kaftans, Spanish women in their becoming black mantillas, ladies of higher rank in bright-coloured shawls, elegant looking young men on foot and on horseback, peasants and porters; all was life and animation.'

At the eastern end of the Alameda is the Parque de Málaga, which despite being tiny (barely 40 metres wide and 800 metres long) and next to a busy road, is a surprising oasis of calm. It is more of a botanical garden than a park, with trees and shrubs from all over the world. Created in 1904, as Spain reeled from the phylloxera epidemic that devastated Spanish vines, it was one of the first attempts by the city authorities to create spaces pleasing to tourists.

Muelles

A *muelle*, in Spanish, is a quay or wharf. Muelle Uno (One) juts out into the Mediterranean on a mole (spit) between the original commercial port and the passenger port. This quay was the first extension of the Port of Málaga beyond the natural shoreline. *Malagueño* merchants petitioned King Felipe II to begin construction and work began in 1588. It was this expansion which, in the late 18th century, allowed the city of Málaga to reclaim some of the territory of the port and develop what is now the boulevard of the Alameda. A clue to the former geography of Málaga is found in the name of the municipal market, the *Mercado de Atarazanas*, meaning 'Market of the Boatyard'. Once on the shoreline, the site is now more than 700 metres from the sea.

At the city end is the polychrome glass cube of the Centre Pompidou

Málaga (the first branch of the gallery outside France), and at the other is the lighthouse: La Farola. Although the Spanish word for lighthouse is *faro*, the Málaga lighthouse is one of only two in Spain to have a feminine grammatical gender (the other is in Tenerife). Constructed in 1817, the current structure replaced a wooden lantern of a century earlier. It once stood at the end of the quay, but successive extensions to the ferry port mean that La Farola is now oddly marooned in the middle of the port area. No longer a working lighthouse, there are plans to use the structure to house a permanent exhibition exploring the history of the Port of Málaga.

The 500-metre-long promenade between the Centre Pompidou and La Farola is now home to dozens of restaurants, cafés, bars and shops, with shaded walkways and palm trees for protection from the sun. Despite having around 25 shops and 30 eateries, the atmosphere is tranquil and it is extremely popular with *malagueños*, especially in the evening and at weekends. Large cruise ships dock further out along the quay, out of sight, and Muelle Uno is now only used by yachts and smaller, luxury craft.

 Muelle Uno is very popular with families, and there are seasonal events and play clubs for children during the school holidays. The best way to find out what's going on is by consulting their Facebook/Meta page: **@muelleuno**.

Muelle Dos (Wharf Two) is the second phase of the 'Special Plan' to have been completed and runs along the waterfront (east-west), perpendicular to Muelle Uno and parallel to the Parque de Málaga. Unlike the commercial Muelle Uno, Quay Number Two is a more tranquil, shaded promenade. The aim here has been to bring together the city and the port by blurring the edges a little. It should be difficult to say where the city becomes the port, and vice versa, because one blends into the other. At the same time, International Maritime Agency rules issued in the wake of the 9/11 attacks, require clear boundaries to berths used by cruise ships. This conundrum — an area that both blends and separates its constituent parts — was the challenge faced by those who entered the public competition to design the project.

The winning entry — a design by the Málaga architects Jerónimo Junquera and Liliana Obal — uses glass, trees and a masonry pergola to provide a barrier between land and sea whilst giving a sense of openness. Visibility is preserved by making the handful of buildings low-rise, and what is effectively a concrete barrier has been fashioned into a canopy of undulating white beams, arranged to recall the swell of the sea and a canopy of palm trees. Even the benches, on closer examination, turn out to do double duty as concrete 'anti-terror' barriers.

La Malagueta

This *barrio*, at the eastern end of central Málaga, is a residential district where you will find the bullring of Málaga (also called 'La Malagueta') and the Playa de Malagueta, Málaga's 'city beach'. This is Málaga's 19th-century seaside resort and it has a handful of high-rise apartment blocks built during the early years of the Spanish tourism boom.

La Malagueta is largely a residential district these days, even if some of those owning apartments here are residents of Sevilla or Madrid for most of the year. It's a pleasant part of town with plenty of decent restaurants and agreeable bars. After work and at weekends, *malagueños* make for the beach to visit a *chiringuito* — a beach barbecue shack. The *chiringuitos* in Málaga are famous for their *espetos de sardinas* — half a dozen fresh sardines threaded onto a skewer — traditionally cane or olive wood — and grilled over a wood fire.

La Malagueta is the location of St George's Anglican Cemetery, the first non-Catholic burial ground established since the *reconquista*. Prior to its opening in 1831, Protestants were buried (though 'disposed of' might be a more accurate phrase) on the beach under cover of darkness. With the (mainly merchant) British community growing in Málaga, the British Vice Consul William Mark sought to address this undignified (and unsanitary) practice when he was appointed in 1824. He secured a plot of ground from the *ayuntamiento* and the relevant Royal Order was granted on 11 April 1830.

La Malagueta is also the site of Málaga's most famous hotel — a hotel which also tells the story of modern Málaga in its own history. Designed by Fernando Guerrero Strachan and standing almost directly opposite the gates to the cemetery, the Gran Hotel Miramar (which translates rather prosaically into English as the 'Grand Seaview Hotel') reopened in 2017 after a €65 million refurbishment and was Málaga's first only true five star or '*gran lujo*' ('great luxury') hotel.

In 1905, King Alfonso XIII stayed in the Ritz in Paris while on his grand tour in search of a wife and keenly felt his own kingdom's lack of luxury hotels. As well as founding the Madrid Ritz, he also decreed that Málaga should have a fine hotel of its own, and in 1926 he officially inaugurated the Hotel Principe de Asturias and spent every winter there until his abdication in 1931 (the Prince of Asturias is the Spanish Prince of Wales, so to speak).

Gibralfaro

North of La Malagueta is the Monte Gibralfaro. 'Mountain' is a rather generous description because the summit is only 136 metres above sea level, but because it is so near the centre of Málaga, Gibralfaro seems to tower above the city. Monte Gibralfaro, like 'River Avon', is tautological because 'gibralfaro' means 'rock of light', formed from the Arabic word for mountain (*jabal*) and the Phoenician word for light (*faro*). Monte Gibralfaro means, therefore, 'Mountain of Light Mountain'.

It is largely for the view that tourists make the journey up the hill to the castle. As a building, the castle's interior is less well-preserved than the Alcazaba (it was used as a military fort well into the 20th century), although the double ramparts are impressive. The entrance ticket, purchased from a touch screen machine, will get you into the castle **and** the Alcazaba, so my advice is to visit the castle for the magnificent view of Málaga and visit the Alcazaba for the architecture.

Though not particularly high, Monte Gibralfaro is steep-sided so the easiest way to reach the top is by bus. You can then return to the city centre on foot or by bus. In 2017 the *ayuntamiento* announced a €530,000 plan to develop the area around the castle on the northern side of the mountain. The small picnic area and *mirador* (viewpoint) were redesigned and modernized, and a children's playground with climbing ropes, climbing walls and a zip-wire created. Three walking trails were due to be renewed and extended. If you have the time, this is the most pleasant route to take either up or down the mountain.

Guadalmedina

Now we look not at a *barrio* but at the river that divides modern Málaga in two; though visitors may question the use of the word 'river' for what is, at best, a sluggish stream flowing alongside an empty riverbed of scrubby grass where children kick footballs and people go jogging and dog-walking. The Guadalmedina was once a mighty, albeit sporadic, river. Rather too mighty, in truth.

Its name comes from the Arabic '*Wadi 'l Medina*' (River of the City), and if you look at a map of Andalucía, you will notice that many of the rivers begin with '*guadal*' (*i.e. wadi 'l*). Málaga's river is not long — only around 47 kilometres, and it rises in the mountains north of Málaga.

A century or so after the *reconquista* many of the mountain forests around Málaga were cleared for agricultural use. For hundreds of years, Málaga suffered regular and catastrophic flooding. After a particularly serious flood in 1907, King Alfonso XIII decreed that a solution needed to be found and the building of a dam and reservoir commenced.

It was an ambitious undertaking, resulting in a reservoir (El Agujero) of 4.5 cubic hectometres, but even this proved to be insufficient. Further works were carried out in the decades following, involving reforestation with Aleppo Pines and the construction of 30 stone dykes. Only in 1983, with the construction of a second dam (El Limonero) was the problem of flooding in Málaga finally solved. So while Málaga's once mighty river is nowadays a rather unimpressive spectacle, it is no longer a constant source of fear and danger for *malagueños*.

El Perchel
(Perchel Sur, Plaza de Toros Vieja & Estación)

Most visitors to Málaga city will pass through the *barrio* known as El Perchel because this is where the railway station is located (though technically it lies a few metres outside the 'Centro' district). A *percha* was originally an article of fishing tackle — a kind of pegged frame upon which nets were hung to dry (it is also the word used in Spanish to mean 'coat hanger') — and the name gives a clue to the historical occupation of the inhabitants of this area.

In the sixteenth century, when El Perchel was a dangerous place to live on account of frequent slaving raids from North Africa, it had a reputation as a den of iniquity. An innkeeper tells Don Quixote that '*los Percheles de Málaga*' are known for 'agility of foot, lightness of hand and a deal of base trickery; pleading with widows, ruining of damsels, deception of children in care, and fame at last in every law-court in the land.' The bad reputation of El Perchel was proverbial. There was even a popular saying,

'Kill the king and run to Málaga'. On the other hand, the beauty of *perche-lera* women was legendary and often celebrated in verse.

Like Triana in Sevilla, El Perchel was once the Gypsy quarter, but the slums were cleared long ago to be replaced by rather unremarkable and often ugly tenements. Comparatively gentrified though it may be, it is probably not a *barrio* that will have you reaching for your camera, but that doesn't mean it should be ignored. There are several modern top-quality hotels and many smaller hotels and *hostales* as well as apartments for holiday rent. Prices here are a bit cheaper than in the very centre even though the Cathedral is only 1.5 km or so from the railway station; less than 25 minutes' walk or a few minutes by bus. The railway and coach stations mean that transport links from El Perchel are very good.

The railway station, Málaga–María Zambrano, is not just a railway station, it also houses a shopping centre. The dining establishments are of the fast-food variety and more likely to be of interest to *malagueño* families who come to visit the multiplex cinema, but the supermarket (Mercadona, closed on Sundays and holidays) is worth knowing about. Not far from the railway station is the Larios Shopping Centre, which is the closest large shopping complex to the centre. It has a very large subterranean supermarket — 'Eroski' as well as a huge branch of Primark. Everyday essentials — footwear, clothing, toiletries, groceries, electronics, repairs etc. — will be considerably cheaper in Larios Centro than in the *centro histórico*.

The presence of the railway and coach stations means that El Perchel is a fairly busy part of town, so there are plenty of places to eat and drink. The huge choice of bars and restaurants in the *centro histórico* might make it unlikely that you will want to make a special journey to El Perchel, but if you happen to be staying in the area, or wish to eat before catching a train, there is plenty of choice. Not far from the station is Los Valle Churros — one of the best and most charmingly traditional places to have breakfast in the whole of Málaga.

Mármoles
(including Perchel Norte)

Mármoles means 'marbles', though do not expect to find this reflected in the architecture. Like most of Málaga west of the Guadalmedina River, the buildings here are mainly 20th-century apartment blocks. The name of the *barrio* comes from the eponymous street — Calle Mármoles — which is itself derived from the marble bollards erected outside the Hermitage of Zamarrilla.

The hermitage is an 18th-century wayside chapel on what was once the main road to Antequera, financed by public subscription in 1757. Those setting off on a journey would pray the rosary here. Like many churches in Málaga, it was badly damaged by rioters in 1931 and its treasured sculptures of Christ and the Blessed Virgin were destroyed. Now sensitively restored, it sits incongruously among modern blocks of flats and is home to a venerable Holy Week fraternity.

The name 'Zamarrilla' is quite secular, however. It is the name of a plant found in southern Spain and North Africa (apparently known as 'Felty Germander' in English), but in the case of the chapel the name comes from the *nom de guerre* of a notorious 19th-century bandit called Cristóbal Ruiz Bermúdez from Igualeja, near Ronda. A number of versions of the legend are in circulation, but the basics are that in 1844, hunted by the Civil Guard, Zamarrilla hid beneath the skirts of the statue of the Virgin in the hermitage. The legend relates that, having evaded the guard, he pinned a white rose to the breast of the statue of Mary (made of wood, in the Spanish style) with his dagger. As he watched, the rose became blood-red and Zamarrilla realized that he had been saved by the redeeming blood of Christ. Like any penitent bandit of legend, he ended his days in a religious community, serving the poor.

The other reason why visitors to Málaga may venture into this *barrio* is for shopping. The nearest branches of Lidl and Aldi to the historic centre are located here, as is the department store El Corte Inglés — the Spanish equivalent of Selfridges (technically, the store is in El Perchel Norte). El Corte Inglés is not the cheapest place to shop, though it does have the virtue of selling almost everything. It even has a newsagent, tobacconist, travel agent and dispensing chemist. Unlike smaller shops, which often close for the siesta, it is open all day.

La Trinidad

North of the Calle Mármoles is the *barrio* of La Trinidad, named after the 16th century Trinity Convent, once home to the Calced (shod) Trinitarian Friars (in contradistinction to the Discalced — or unshod — Trinitarian Friars) and dedicated to St Onuphrius (*Onofre*), a rather obscure 4th-century Egyptian saint popular in Spain. This *barrio* is now one of the most populous districts in Málaga. The city's main acute and maternity hospitals are located here. The convent is in a state of near-ruin having been seized by the state in 1835 and subsequently used as a military barracks. The nearby church dedicated to the Trinity is of 19th-century construction. In 2019, the Mayor of Málaga, Francisco de la Torre, floated the idea of restoring the ruined convent for use as Málaga's archaeological museum, but in 2023, work had still not begun.

However, La Trinidad is a neighbourhood with a great sense of local identity and community and they have their own annual *feria* distinct from the main city-wide fair in August. This *feria* has declined somewhat and is now little more than a procession in the parish of San Pablo, but between the 1950s and 1980s, it was a huge event spanning three or four days. La Trinidad is also known for its *corralones* — a local style of domes-

tic architecture also found in Mármoles and El Perchel. Like the innovative Polish Flat in the US or the Tyneside Flat in the UK, the *corralón* is an imaginative style of low-cost housing. Small apartments with cantilevered walkways are arranged around a central courtyard (often with a fountain or well). This is the multi-occupancy version of the traditional *andaluz* house built around a *patio* of the sort that can be seen in Málaga, and to an even greater extent in Córdoba and Sevilla.

North of the Centro Histórico
La Goleta, San Felipe Neri, El Molinillo & Capuchinos

The *barrios* north of the *centro histórico* are part of the '*Centro*' district but have more of a local feel, with fewer shops and no branches of Zara or The Body Shop in sight. These *barrios* are more residential than the *centro histórico*, but none is short of interesting shops, beautiful churches, shady squares, pleasant bars and restaurants. These were originally the suburbs of Nasrid Málaga, being outside the city walls. The enlargement of the city was constrained to the south by the sea, to the east by the Monte Gibralfaro and to the west by the river (back when it really was a river) so it most naturally expanded north. This, then, is 'old' Málaga — just not quite as old as the *centro histórico*.

La Goleta means 'the schooner' and the area takes its name from a maritime academy that once operated here. In Nasrid times, it was known as the suburb of Funtanalla (or Fontanilla) and was connected to the city proper via the Bab Al-Funtanalla, later Christianized as the Puerta de Granada. The gate itself was demolished in 1821 and the only reminder of it now is found in the name of a street (Calle Granada) that leads north from the Plaza de la Constitución. La Goleta is a somewhat down-at-heel part of town and although perfectly safe for visitors it is known to have had something of a problem in the past with *yonquis* (junkies) and *camellos* (drug dealers).

La Goleta has its fair share of churches and convents. The Convent of San José is still home to nuns who still support their life of cloistered prayer by making items used by churches in Málaga, such as linen and hosts (the 'wafers' used for Mass), so they would probably be surprised to learn that Wikipedia thinks they moved out years ago. Other convents have been converted for different uses. One of these is the Franciscan Friary of San Luis El Real (Bishop of Toulouse). It was founded in 1489 and survived until its confiscation in 1836. The name is recorded in the Plaza San Francisco (another of those Spanish squares created by the destruction of religious buildings).

59

The Convent of the Mercederías has also been converted to another use, although the Mercederian nuns only built their convent (or, to be strictly accurate, monastery) in the late nineteenth century, many decades after the confiscation. The sisters themselves remain in Málaga, though in reduced numbers and surviving thanks to overseas members (their Mother Superior in 2023 was from Guatemala). The church is still in use. The attached buildings have been made into a museum to display the works of the *malagueño* neo-expressionist painter Jorge Rando.

East of La Goleta is the tiny *barrio* of San Felipe Neri, named after the parish church at its heart. The *barrio* is home to the Gaona Institute (now officially called the Instituto Vicente Espinel) which was the first public high school in Málaga, inaugurated in 1846 (in the former Oratorian House of Studies), and the only one in existence in the province until 1928, when another was opened in Antequera. Aspiring to be a sort of mini-university, it featured a natural history museum, a botanical garden, a weather station, and a provincial library. Pablo Picasso studied here, as did other luminaries such as the poets Vicente Aleixandre and Emilio Prados, the philosopher José Ortega y Gasset and the crusading Republican lawyer, Victoria Kent. Also in the *barrio* is perhaps Málaga's most unusual and fascinating museum, the Museo del Vidrio y Cristal (Glass and Crystal Museum), occupying a rather grand 18th-century former inn.

El Molinillo ('The Mill' — a number of mills were established here after the San Telmo aqueduct was completed) is north of La Goleta and San Felipe Neri, and visibly scruffier. Once a thriving local neighbourhood, residents now complain of being left behind as the historic centre grows and thrives. One can see its past glories in the architecture, like the impressive *neomudéjar* Salamanca Market. Tourism is not a panacea, but one may hope that it can play its part in rehabilitating this area without forcing out local residents.

Capuchinos is another *barrio* that grew up after the *reconquista*, around the first convent of the Capuchin Franciscans in Málaga, erected on an extensive hill in the north-west of the old city, where previously a hermitage dedicated to Santa Brigida stood. During the 19th and 20th centuries, Capuchinos was a lower and middle-class neighbourhood. According to the 1845 census, it seems that Calle Capuchinos was still a road on the northern edge of the city. The area was occupied by orchards and plots growing potatoes, vegetables and flowers, and by dairy farms (the district to the north of 'Centro' is still known as Ciudad Jardín — 'City Garden'). Little by little the orchards began to disappear, although some still remained at the beginning of the 20th century, coexisting with bakeries, pottery factories, tanneries, and other craft industries.

North-west of the Centro Histórico

La Merced, La Victoria, Lagunillas, Cristo de la Epidemia & El Ejido

La Merced is the *barrio* to the north-east of the *centro histórico* and takes its name from the church and priory of La Merced (dedicated to Our Lady of Mercy) founded by the Mercedarians — a Catholic mendicant order of friars (and later, nuns) founded in 1218 in Barcelona by St Pedro Nolasco to redeem Christians taken into slavery by the Islamic polities of North Africa and Southern Europe.

Recent years have seen the publication of a stream of books celebrating the culture of Southern Spain before 1492, for example María Rosa Menocal's *The Ornament of the World: How Muslims, Jews and Christians Created a Culture of Tolerance in Medieval Spain*. The gist of most of these books is that a flourishing, cosmopolitan and liberal culture fostered by Spain's Moorish rulers was senselessly destroyed by the fundamentalist Catholic forces of Fernando and Isabel who ushered in a period of oppression, typified above all by the Spanish Inquisition. From our twenty-first-century standpoint, we might find much to criticize about the Catholic Monarchs — the forced conversions and the expulsion of Jews to name just two — but it does not follow that the rulers they overthrew were paragons of enlightened virtue.

However attractive the idea of a lost paradise of *convivencia* (living together) under the Moors might be, the truth is probably closer to the '*coexistencia precaria*' suggested by Dario Fernández Morera in his book *The Myth of the Andalusian Paradise: Muslims, Christians, and Jews under Islamic Rule in Medieval Spain*. Muslims, Christians and Jews may indeed have coexisted at times, but it was unlikely to have amounted to a real 'living together'. These groups remained distinct in terms of religion, culture and, crucially, power.

61

For much of its time under Moorish rule, Andalucía was a region at war — martial, religious and intellectual — and this was part of the background against which the Mercedarian Order was founded. When they first came to Málaga in 1499, the friars were installed in a small hermitage near the port by a Christian noble called Alonso Fernández de Ribera. However, the location proved insecure due to frequent raids by Berber pirates and the friars looked for land closer to the city walls.

The first Mercedarian church was a modest, *neomudéjar* building about which very little is known because it was demolished and rebuilt in the late eighteenth century. Construction of the second, larger, church of the Merced was begun in 1792 in a more austere, neoclassical style. Less than 40 years later the convent was seized by the state as part of the programme of confiscations inaugurated by Juan Álvarez Mendizábal during his tumultuous six-month tenure as Prime Minister of Spain.

In 1836 the priory of the Mercedarians was confiscated and the friars evicted. The church was handed over to the Bishop of Málaga and soon fell into a poor state of repair despite successive attempts to improve its physical state. In 1881 a new bell was hung — a significant moment because it had been cast in Málaga at the Ferrería Heredia, then one of the most modern ironworks in the world. The bell tower, however, had to be demolished after being damaged in the earthquake of 1884 and, seven years later the furnaces of the Heredia were extinguished when extortionate tariffs on British coal rendered their operation unprofitable. The bell is now on display in the Málaga Museum.

The church was badly damaged in the *quema de conventos* (the Burning of Convents) in 1931 and for the next 30 years stood in ruins, serving as a reminder of the excesses of anti-clerical zeal. Only in 1963 did the diocese of Málaga agree to its demolition to make way for housing. This volte-face almost certainly came about due to the discovery that a local priest, the infamous Hipólito Lucena Morales, had been using the ruined church for irreligious 'liturgies' celebrated with a community of women that had gathered around him. It had come to light that Father Hipólito's 'community' was less a spiritual support group and more a sex-centred cult.

Since 1842 the Plaza de La Merced has been dominated by the obelisk monument to another opponent of the absolutism of Fernando VII: General José María Torrijos. After a period of exile in London, Torrijos returned to Spain in 1831 along with 60 men hoping to overthrow the king. He was caught and later executed on the San Andrés beach along with 48 of his fellow revolutionaries.

The most famous former resident of the Plaza de La Merced is undoubtedly Pablo Picasso. He was born in a second-floor flat at number 36 in 1881, and shortly afterwards his family moved to the apartment next door. His father José Ruiz & Blasco, also an artist, was professor of drawing at the San Telmo Royal Academy of Fine Art and curator of the Art Museum in Málaga. After landing a more secure position at the Fine Art School in La Coruña, he moved there with the ten-year-old Pablo and the rest of the Ruiz & Picasso family. (Picasso later adopted his mother's surname, perhaps because Ruiz is the eleventh most popular surname in Spain.) Although the Ruiz & Picasso family returned for holidays in the 1890s, Pablo never returned as an adult. Thus, many people find it strange (or even desperate) that the city of Málaga makes such a fuss of its long-absent son.

Yet we know from Picasso's family that he continued to think of himself as a proud *malagueño* and often expressed the hope that a permanent exhibition of his works would one day open in Málaga. Although his first public exhibition was in La Coruña (when he was 13 years old), he pined for Málaga, as did his father, and he lamented that La Coruña was 'Neither Málaga, nor bulls. No friends, no nothing!'. One of Picasso's earliest known works, *La Picador Amarillo*, depicting a mounted bullfighter, was painted after attending a bullfight in the bullring of Málaga in 1890, shortly before his ninth birthday. He enjoyed playing '*toros & toreros*' (bulls and bullfighters) with other children in the square. His friends and family recall that he talked constantly of Málaga and remained convinced that Málaga wine was the secret of his productivity. On his deathbed in the South of France, he called his nephew close and gestured towards the window, saying, '¡*Mira, allí, al sur, está Málaga!*' ('Look, there, to the south, is Málaga!'). Like many memories of childhood, Picasso's recollection of Málaga was perfect and idyllic — perhaps the reason that he never returned was the fear of discovering that the city was not as he remembered it.

The oval-shaped *barrio* of El Ejido ('The Common') is occupied by university faculty buildings (though the new campus in Teatinos is where most of the university is now located). In Moorish times, the cattle that provided meat and milk to the city grazed here and later it was a clay-pit and the site of brickworks. The economic crisis suffered by the Province of Málaga as a result of the phylloxera infestation and the collapse of the steel industry at the end of the 19th century turned El Ejido into a shanty town where immigrants from rural areas settled. Because of the soft clay, many of these families dug caves into the hill and there were cave-dwellers in Málaga as recently as the 1950s. Unless you attend a concert at the Music Conservatory or the Cánovas Theatre, there is little of interest to the visitor here.

North-west of El Ejido is the *barrio* of Cristo del Epidemia. This area, with the same clay deposits as El Ejido, was the centre of brickmaking in the Moorish period. The *Reyes Católicos* set up their camp here, which is why the Basilica of Our Lady of Victory (*Nuestra Señora de la Victoria*) is now located here (confusingly, the Church of La Victoria is not technically in the *barrio* of La Victoria.) The name of the *barrio* comes from the area's association with a couple of miracles of deliverance from epidemics.

Between Cristo de la Epidemia and La Merced are the small *barrios* of Lagunillas and La Victoria. Lagunillas means 'little lagoons' because clay extraction in this area would leave behind water-filled trenches. Another local name for this *barrio* is 'Cruz Verde' because the 'green Cross' (in the sense of living, rather than green-coloured) was the emblem of the Spanish Inquisition and this is where *autos de fe* were held. It is one of the more deprived *barrios* in '*Centro*' but, like anywhere in Málaga, there are plenty of interesting little shops and good bars serving excellent food and drink, so do explore!

The *barrio* of La Victoria began to take shape after the *reconquista* when the land located between the old Plaza del Mercado (the current Plaza de La Merced) and the basilica and Royal Sanctuary of the Victory began to be occupied. In the mid-19th century, La Victoria became known as an area of petty bourgeoisie: dressmakers, owners of washing and ironing workshops, small merchants and administrative employees.

The church of San Lázaro, founded by the *Reyes Católicos* in 1491 was initially constructed as a chapel for the hospital that was also located there, intended to treat lepers. Today only the chapel remains since the rest of the facilities suffered extensive damage during the floods of 1628. The nearby Water Chapel, also known as the Rescue Chapel, the Corner Chapel or the 'Victoria Lighthouse', was commissioned in 1797 by some residents of Calle de la Victoria and designed by Marcos López and José Miranda.

Getting Around Town

Apps & Websites

In my opinion, **moovitapp.com** is the most reliable urban mapping app available (at the time of publication at least). Its coverage and reach are wider than Google's and it generally seems to have the most up-to-date information (though for the app to report accurate information, the local transport companies need to ensure their online feeds are updated). If the ads bother you, it's possible to buy a one-month subscription. The very popular **citymapper.com** app recently added Málaga to its list of locations, but the coverage is not as extensive as Moovit's. It's fine for journeys in the city centre, but patchy beyond.

For travel outside city limits, the website **rome2rio.com** pretty reliably tells you your options to get from **A** to **B** anywhere in the world. However, beware! Sometimes the information updates lag, especially after timetable changes, and Spanish travel timetables vary seasonally, so **always** double-check the information with the transport provider. Even if their information is not up to date, **rome2rio** will usually be able to tell you who the bus providers are. The main operator in Andalucía is **ALSA** (**alsa.com**), closely followed by **Avanza** (**avanzabus.com**). ALSA is a subsidiary of the UK company National Express, but don't let this put you off. ALSA buses are a very comfortable way to travel and, given that vast tracts of Spain have little railway infrastructure, they are used by 'normal' travellers, not just impecunious students.

busbud.com is also a useful site (and smartphone app) that will allow you to book and buy tickets for most bus journeys in Spain. However, it is usually slightly cheaper to use the ALSA or Avanza smartphone apps for booking tickets where possible.

renfe.com (**RRen**-fay) is the Spanish national railway site where you can plan journeys and buy tickets. There is also an app for e-tickets. Most tickets can be purchased on the UK **thetrainline.com** site, which has recently improved considerably and will often give you a wider choice of tickets than the official RENFE website, including options for the ouigo (**we**-go) and iryo (**eer**-yo) operators. All operators and agencies have smartphone apps that can be used for e-tickets. They also send you a confirmation email which includes links to add tickets to Google or Apple Wallet, or print conventionally.

Buses

If you are staying in the *centro histórico* or the *barrios* immediately surrounding it, then most of the main sights are easily walkable, but you may want to take the bus to get to and from the railway station, especially if you have luggage to carry. Other sights, such as the Russian and Automobile Museums, are an easy bus journey or rather a long walk. If you fancy a long walk along the beach (either east towards El Palo or southwest towards the Guadalhorce estuary) then taking a bus in one direction might be a good option to save time and shoe leather. Take a bus out and walk back, or walk until you get tired and take a bus back to the centre.

EMT Málaga is the local bus company's official app:

  Android   iOS

City buses are operated by a company owned by the *ayuntamiento* called **EMT (Empresa Malagueña de Transportes)** and they are cheap and easy to use. Most of the main bus routes pass along the Alameda Principal or the Avenida de Manuel Agustín Heredia (Soho), which is convenient for the *centro histórico*. Many have stops near the María Zambrano Railway Station if you are staying west of the river. The 'Directions' feature of Google Maps (and of iOS Maps) is linked to the EMT database and gives reasonably accurate results (select 'Public Transport' to see options by bus, train and metro). A free app (EMT Málaga) is available for Android and iOS and provides real-time information and route planning; however, the Moovit app is probably easier to use for tourists who may not know the name of the place they are going to and would rather click a location on a map. The EMT website (emtmalaga.es) is in Spanish but offers a Google Translate option in the top-right-hand corner. It gives information about lines and timetables and also features a route planner. Most bus stops in the city centre have live bus information displayed, which is usually accurate to within a couple of minutes.

Buses are boarded from the front door, with the middle and rear doors for disembarkation only. Bus drivers are usually able to give change but will refuse notes larger than €5, so try to have coins or, at most, a €5 note.

Contactless payments by debit card have become a feature since COVID, with 80% of the fleet already fitted with contactless payment points. A bit of language comes in handy. A phrasebook might advise you to ask for '*un billete sencillo, por favor*', but this will make you sound like an over-eager exchange student. Most people just hand over the money. You could say '*uno*' (**oo**-noh) if you like, though if you want more than one ticket for others in your party then say the number: *dos* (**doss**), *tres* (**tRRayss**), *cuatro* (**kwat**-RRoh), etc. Like English buses, there are seats for the elderly and disabled clearly indicated (mostly towards the front). All buses in Málaga are air-conditioned, though older vehicles sometimes struggle to keep cool, especially when impatient passengers insist on opening the windows!

If you (and your travelling companions) are likely to take more than four or five journeys (in total) during your visit to Málaga then it is worth buying a ten-journey pre-paid ticket called a ***tarjeta bus*** (or *bonobús*), dramatically reducing the journey price. It's valid on any EMT bus journey except the Airport bus. You can purchase these cards from ***estancos*** (tobacconists) or ***quioscos*** (newspaper kiosks). You can also buy them from the information desk on the main concourse of the María Zambrano railway station. A 10-journey ticket is sold as a plastic smart card and includes a deposit for the card itself — just ask for *tarjeta bus* (tar-**khay**-ta booss). If you need more journeys then you can top up the card at any *estanco* or *quiosco*. The minimum top-up amount is 10 journeys. A map of charging points can be viewed here: **bit.ly/MalagaBusCharge**, or scan the QR code. Remember that most *quioscos* and *estancos* close for the siesta (usually 1400–1800).

The *tarjeta bus* can be used by multiple travellers. So if you are a couple or a family, you only need one card. To use the card on the bus, tap it against the reader, once for each traveller (up to a maximum of fifteen). Another advantage is '*transbordo*' (transfer). If you catch another bus within an hour you still need to tap in, but your card will not be charged. This is standard on most bus transport in Spain. *Transbordo* only works when you change buses, so if you take the same number bus again, even in a different direction, you will be charged.

The card itself does not expire, though the loaded balance expires 365 days after purchase/top-up. However, these expired journeys will be reactivated at the next top-up. As the *tarjeta bus* is not personalized, it is transferable, so you can give or lend it to someone you know who is going to be visiting Málaga.

⚠ Bus ticket prices were substantially lowered in September 2022 as part of a government package of measures to help with the 'cost of living crisis', with the cost of ten bus journeys dropping again in 2023 to €4.20

(¢42 per journey). Although this is a temporary 'special offer', the previous price had been less than €10, still representing a significant saving on buying individual tickets. Thus, when the price inevitably increases again, the *tarjeta bus* will still be the cheapest way to travel around Málaga. Scan the QR code for the latest ticket prices. Children under the age of 3 travel free as long as they do not take up a seat.

Ⓜ Metro

 It is unlikely that, as a visitor to Málaga, you will need to make much use of the **metromalaga.es**. The line going north-west from the metro station near the María Zambrano Railway Station (**El Perchel**) passes through residential suburbs and through areas where a number of the university faculties are located. The line going south-west might look handy for Málaga's southern beaches (like San Andrés) or attractions such as the Automobile Museum, but buses are usually more convenient from the city centre.

However, with the opening of the **Atarazanas** metro station on the Alameda Principal in 2023 (it was due to open in 2022, but there were delays), visitors may well make greater use of this option, just two stops from **El Perchel** station, which is located between the Bus and Train stations. Eventually, the city centre terminus is due to be located at the Plaza de la Marina, forming a combined Metro and bus subterranean interchange.

 The EMT Bus card cannot currently be used on the Metro, but single and multiple-journey tickets may be purchased from the machines at stations. The simplest ticket is called the **Billete Ocasional**, but if you are likely to make more than a couple of return journeys, then a better option is the **Tarjeta Monedero Metro de Málaga**. As long as there are sufficient funds loaded onto the card then several people can travel together on the same card. For the current ticket prices scan the QR code.

⚠ It might seem like the green **Tarjeta Monedero Consorcio de Transportes** (Málaga Transport Consortium prepaid card, which covers travel on intercity buses, urban buses, 🚆 *Cercanías* trains and the Metro) is the best deal of all, but it isn't really suitable for visitors. Unlike London's Oyster card, which is a multi-network pre-paid card, the Consortium card is personalized, like a season ticket. It's only a money-saver if you need to make multiple journeys using the same combination of train, metro and bus on the same route.

🚕 Taxi

Taxis are a fair bit cheaper in Spain than in the UK, and much cheaper than in London. All taxis have meters and prices are regulated by the *ayuntamiento*. For travelling around town, the standard rate (**in 2023**) was €0.88 per km on weekdays between 0600 and 2200. The higher rate (2200–0600, weekends, and holidays) was €1.07 per km. The standard minimum charge was €3.85, or €4.75 at the higher rate. The same rates apply to journeys to and from the airport plus a €5.50 supplement (in 2023 the **average** taxi fare from/to the airport was around €28). Check the latest tariffs here: 🆓**free-now.com/es/tarifas-malaga**.

 Taxis are plentiful, so you are unlikely to wait long, wherever you are. To locate the official taxi ranks, consult the '**Callejero**' app (QR code left) and select '**Transporte**' and '**Paradas de Taxi**'. **Uber** and **cabify** now operate in Málaga. I would also recommend the PideTaxi App:

The **pidetaxi.es** app is very useful as it works right across Spain by linking with local radio-taxi and minicab firms. This means that you can use it in Málaga, but also in most other Spanish towns and cities. Non-Spanish bank cards tend not to work with the app, though, so you will probably have to pay cash. Booking with PideTaxi is slightly cheaper than hailing a cab in the street or picking one up from a rank. It's also handy for when you need to pre-book a taxi at a particular time.

🚲 Bicycle

Málaga is mainly on the flat and is fairly compact. There are a few bicycle paths but the network remains, to say the least, 'incomplete'. Like almost every other city in Europe, Málaga until recently had its own public bicycle hire scheme (called MálagaBici). However, that bicycle hire scheme has now been discontinued and the *ayuntamiento* has invited tenders from private companies to run similar schemes. Keep your eyes peeled and use the QR codes displayed on hire bikes to visit the relevant app with terms and conditions as the operating companies can change quickly.

Serious cyclists who want a high-end road bike to explore the city or even something suitable for the mountains (or anyone wanting to make more than a short journey) should book ahead online with **bike2malaga.com** (prices are on a sliding scale, getting cheaper the longer the hire period). They also have road bikes, hybrids, e-bike hybrids and both hardtail and full-suspension mountain bikes for hire, all of which are very well maintained.

Other bike hire companies in the centre of Málaga include:

malagabiketours.eu, **biketoursmalaga.com**, **www.rentacarprima.com**, **labiciclettabikerent.com**, **alikindoi.org/en/home**, and **eatsleepcycle.com**

all of which are excellent. However, new establishments are opening all the time, so search online for maximum options.

🚶 On Foot

Málaga is a compact city and very easy to explore on foot. Apart from the Botanical Gardens and Russian Museum, none of the main sights is really more than 20 minutes' walk from anywhere else. Another exception to this rule of thumb is the Castillo de Gibralfaro which is not far as the crow flies, but quite a steep climb.

If you are visiting Málaga during the summer (June-August) remember that walking is far more pleasant an activity in the shade than in the full glare of the sun. You'll notice that on a particular street, everyone walks on the same side — locals always choose the shady side!

Other options

Horse and carriage rides are popular throughout Andalucía. The owners and operators are mainly *gitanos* (Romani), many of whom go from town to town according to the cycle of local fairs. During the *feria*, the most stylish way to be seen at the *recinto ferial* or arrive at the bullring is by horse and '*carruaje*' and the carriage drivers will often be wearing full *andaluz* riding gear of high-waisted trousers, short jacket and wide-brimmed hat. But for the rest of the year the 'uniform' is flat cap and cardigan. The prices are regulated by the *ayuntamiento* and represent good value. The horses are well cared for. The main 'carriage rank' is the Plaza de la Marina, at the city end of the Parque de Málaga.

Segways® can be hired from a number of outlets in Málaga including, for example, **Segway Málaga Experience** on Muelle Uno. Search **bit.ly/SegwaysMLG** for more options. Segways are only hired out as part of a tour (one guide for 8 people). Helmets and high-vis vests (provided) are required, so these tours are not for the self-conscious, or stylish.

🚌 Provincial Buses

Longer bus routes outside the city of Málaga are operated by the *Consorcio de Transporte Metropolitano del Área de Málaga* (Metropolitan Transport Consortium) with their distinctive green and cream livery. They have a user-friendly website in English: **bit.ly/ctmamalaga** (or scan QR code).

☂ Tours

As in any city, there are plenty of walking tours on offer every day. Some of the pricier options (*e.g.* those organized by **welovemalaga.com**) start at €45 (2023 prices) for a walking tour, almost doubling if drinks and *tapas* are included, though they are highly rated. As is increasingly the case, many tours on offer are 'free' and last 1.5 or 2 hours. The guide is paid through tips at the end of the tour. You do not have to pay anything at all, but it would be fair to give what you think is reasonable for the length of the tour, taking into account the number of people sharing the same tour. Operators offering both free and paid tours include: '**Explore Málaga**', '**Málaga a Pie**' (Málaga On Foot), and '**Málaga Adventures**'. All the guides are officially registered and speak good English. The websites **freetour.com/malaga** and **guruwalk.com/malaga** list a variety of possibilities as well as the ability to book in advance online.

If you would rather cover a bit more ground by bike then **biketoursmalaga.com** offer very good value guided tours which last for 3 hours, bicycle hire included. Tours run every day, morning and afternoon, and it's possible to book online.

The *ayuntamiento* has a fascinating page on its website, with a map, for a self-guided route showing the main points of archaeological interest (from the Roman, Phoenician/Punic, and Moorish periods) in the old city at **rutasarqueologicas.malaga.eu**. The main site is in Spanish. However, the points of interest all have a link to '*más información*' (more information) and this is provided in Spanish and English. You could use this resource to guide you around a historical route, often past features you might not otherwise notice. A dozen of the more visitable locations are shown on the **MÁLAGA History** layer of the companion Google map (**bit.ly/MalagaMap**).

Málaga in 3 Days! The Top Ten of Everything

Any Google search (other search engines are available) will serve up no end of results for 'Málaga in a Day', 'Málaga in 3 Days', 'A Week in Málaga' etc. Some of these web pages are interesting and useful, written by bloggers who have actually visited and know the city well. Some are written by genuine, resident experts like Alejo Tomás (**malagatop.com)** or Joanna Styles (**guidetomalaga.com**). On the other hand, some of the guides that appear in national newspapers are imaginative works of fiction.

The other problem with these 'What to Do in Málaga in X-Number-of Days' articles, handy though they may be, is that we are all different. Some travellers are culture vultures, keen to tick off the maximum number of museums and galleries. Others are foodies or *bons vivants*, focusing on bars and restaurants. For some, the pleasure is more ontological and about simply imbibing the *ambiente*. **You can pick up leaflets from the *turismo* that suggest itineraries for 1, 2 or 3-day stays, plus walks, nature routes, food routes, guides to particular neighbourhoods etc. They are all excellent:** bit.ly/MalagaRoutes. But for what it's worth, here's my list of two dozen things to do, see, eat and drink in the City of Málaga:

👀 Get a good view

A good way to see the lie of the land is to take in the views from the Castillo de Gibralfaro. Other locations with commanding views are the Alcazaba, the roof (*cubiertas*) of the Cathedral and any one of the many rooftop bars in the city.

🏬 Go to market

Spanish municipal markets are always interesting to visit with their beautiful displays of every kind of food imaginable. Try to buy something, though — a smoothie or some fruit, a handful of Málaga's famous almonds or raisins, or a few slices beautiful ham to take home with you.

🐚 Enjoy some *conchas finas*

The *concha fina* is a smooth shell clam eaten raw with lemon juice, salt and pepper and, ideally accompanied by a glass of dry white wine. They are served in dozens of bars, but perhaps the most atmospheric place to enjoy them is the Mercado Atarazanas.

🏛 Discover Moorish Málaga

A visit to the Alcazaba is the most obvious way to get a feel for Málaga's Moorish past. Call into the Roman *Teatro* at the same time.

🎨 *Málaga Picassiana*

Pablo Picasso may not have returned to Málaga as an adult, but he never forgot it. You have a couple of options to immerse yourself in the life and work of the great artist: the large Museo Picasso, or the more intimate Museo Casa Natal (birthplace museum).

🍷 Drink a Very Old Tear

A popular local wine is called *lágrima trasañejo* ('very old tear'). The fortified wines of Málaga were once hugely popular in Britain but are little known these days. The iconic bar in which to sample a good range of wines from the barrel is Antigua Casa de Guardia. To find out more about the winemaking of the region, pay the Museo del Vino a visit.

🖼 Go to a Gallery

The most famous and high-profile art gallery is the Carmen Thyssen, though if you'd prefer to see more contemporary art, try CAC Málaga or the Centre Pompidou.

🍴 Breakfast like a *Malagueño*

As in the rest of Spain, *churros* are a popular morning snack, but in Málaga, they are called *tejeringos*. Plenty of cafés serve them, and few feel more authentic than Los Valle.

☕ Stop for Coffee

If you didn't have one with your *tejeringos*, make sure you take the opportunity to order a coffee in the traditional fashion. Enjoy your *mitad*, *semi largo*, or *sombra* and watch the world go by.

⛪ Go to Church

The Cathedral is well-known, but there are lots of other churches in the city centre, all of which have interesting features. Most are open in the morning and early evening.

☕ The *Hora del Vermú*

No one sits down for lunch until 2 pm, but the bars are full long before this with people enjoying an aperitif. *Vermú* (vermouth, often spelt '*vermut*' in the Catalan fashion) has enjoyed a resurgence in recent years, shrugging off its formerly fusty reputation. Most traditional bars serve *vermú*.

🍴 And Now Lunch...

You will never be stuck for a lunch stop in Málaga, but a typically Spanish approach is to have a *menú del día* — a great value two or three-course set lunch, including a glass of wine or beer. Keep your eyes peeled when out and about because *menú del día* options usually appear on blackboards outside bars.

🍦 Have an Ice Cream

Rather than rounding off a meal with one of the rather dull puddings one tends to find on Spanish menus, go for ice cream. Try Casa Mira and enjoy your ice cream in the shadow of the Cathedral or on Calle Larios. Try a flavour that you won't find at home, like *cuajada con miel* (sheep milk curd with honey) or, of course, *Málaga* (wine and raisin).

🦑 *Ir a tapear*

If you've had a decent lunch then enjoy Málaga's *tapas* scene in the evening. While you can easily enjoy an entire *tapas*-based meal in a single bar, the authentic way to do it is to go on a crawl (*rastreo*), sampling the speciality of the house at each stop.

🏺 Take in a Museum

Málaga's largest museum, the Museo de Málaga, is near the Alcazaba and has a huge variety of exhibits on display, including works of art. Also in the shadow of the Alcazaba is the more intimate Museo del Patrimonio Municipal (MUPAM).

👫 Enjoy the *Paseo*

The afternoon or early evening stroll (*paseo*) is a Spanish institution when sleepy parks and streets suddenly fill with people. The quayside (Muelle Uno and Muelle Dos) is an ideal place for a pre-dinner perambulation.

🌳 Go to the Park

You could begin your afternoon *paseo* by walking through the quiet and cool Parque de Málaga, only metres from the hustle and bustle of the city centre but a real oasis of calm. Alternatively, take a bus to the stunning La Concepción Botanical Gardens.

🏖 Go to the Beach

Málaga's 'city centre beach' is La Malagueta, just beyond the bullring, but you could hop on a bus to El Palo or Pedregalejo, or walk along the Promenade 'Antonio Banderas' south-west of the railway station where the beaches are busy with local families.

🍢 Try an *Espeto*

Grilled skewers of sardines called '*espetos*' (eaten all year round, but at their juiciest, fattest best from May to August) are enjoyed all along the coast of the Province of Málaga, prepared in beach restaurants known as *chiringuitos* or *merenderos*. Every beach has at least one.

🏛 Visit a Small Museum

As well as the big crowd pullers, Málaga has plenty of small and unusual museums. Two of the most enjoyable are the Glass Museum and the Museo de Artes y Costumbres Populares (Museum of Popular Arts and Customs).

🍽 Cool Down with a Cold *Tapa*

Málaga's signature salad is a cool and refreshing mix of cod, potato, orange and olives. If you're not a fish lover, look out for *ajoblanco*, a delicious chilled almond soup.

🏃 Venture Beyond the Centre

There's plenty to keep you occupied in the historic centre of Málaga, but there is much to be said for wandering further afield and discovering that fabulous local bar before anyone else.

🥪 Try *Salchichón de Málaga*

Málaga's local sausage is not quite like any other salami you've tasted, being only very mildly cured. Bar Diamante is a good place to order it in a *pifuto* (little sandwich).

🐟 Eat *Boquerones*

Málaga is famous for its fresh anchovies, available from January to November. Enjoy them marinated in lemon or vinegar, or else quickly fried in crunchy batter. Eaten whole.

Gastronomy

The variety of establishments devoted to eating and drinking, and the nomenclature thereof, can be confusing. You can order breakfast in a bar, have a beer in a *cafetería*, a three-course meal in a *taberna*, and *tapas* in a *restaurante*; so the following attempt at a taxonomy may be enlightening.

Restaurante

Unsurprisingly, a restaurant, but in a world where McDonald's and The Ivy are both 'restaurants', this is not always a very instructive description. A place that calls itself a *restaurante* should, at least, have a dedicated dining area with table service.

Asador

An *asador* (**ass-a-dor**) is a *restaurante* specializing in roast meat, which in most of Spain tends to mean lamb or pork (an *asador* is the spit upon which meat is roasted). Most are quite traditional establishments.

Mesón

Mesón (**may-sonn**) is a rather old-fashioned word for an inn. Do not expect to encounter avocado foams or carrot gels; the vibe here is more Don Quixote than Ferran Adrià.

Parrilla

(**pah-RReel-ya**) *Parrilla* can mean a flat-top grill (more accurately known as a *plancha*), or it can mean a real grill over charcoal. Any restaurant or bar calling itself a *parrilla* is more likely to be cooking on the latter.

Marisquería

Mariscos is the term used to refer to seafood, so a *marisquería* (**mah-riskay-RRee-ah**) is a fish and seafood restaurant. **A** Although fish are *pescados*, *pescaderías* are fishmongers, not dining establishments.

Chiringuito

A *chiringuito* (chee-reen-**ghee**-toh) is a typically *malagueño* establishment that combines the *marisquería* (seafood restaurant) and the *parrilla* (grill) outdoors. *Chiringuitos* (sometimes called *merenderos*) are near, or on, the beach. Some are little more than shacks with outside seating, while others are smart, air-conditioned restaurants with terraces. What they have in common are their barbecues, or charcoal grills, over which most of their fish dishes are prepared. The most typical and emblematic preparation is the *espeto* — an olive wood, cane or metal skewer of fresh sardines. Going to Málaga and not eating an *espeto* would be like going to Naples and not eating pizza.

Taberna

A *taberna* (tab-**air**-nah) is a bar. Primarily drinking establishments, *tabernas* usually also serve good quality food: *tapas* and sharing plates at the very least, and sometimes full sit-down meals.

Pub

If a place is called a 'pub' (poob) it's a pretty safe bet that an attempt has been made to recreate an English (or an Irish) pub. Usually overpriced.

Cafetería

A *cafetería* (kaf-ay-tay-**ree**-ah) could be a coffee-shop, a bar or a restaurant. It could be primarily a café selling coffee, cakes, ice cream and snacks, but unlike similar establishments in the UK, it will almost certainly have draught beer and a selection of wines and spirits. Alternatively, it might just be a bar with a good kitchen and a reputation for good coffee and breakfasts. A pure coffee and cakes sort of place could also be called a *panadería*, *pastelería*, *confitería*, or just a *café*. The precise boundary between a *cafetería* and a bar is loose and fluid, but a *cafetería* always serves food. *Cafetería* is one of the few *castellano* words to have entered the English language (along with embargo, canyon, cargo, patio, bonanza, breeze, etc.).

Bar

A bar can be many things, but it always has an actual bar across which drinks are sold. Some bars serve very little apart from drinks and a few *tapas*. This is the baseline. Almost every bar serves coffee and those open in the morning will offer breakfast (coffee, fresh orange juice and toasted bread with tomato, ham, cheese, or jam). Some offer a *menú* at lunchtime. In plenty of bars, it is possible to have a full meal. Some bars have a separate *comedor* which means that they are also *restaurantes*.

Bodega/Vinoteca

A *bodega* is technically a wine merchant (derived from the Greek word for 'storehouse' — *apotheke* — which also gives us 'boutique'). Nowadays almost all *bodegas* in the city are basically bars, but you should expect a decent choice of wines, beyond the house *tinto*, *blanco* and *rosado*.

Cervecería

(ther-bay-thay-RRee-ah) Technically a brewery (of beer, *cerveza*) but these days often just a bar. Every bar serves draught beer, but a *cervecería* will usually serve more than one variety.

Bar de Copas

This is a cocktail bar and is principally about the consumption of spirits and cocktails. Beyond crisps, olives and nuts, do not expect much in the way of food. Most *bares de copas* tend to open later in the evening.

Using TripAdvisor and Other Websites

Google > TripAdvisor: TripAdvisor is primarily a travel and tourist app so only the most 'touristy' attractions rise to the top. Google reviews are more useful as they are more likely to come from locals.

Price Categories: The classification of establishments by price is always vague and comparative rather than quantitative. A €9 *tapa* is pricey; a €9 *menú del día* is a bargain.

Make use of online booking features: Part of the fun of choosing a restaurant is wandering past, having a look at the menu, peering inside and deciding whether you like the cut of its jib, but securing a booking is often a good idea at weekends when the most popular establishments will be heaving.

Read between the lines: A handful of bad reviews might set alarm bells ringing, but often they can say more about the diners than the dining establishment. I have seen bars marked down for a 'poor choice of beers' even though almost no bar in Spain has more than one beer on tap.

What do Spaniards think? A sensible rule of thumb is to prioritize the opinions of Spanish reviewers. This is not because Spaniards are more discerning than other nationalities, or have superior palates, but because they have the context necessary to make a fair judgment.

What does the manager say? Look to see whether the bar or restaurant replies to reviews, either to acknowledge a good review or to address an issue raised in a poor review. This is usually a sign of a place that takes quality and service seriously, even if they sometimes miss the mark.

Make your own contribution: If you had a great experience, leave a review and try to make it helpful. What was especially delicious? Was there anything you'd avoid were you to visit again?

Have a look at the website: A slick, professionally produced website may look impressive, but not if the most recent menu (*carta*) was uploaded four years ago. On the other hand, plenty of smaller establishments have no website, but their Facebook/Meta or Instagram page is frequently updated with the latest *menú del día* and photos of dishes that they are proud of. User-submitted photos on Google reviews can also tell you a lot about a place.

Making Bookings

An increasing number of venues have online booking forms on their own websites, **thefork,** and/or **Google**. This makes booking tables easy. But don't be nervous about booking by email, even if you don't speak *castellano*. As long as your message is simple, Google Translate will do a reasonable job of rendering it in Spanish (and translating the reply into English). If you are staying in a hotel (rather than a *hostal*), you can ask the concierge or front desk to make bookings for you.

Some great bars in Málaga do not take reservations because they are so small. Others only accept bookings by phone and in person. If you don't speak *castellano* there is no cause for fear. Bars and restaurants take bookings because they want your custom.

🍢 Tapas, ⓘ Raciones & 🏮 Menús del Día

A *tapa* is traditionally a morsel accompanying a drink, of the sort and size that might be given away free — a few olives, a handful of crisps, a single *croqueta*, a slice of ham on a small piece of dry or toasted bread. The word *tapa* comes from the verb *tapar* 'to cover', and it seems likely that *tapas* were originally placed on the tops of glasses to keep out the dust, flies, and other sources of contagion. Outside Granada and Jaén, *tapas* are not usually handed out for free.

You will also encounter the *ración* (ration), which is a plate or large portion of *tapas*, enough for a few people to share. In between the *ración* and the *tapa* is the *media ración*. Many options on the *carta* will be available as *tapas*, *raciones* or *medias raciones*, priced accordingly.

Raciones always come with a little basket of bread and strangely moreish tiny breadsticks ('breadtwigs', perhaps?) called *picos*. Feel free to order something to share (*para compartir*) — this is how the Spaniards do it. But — and this is important advice — try to resist the temptation to order everything that you want to eat at once. Go with the flow. In Spain, eating is not something to be rushed.

It is perhaps worth saying that the starter/main/dessert shape of the normal restaurant meal in the UK is only loosely adhered to in Spain. Even in restaurants, ordering something to share (*para compartir*) is normal and expected, especially for starters. A lot of restaurant menus (*cartas*) list main courses that are fairly obviously dishes for one person — a duck leg, a burger, a veal steak, etc. The temptation, then, is to assume that the dishes listed in the section before that are conventional 'starters'. '*Entradas*' may literally **mean** 'starters', but only in the poshest restaurants will they be starters suitable for one person. If there are four people in your party, order two dishes to start, to share. If there are two of you, order one. If you are on your own, order something light, like *gazpacho* or a *tapa*.

🍰 Smurfs, Fleas and Viennas

In Málaga, the names of sandwiches are slightly different from the standard Spanish names. A *bocadito/mondatido* (tiny sandwich) is called a ***pulga*** ('flea') or ***pulguita*** ('little flea'), a *bocadillo* (standard-sized roll) is a ***pitufo*** ('smurf'), and the large *bocata* is a ***viena*** ('Vienna').

Málaga's other local sandwich is the ***campero*** (meaning 'country style'). It's a large sandwich made in a '*mollete*' (a soft muffin typical of Antequera), originally containing lettuce, tomato, 'York' ham, cheese, mayonnaise, ketchup, and mustard, though nowadays one can choose from many other fillings. It is prepared like a *panino* on a grill.

🍽 *El menú del día*

This is a daily lunch menu offered by many bars, cafés and even traditional restaurants. You will get a *primer plato* (starter) and a *segundo plato* (main course). The choices for these two courses will be listed on a blackboard or printed menu and there are usually 3 or 4 options for each. Mains usually include at least one chicken/meat and one fish/seafood choice. A drink (*bebida*) is generally included, as is bread (*pan*). If the menu says *vino*, that usually might mean a glass, but it can be a carafe or half a bottle in some restaurants. It also means that you can choose beer or water instead. Most *menús del día* give you the choice of either pudding or coffee (*postre o café*).

How to Eat

You may be the sort of person who normally has a very light lunch with a main meal in the evening, in which case the *menú del día* is probably not going to suit you. But if you are prepared to go native, remember that Spanish lunches are long and unhurried and can be followed by a siesta and then a restorative *paseo* (stroll). The lunchtime *menú*, providing you find one that appeals, is the cheapest way to eat in the middle of the day, so give it a go if you can. It's also a very cost-effective way of eating in more expensive restaurants.

Going to a restaurant in the evening can be a very pleasant experience, but I would recommend giving the pastime of *tapear* (to go for *tapas*, especially bar to bar) a shot too. It won't cost any more than going to a restaurant and enables one to try a greater variety of eateries and dishes. Start off in a promising-looking bar and order a *tapa* of something that sounds delicious, especially if you see people around you eating it. Move on somewhere else. The walk between the first and second bar will reanimate your appetite. Repeat until you are full, or ready for bed. If the mood takes you, have something more substantial in the form of a *ración* or *media ración*.

Tapas Bar Favourites

In Spain, some dishes are ubiquitous. There can hardly be a bar in the country that does not prepare *tortilla española* every day, just as every bar has a *jamón* (cured leg ham) on the go, with others hanging above in readiness for the knife. The *tapas* listed below are likely to be found in almost every bar in Spain:

Croquetas (kro-**kay**-tass) — Crumbed, fried ovoids of flavoured *béchamel* — the main types are cheese, ham and cod (*bacalao*).

Queso (**kay**-soh) — Cheese. It's usually *manchego*, a sharp and tasty ewe's milk cheese from La Mancha, but there are many other kinds. The soft and blue varieties are mainly found in the north (where most of the dairy herds are), getting harder as one moves south.

Jamón (кнam-**on**) — Without doubt the finest ham in the world, and very possibly the finest single food item in the world. Smell it, touch it, rub it on your lips and then taste it. Garnet red flesh and rich, yellow fat, three years in the making. British boiled or baked ham (known as *Jamón York* in Spain) can be a fairly insipid product, but *jamón* is rich, unctuous and deeply 'piggy'. The truth is that even the cheap stuff is pretty good, but the very best is *Jamón Ibérico de Bellota* (*bellota* means 'acorn', the main diet of the fattening pigs), often called *pata negra* (black foot).

Bacalao — (bakka-**laow**) Dried salt cod, and tastier than one might think. It is often found in *croquetas*.

Gambas — (**gam**-bass) The most common name by which prawns are known. Prepared in a variety of ways, one of the most popular is *gambas al ajillo* (sizzling in olive oil with garlic).

Mini hamburguesas (**mee**-nee am-bor-**gay**-sass) — These sound naff, but they are a popular *tapa*. Expect a beautifully tender, well-seasoned veal burger in a tiny soft bun, perhaps with *confit* onions and cheese.

Albóndigas (al-**bonn**-dee-gass) — Small meatballs, usually made from pork and served in a tomato sauce. The origin of the name is from the Arabic *al-bunduq*, meaning 'hazelnut'.

Aceitunas (a-тнay-**toon**-ass) — Olives. Green, sometimes stuffed, but always fresher and juicier than anything available in the UK.

Boquerones (bo-kay-**rown**-ayss) — Fresh, white, and either grilled or fried; or marinaded in lemon (or wine vinegar) and olive oil. There cannot be a bar in Spain that does not serve *boquerones*, but the natives of Málaga are convinced theirs are the best. In fact, the nickname given to the natives of Málaga is '*boquerones*'.

Calamares (calah-**mar**-ayss) — Squid, of course; but often called *rabas* (served in strips, not rings) on *tapas* menus, like battered squid chips with masses of lemon and salt.

Mejillones rellenos (meh-кнil-**yoh**-naiss rell-**yay**-noss) — Stuffed mussels; diced and mixed with a piquant tomato sauce, then put back into the shell and often gratinéed with *béchamel* and breadcrumbs. Sometimes called *tigres* because of the (very) slightly spicy sauce.

Patatas bravas (pah-**tah**-tass **brah**-vass) — Fried potato served with a spicy tomato sauce. What passes as 'spicy' (*picante*) in Spain is likely to be fairly mild to English tastes, with the 'heat' coming from paprika (*pimentón*) rather than chilli.

Pimientos de Padrón (pim-**yen**-toss day pad-**ron**) — Mild, green, thumb-sized chilli peppers (sometimes dusted with cornmeal) and either quickly fried or chargrilled. Padrón is a small town near Santiago de Compostela, famous for growing these peppers.

Tortilla (tor-**teel**-ya) — Good old Spanish omelette: potatoes and onions cooked very slowly in oil as for a confit, before the addition of eggs. Sometimes *jamón*, *chorizo*, etc. is added.

Paella (pah-**ail**-ya) — Not usually to be recommended outside Valencia or a *valenciano* restaurant. Authentic paella should have beans, rabbit and snails (*caracoles*) but one also encounters seafood paella.

Ensaladilla rusa (en-salla-**deel**-ya RROO-sah) — 'Little Russian Salad'. This embellished potato salad is always based on diced, boiled potatoes, vegetables and mayonnaise. The Spanish version usually contains tuna, prawns or surimi (crab sticks). Since 2022, it has been renamed *ensaladilla ucraniana* in most establishments, for obvious reasons.

Morcilla (mor-**theel**-ya) — Spanish black pudding, of which there are many regional varieties. Most contain paprika and are more highly seasoned than the English kind. In Andalucía, cumin, onions, rice or pine nuts are often added. It is a popular sandwich filling.

Chorizo (choh-RRee-thoh) — A pork sausage flavoured with paprika. Like *morcilla*, there are dozens of varieties and it features in many dishes as a way of adding paprika and pork fat. The juicy, fat, soft *chorizos* are added to cooked dishes, whereas the drier, firmer *chorizos* are sliced and eaten like salami. You might occasionally see a particular dish, such as *fabada* — a bean stew — described as '*con todos los sacramentos*' (with all the sacraments). This means 'with all the trimmings', in other words: *morcilla*, *chorizo* and *tocino* (pancetta).

Empanadillas (em-pa-na-**deel**-yas) — small, hot-water-crust pasties (meat, fish, vegetables or cheese, with tuna being the most popular filling).

Garbanzos con espinacas (gar-**ban**-thos kon ess-pin-**ack**-ass) — chickpeas stewed with spinach, garlic, spices and vinegar. This dish is often ignored by foreigners because it sounds somewhat dull. It's not.

Huevos rotos (**way**-voss **roh**-toss) — literally 'broken eggs': a dish of fried potato and usually one other ingredient (ham, sausage, *morcilla*, elvers, etc.) topped with a fried egg or two.

Tortillitas de camarones (tor-teel-**yee**-tass day kah-mar-**oh**-nayss) — A pancake-like fritter made from chickpea flour batter enriched with garlic, parsley and tiny shrimp, fried into crisp, lacy galettes. A speciality of Cádiz, nothing accompanies a cold beer quite like *tortillitas de camarones*.

📖 Understanding *cartas*

The days of phrase books and dictionaries are largely over, thanks to the smartphone and cheaper roaming charges. Download the Google Translate (or similar) app for your iOS or Android phone and use it to check translations of items on *cartas* and *menús* in Spanish. The following is a list, by no means exhaustive, of typical *andaluz* dishes (if any is associated with a particular province, this is indicated), some of which will probably not be in any phrase book and might flummox a translator app.

🍲 *Entrantes, Sopas & Cocidos* (Starters, Soups And Stews)

Aceitunas aliñás — Olives marinated with bitter orange, red pepper, fennel, thyme, oregano, etc.

Ajoblanco (Granada & Málaga) — The forerunner of *gazpacho*; chilled garlic and almond soup.

Arroz Caldoso Marinero (Málaga) — Imagine paella in soup form. My advice is to ignore *paella* in Málaga (go to Valencia if you want to try it), but order this if you see it on the menu.

Berza Malagueña (Málaga) — A hearty thick soup with *pringá* as the main flavour, plus green beans and carrots.

Caldillo de pintarroja (Málaga) — A spicy and savoury marine winter soup using dogfish (aka 'Morgay'). Traditionally eaten by Málaga's fishermen to warm up before (or after) sailing out to sea and a favourite in the many traditional taverns.

Cazuela de Fideos (Málaga) — A spicy fish soup made from whichever fish is available (or leftover) that day, with the addition of *fideos* (short noodles).

Ensalada/Ensaladilla malagueña — The signature salad of Málaga is made with potatoes, cod (sometimes tuna), oranges (traditionally *cachorreña* or sour oranges) and green olives. It is sometimes called '*salmorejo*' in Málaga which, confusingly, is also the name of a completely different dish (a thick, chilled tomato soup from Córdoba).

Garbanzos con bacalao — Chickpeas stewed with salt cod.

Gazpacho — A chilled and blended soup of tomatoes, peppers, cucumber, garlic and sherry vinegar.

Gazpachuelo (Málaga) — Quite different from *gazpacho*! A *malagueña* bouillabaisse thickened with mayonnaise served hot or warm, not chilled.

Habas con calzones — Runner beans with ham (*lit.* 'beans in their pods')

Habas fritas con jamón (Granada) — Haricot beans cooked with ham.

Migas (Córdoba, Granada, Málaga, & Almería) — Breadcrumbs fried with garlic and served with one or more toppings — sausage, ham, egg, fish, shellfish, grapes, cheese, etc.

Migas de harina (Granada) — A thick wheat porridge with garlic.

Porra (Málaga) — *Gazpacho* is ubiquitous throughout the Iberian peninsular, but this is the version from Antequera, in the Province of Málaga. A thick *gazpacho* eaten with a spoon rather than drunk from a glass, and often garnished with tuna or cod.

Puchero andaluz — A rich stew (chicken, beef, lamb, pork, etc.) with potatoes, chickpeas and vegetables. Quite similar to *cocido madrileño*.

Remojón/Picadillo de naranjas (Granada, Málaga) — Orange salad, often with onions, olives, cod, etc.

Salmorejo (Córdoba) — A thicker version of *gazpacho*, more like a sauce than a soup and often used as such.

Sopa cachorreña — A cream soup made from *cachorreña* (sour) oranges, garlic, tomato, cumin and paprika. Often garnished with flakes of cod.

🌱 *Verduras* (Vegetables)

Alboronía — The *andaluz* version of ratatouille (or *pisto* as it is known in Spain).

Berenjenas con miel (de caña) — Popular throughout Andalucía, but this dish of fried aubergine slices or batons drizzled with 'cane honey' (*viz.* molasses) really belongs to Málaga because it is the centre of sugar cane production.

Habas a la rondeña (Ronda, Málaga) — A hearty casserole of broad beans and ham or gammon; beautiful with crusty bread.

Pipirrana — Another dish found all over Andalucía, made from finely chopped red pepper, green pepper, tomato, onion, olives, tuna, and mussels or other seafood dressed with extra virgin olive oil and sea salt.

Piriñaca (Cádiz) — This is basically unblended *gazpacho*, more like a salad than a soup.

🍖 *Carnes* (Meat)

Chivo Lechal Malagueño (Málaga) — Roast suckling goat (kid). Málaga is famous for its goats, and the La Axarquía region of the province is famous for this dish. Often served with '*pastoril*' sauce made with bacon and almonds, and accompanied by the offal, either fried with onions or made into a pate.

Flamenquín (Córdoba) — A slice of ham or pork rolled around cheese, crumbed and fried.

Huevos a la flamenca — Eggs cooked in *pisto* (ratatouille).

Manteca colorá (Málaga) — Literally 'coloured lard'; pork loin in lard and paprika enjoyed cold on toast or in a sandwich.

Pan de Pollo (Málaga) — This translates as 'chicken bread' — a *pâté* or terrine of chicken, pig's liver and pork belly.

Pepitoria de Pollo (Málaga) — Chicken with almonds, a kind of non-spicy chicken korma.

Plato de los montes (Málaga) — Pork loin in paprika-flavoured lard, served with fried potato, onions, peppers, black pudding, etc. A very hearty 'mountain' dish.

Pringá — Comes in different forms depending on which meat was used (it can be made from beef, pork, *chorizo* or *morcilla*), but it's what we would call 'pulled' in English; slow cooked and tender, almost rillettes. Similar to *zurrapa*, but more meat than fat.

Tartar de Salchichón (Málaga) — A recent addition to the culinary patrimony of Málaga. '*Salchichón de Málaga*' is a very lightly cured sausage that has the soft mouthfeel almost of raw pork, so this is a take on the classic steak tartare using Málaga's native charcuterie.

Zurrapa (Málaga) — Another pork and lard dish, this time of shredded pork in seasoned lard (without paprika) and spread on toast. Very 'porky' and quite delicious.

🐟 🦑 *Pescados & Mariscos* (Fish & Seafood)

Araña — Not a dish, but a kind of fish (and not a spider as Google will translate it) — the weever. The spines are venomous, but it is a good eating fish, with a flavour similar to sole.

Atún mechado (Málaga) — Tuna braised with white wine and bacon.

Cazuela de arroz a la malagueña (Málaga) — The *malagueño* version of paella. Also known as **Arroz a la Parte**.

Espeto de sardinas (Málaga) — Up to half a dozen sardines grilled over wood/coals on a skewer. The origin of these sardine skewers is associated with open-air beach bars.

Fritura Malagueña (Málaga) — Every coastal town in Andalucía has its own version, but the basics are the same: small fish and pieces of larger fish, dredged in chickpea flour and quickly fried to achieve a 'good fry' (*viz.* not too greasy or heavy). The difference in Málaga is that you will find more anchovies in your *fritura*. See also *pescaíto frito*.

Pescado adobado/Bienmesabe — Fish which has been marinated in vinegar, bay, cumin, paprika and garlic before cooking. **A** *Bienmesabe* just means 'it tastes good' and is also the name of a pudding made from honey, egg yolks and almonds!

Pescaíto frito — Fried fish, first dusted in chickpea or pea grass flour. The Spanish word is actually *pescadíto* but because *andaluces* are famous for swallowing their consonants, the 'd' has been completely dropped over time.

Pescado en blanco (Málaga) — A simple country cousin of the *grande bouillabaisses* of the French littoral, made with fish and potatoes.

Rosada — A catch-all term for a few kinds of firm-fleshed white fish. Often, it's 'Kingklip' (Cusker Eel), fished in the Southern Atlantic and Indo-Pacific oceans. In other words, it's what Spanish restaurants have in their freezers (so it's fine to order on a Monday). It's a good-eating fish, a little softer than monkfish with large, firm flakes and a mild flavour.

☙ *Postres & Dulces* (Puddings & Pastries)

Alfajores — Pastries made from a paste of almonds, nuts and honey.

Borrachuelos (Málaga) — Especially popular at Christmas and Easter, these pastries are flavoured with wine and *anís*, filled with candied sweet potato or pumpkin jam, and usually dipped in honey syrup.

Granizado de almendra (Málaga) — A frozen dessert made from almonds, sugar and cinnamon.

Hojaldrina — A crumbly cookie.

Pan de higo — Dried figs pressed into a cake and eaten with cheese.

Pestiños — Crumbly honey wafers a little like substantial brandy snaps.

Peras estofadas (Málaga) — Pears poached in wine with honey and cinnamon.

Tarta Malagueña (Málaga) — A cake made with ground almonds and Málaga sweet wine, as well as apricot jam.

Tocino de cielo — 'Heaven's bacon'; a tooth-shatteringly sweet confection of caramelized egg yolks.

Tortas de aceite — Thin, crisp, round wafers made with flour, olive oil, aniseed and sesame.

Tortas Locas (Málaga) — 'Mad Cakes' were invented in the 1950s to bring a little sweet luxury to ordinary *malagueños* who could not afford rich cream cakes. These are sandwiches of puff pastry filled with custard and iced with orange frosting, topped with a glacé cherry.

Yemas del Tajo (Málaga) — A version of *Yemas de Santa Teresa* made by nuns in Ronda.

🥕 Vegetarian Options

If you're a vegetarian who eats and enjoys fish, then Spain is an Omega-3-rich gastronomic paradise. If you don't eat fish, you'll need to be more careful in your choices, especially in Andalucía. Larger restaurants (the sort with tablecloths and *cartas* in several languages) will be used to dealing with vegetarians and those with other dietary requirements, like gluten-free dishes, but smaller bars might not be so up to speed. The following is a list of some (usually) safe options you are likely to find on many, or even most, *cartas* (Ⅴ denotes vegan):

queso — cheese ■ *tortilla* — omelette, and just eggs, potatoes (and onion) unless indicated otherwise Ⅴ*gazpacho* — this is vegetarian but sometimes comes with diced ham as a garnish Ⅴ*pisto* — Spanish ratatouille, but check it contains no meat Ⅴ*porra/salmorejo* — the thicker variants of *gazpacho* often come with ham/fish garnishes, so ask for it '*sin guarnición*' (sin gwar-nith-**yon**) ■ *croquetas* — often just cheese flavoured *béchamel*, but can also contain cod/ham; other popular flavours are *Cabrales* (blue cheese), *espinacas* & *piñones* (spinach and pine nuts), *roquefort* & *nuez* (blue cheese and walnuts), and *setas* (wild mushrooms) Ⅴ*zanahorias aliñadas* — carrots marinated in garlic, cumin, oregano and paprika ■ *espárragos con huevos* — asparagus with diced hard boiled egg (a common alternative term for asparagus is *trigueros*) Ⅴ*espinacas con garbanzos* — spinach and chickpeas Ⅴ*berenjenas* — aubergines, fried and often drizzled with *miel de caña* (molasses) Ⅴ*ajoblanco* — almond and garlic soup Ⅴ*patatas bravas/arrugadas* — sautéed/boiled potatoes with spicy tomato or other sauces ■ *patatas con alioli* — potatoes with garlic mayonnaise (real *alioli* is actually vegan but rarely encountered) Ⅴ*pimientos de Padrón* — fried/grilled peppers ■ *pimientos del piquillo* — sweet red peppers, but check if they are stuffed, and with what (it's usually cream cheese) Ⅴ*setas/hongos/champiñones* — generic terms for mushrooms, though *champiñones* are generally button mushrooms Ⅴ*tostada con tomate* — toasted bread with tomatoes, garlic and oil ■ *huevos* — eggs: *rotos* are fried with potato (but check what else), *revueltos* are scrambled, often with ham or prawns, but also commonly with white *espárragos* or *ajetes* (garlic shoots — especially delicious) Ⅴ*tomates aliñados* — tomato salad, which sounds dull, but in Spain rarely is Ⅴ*ensaladas* — *ensalada mixta* is a plain salad, but check for any other kind of salad as ham and/or fish often creep in.

⚠ Even what looks like a plain lentil stew may be prepared with a base of meat stock, and most traditional Spanish biscuits are made with lard!

🥐 Breakfast

The breakfast (*desayuno*) eaten mid-morning throughout Spain consists of toasted bread (*tostada*), with olive oil (or for more traditional *andaluces*, paprika-infused lard) and topped with tomato and salt. The bread used in Málaga is either a crusty white roll or a *mollete antequerano*, a roll from Antequera with the consistency of an English muffin. In most bars it is possible to order your *tostada* with cheese, ham, *chorizo*, pâté ('*foie*') or jam ('*mermelada*') and this 'breakfast' is usually served until lunch so it can make a reasonable midday snack if you can't manage to hang on until the Spanish 'lunchtime' of 2 pm or so.

Most people outside Spain are now familiar with *churros* — deep-fried tubular doughnuts to be dipped into chocolate. They are especially popular in Málaga, although they are piped into the oil from a round nozzle instead of a star-shaped one, giving them a smooth but slightly lumpy appearance. In Málaga they are called *tejeringos* (teh-кнeh-**rin**-goss) after the implement used to pipe the dough into the hot oil, which looks like a syringe ('*jeringa*').

💬 Useful Phrases

Hi! / Hello!	*¡Hola!*	**oh**-la
Excuse me / Sorry	*Disculpe*	diss-**kool**-peh
Yes / No	*Sí / No*	see / noh
Do you have …?	*Tiene …?*	**tyen**-neh …?
Does it have … in?	*Lleva …?*	**yay**-ba…?
Fish	*pescado*	pes-**ka**-doh
Meat	*carne*	**kar**-nay
Dairy	*lácteos*	lak-**tay**-oss
Nuts	*frutos secos*	**froo**-toss **say**-koss

I'm allergic to ...	*Soy alérgico a ... (m)*	soy al-**air**-kheeko ah ...
	Soy alérgica a ... (f)	soy al-**air**-kheeka ah ...
Without ...	*sin ...*	sin...
I can't eat…	*No puedo comer…*	noh **pway**-do kom-**air**
Do you have a menu	*Tiene una carta*	**tyen**-neh **oo**-na **kar**-ta
(in English)?	*(en inglés)?*	(enn een-**glayss**)?
How much does it cost?	*¿Cuánto cuesta?*	**kwan**-toh **kwess**-tah?
The bill, please	*La cuenta, por favor*	la **kwen**-tah, por fav-**ORR**
Thank you (very much)	*(Muchas) Gracias*	(**moo**-chass) **grath**-yass
You're welcome	*De nada.*	day **nah**-dah
Where is ...?	*Dónde está ...?*	**donn**-day ess-**stah** ...?
Goodbye	*Adiós*	add-**yoss**
I don't know	*No sé*	noh say

🥩 Cooking of Meat

Useful vocabulary for ordering steaks, burgers, etc.:

Very rare/blue	*muy poco hecho*	moy **poh**-ko **ech**-oh
Rare	*poco hecho*	**poh**-ko **ech**-oh
Medium rare	*en punto*	enn **poon**-toh
Medium	*punto pasado*	**poon**-toh pah-**sah**-doh
Medium well	*hecho*	**ech**-oh
Well done	*bien hecho*	byenn **ech**-oh

Bebidas (Drinks)

☕ Chocolate

Spain was the first place in Europe where chocolate was consumed (as a beverage). Although Columbus brought cocoa beans back to Spain in 1504, it was not until Spanish settlers in what are now Mexico and Guatemala developed a taste for drinking chocolate that it began to be consumed in Spain. When solid chocolate was perfected in 1847 (by Fry and Sons in Bristol, UK) that, too, would take Spain by storm.

Drinking chocolate (*chocolate a la taza*) is powdered bitter-sweet dark chocolate that is mixed with hot milk and sugar and, usually, thickened with cornflour and enjoyed with *tejeringos*.

☕ Café

Visitors to Spain either love the coffee or hate it. The two main kinds encountered are '*natural*' and '*mezcla*' (a mix of natural and '*torrefacto*'), the latter being the more traditional and widely consumed of the two. *Mezcla* blends are a result of the '*torrefacto*' process in which the raw beans are sprayed with a fine mist of sugar solution before roasting.

The most common coffee orders in Spain are:

café solo — an espresso/lungo shot; if you ask simply for '*un café*' this is what you'll get.

café con leche — espresso topped up with milk, but stronger than an Italian latte. You may be asked whether you want cold (*fría*), room-temperature (*templada*), or hot (*caliente*) milk.

café cortado — espresso with a smaller quantity of milk; stronger than a flat white.

café Americano — an espresso shot diluted with hot water (can also be *con leche*)

Fed up with wasting cups of coffee not precisely to a customer's taste at a time when coffee, milk and sugar were extremely expensive, in the 1950s the owner of Málaga's Café Central devised nine basic ways to order a coffee. The clientele got used to it and years later they were captured in tiles by the artist Amparo Ruiz de Luna (who added a humorous tenth option). These names are now used throughout Málaga, though if you try to order an '*entre corto*' anywhere else in Spain, you'll receive a puzzled look.

Every cup of coffee in Spain (at least in traditional bars and cafés) will come with a sachet of sugar that contains up to three or four teaspoons of sugar. If you want artificial sweetener, the word is *edulcorante* (ay-**dool**-ko-**ran**-tay). The word *sacarina* is also widely used.

	Name in Málaga	Translation	Coffee	Milk	Similar to:
	Solo	'just' coffee	100%	0%	*espresso, lungo*
	Largo	long	90%	10%	*macchiato*
	Semi Largo	half long	75%	25%	*macchiatone*
	Solo Corto	short *'solo'*	60%	0%	*ristretto*
	Mitad	half (& half)	50%	50%	*cortado*
	Entre Corto	inter–short	40%	60%	'flat white'
	Corto	short	30%	70%	*caffè latte*
	Sombra	shadow	20%	80%	
	Nube	cloud	10%	90%	
	No me lo ponga	'Don't give me any'	0%	0%	

♪ *Vino* (Wine)

Viticulture has been practised in Spain for what seems like forever, and this is not much of an exaggeration. There is evidence to show that vines grew in the Peninsula as far back as the so-called Tertiary Period (which ended 2.6 million years ago), and that these grapes were cultivated some-time between 4000 and 3000 BC, long before the Phoenicians founded Cádiz around 1100 BC. It is thought that grapes for wine were first grown in the Province of Málaga in the sixth century BC. The Carthaginians, armed with the Punic texts of the agriculturalist Mago, improved on the wine-making techniques of the Phoenicians, but real wine history and culture began after the Romans won the Punic Wars against the Carthaginians and the Peninsula became 'Hispania'. Indeed, the oldest archaeological evidence of winemaking is from the late second century AD — a fermentation tank uncovered in the town of Cártama, about 25 miles from the city of Málaga.

Spanish Wine Classifications

Spanish wines are still frequently described as coming from a par-ticular '**DO**' (*denominación de origen* — 'designation of origin'). The term is still used, but in 2016, Spain began using the EU system of designation based on the '**DOP**' – (*denominación de origen protegida* — 'protected denomination of origin'). This designation covers not only wine but fruit, ham, cheese, honey, seafood, rice, and much more.

In the case of wine, a **DOP** may be **DOCa/DOQ** (denomination of qualified origin, *viz.* Rioja and Priorat), **DO** (*e.g.* Málaga), **VP** (*vino de pago* or 'estate wine') or **VC** (*vino de calidad*, quality wines with a geographic indication). Below the **DO** level are **IGP** wines (*indicación geográfica protegida*, protected geographical indication), and many of these are excellent quality. The lowest classification is **VdM** (*vino de mesa*, that is, table wine) — usually blended bulk wine, but occasion-ally it could be a very fine wine that simply does not satisfy the rules of the DO (because of the use of an unapproved grape variety, for example). This complex hierarchy of classification can be confusing, to say the least.

🍷 Málaga Wines

If a viticulturist in the Province of Málaga wants to join an appellation (DOP), he or she has several options. They could join DOP Málaga by fol-lowing its regulation. Another option would be to join DOP Sierras de Málaga (Málaga Mountain Ranges DOP) which has a different regulatory structure. These two wine regions overlap, so the regulation differs while the geographical area is exactly the same. In the subzone of Manilva or Axarquía, a viticulturist could join the DOP Pasas de Málaga (Málaga Raisins DOP) though this focuses on table grapes, not grapes for wine-making. Yet another option would be to join two DOPs (or even all three of them) by registering different vineyard plots to different appellations. This means that the Regulatory Council that controls the three DOPs will supervise each plot depending upon to which DOP it has been assigned. The two wine DOPs cover 3,800 ha (9,390 acres) and produce almost 2.5 million litres annually. The main varieties cultivated are still Moscatel de Alejandría and Pedro Ximénez (often known as Pero Ximén in the Málaga region), reflecting the historical importance of sweet wines.

When it comes to wine, not raisins, DOP Sierras de Málaga makes more conventional table wines (reds, rosés, whites; *tintos, rosados, blancos*) whilst DOP Málaga makes sweet and fortified wines or *vinos generosos*. The traditional wine style of Andalucía is the sweet or dessert style, and the familiar red/rosé/white styles are more recent, with a number of *bodegas* (wineries) switching to table wines in recent years. Though if we go back even further, the wines of the area were probably lighter and drier than those produced now, with the fortified style being developed because it maintained its quality for export (a long sea voyage) and appealed to British tastes (a big export market).

History

After the *reconquista*, the Brotherhood of Viñeros de Málaga was created in 1487. Some years later, on 12 January 1502 in Seville, the *Reyes Católicos* confirmed the creation of the Fraternity of Vintners by Royal Decree. The guild privileges were confirmed again by their daughter Queen Juana (of Castilla) in 1513.

Although soon eclipsed by Sherry, Málaga wine was once hugely popular in Britain and throughout Europe. In 1791, Miguel de Gálvez y Gallardo, the Spanish ambassador to Moscow, presented Catherine the Great with some cases of Málaga wine, and we assume that it met with her approval because all shipments of wine controlled by the Fraternity of Vintners were soon afterwards exempted from Russian tariffs.

One assumes, too, that Málaga wine enjoyed some popularity in Russia generally because it is mentioned by Fyodor Dostoevsky in his novella *The Dream of a Ridiculous Man*. Throughout the 18th century, Málaga wine grew in popularity, while Sherry declined. In the 19th century, the situation was reversed, largely due to the commercial preferences of British merchants. It was not Málaga wine that filled colonial decanters in Madras, Melbourne and Mombasa, but Sherry wine.

More recently, there has been a modest resurgence of sweet wine and

Málaga wines are beginning to rediscover their position in the world. Twenty years ago, many were convinced that the most traditional bars in Málaga would have to shut their doors as the thirst for sweet wine declined. So far, this has not happened. If anything, there has been a revival.

▦ Subzones

There are five geographical sub-areas within the Málaga, Sierras de Málaga, and Pasas de Málaga DOPs (remember that they overlap): Axarquía, Costa Occidental-Manilva, Montes, Norte and Serranía de Ronda.

Axarquía

Axarquía (from the Arabic, *al-sarqiyya*, 'the east') is located in the eastern part of the province and it extends from the coast up into the mountains. Here, Moscatel de Alejandría (Alexandria Muscat) has been grown for more than two thousand years. Another high-profile grape is the indigenous Romé (used to make *blancos* and *tintos*) which is well adapted to the subtropical conditions of mild weather and little rainfall alongside considerable moisture due to proximity to the sea. The whole area is famous for its raisins (*pasas*).

Costa Occidental-Manilva

The wines from the western coastal area have had to compete with bricks and mortar with the growth of the tourist resorts along the Costa del Sol. Nonetheless, wine varieties, table grapes and raisins are still produced here. The main variety is (as usual) Moscatel de Alejandría, but Cabernet Sauvignon, Merlot, Syrah and Tempranillo also have increasing shares.

Montes

Málaga's municipality is surrounded by a steep hill range with very diverse vine-growing conditions, which allows wineries to make a wide range of table wines (*tinto*, *rosado* and *blanco*), sweet wines, and liqueur (fortified) wines. Two famous local *bodegas* are Antigua Casa de Guardia (also the name of a tavern on the Alameda Principal in Málaga) and Quitapenas. The main varieties are Pedro Ximénez (or Pero Ximén as it is known here) and various varieties of Moscatel (Muscat). In its heyday, Montes was known for producing the finest examples of Málaga wine and in the 18th century many British decanters had silver labels engraved with the name 'Mountain'. Dark (*tinto*) wines were anglicized as 'Tent'.

Norte

The little-known Doradilla grape variety is indigenous to this subzone, although Pero Ximén is also very common. Unlike areas such as Axarquía or Montes, the vineyards are planted in fertile soils and on largely flat ground. The climate is continental, rather than subtropical.

Serranía de Ronda

Almost half of the wineries belonging to the DOP Sierras de Málaga are situated in the Serranía de Ronda ('Ronda mountain range'). At an altitude of over 700 m, the focus in this zone is more on table wines than on traditional sweet and fortified wines. As a result, 'new' (to Spain, or to the region) varieties like Chardonnay, Cabernet Sauvignon, Merlot, Syrah and Tempranillo have become more and more common. Some of Málaga's best quality wines come from here.

DOP Sierras de Málaga

Types Of Wine

DOP Sierras de Málaga covers 'still wine' production. Red, Rosé and White (*tinto*, *rosado* and *blanco*) types are produced.

The authorized white grape varieties are Pero Ximén (Pedro Ximénez), Moscatel de Alejandría (Alexandria Muscat), Small Berry Muscat (Morisco), Chardonnay, Colombard, Doradilla, Airén, Gewürztraminer, Macabeo (Viura), Riesling, Sauvignon Blanc, Verdejo and Viognier.

The permitted red varieties are Romé, Cabernet Franc, Cabernet Sauvignon, Garnacha (Grenache), Graciano, Malbec, Merlot, Monastrell (Mourvedre), Petit Verdot, Pinot Noir, Syrah, Tempranillo and Tintilla (Tintilla de Rota).

Classification according to the ageing process is the same as for all Spanish table wines:

- **Crianza** ('ageing'): At least 2 years ageing between both oak barrel and bottle. The barrel ageing should last for at least 6 months.

- **Reserva**: At least 3 years ageing between both oak barrel and bottle. The barrel ageing should last for at least 12 months.

- **Gran Reserva** (for red wines): At least 5 years ageing between both oak barrel and bottle. The barrel ageing should last for at least 24 months.

- **Gran Reserva** (for white and rosé wines): At least 2½ years ageing between both oak barrel and bottle. The barrel ageing should last for at least 6 months.

DOP Málaga

DOP Málaga produces both 'liqueur wines' and what, to most British palates, seem like 'sweet' wines, even if some are officially 'dry'. There are multiple ways of classifying and describing wines of this DOP, reflecting its very long history of winemaking. Málaga wines are known by many different names as they can be classified in different ways:

Classification according to ageing in oak:

- *Málaga Pálido* ('Pale Málaga'), up to 6 months, but usually unaged.
- *Málaga* from 6 to 24 months.
- *Málaga Noble* ('Noble Málaga'), from 2 to 3 years.
- *Málaga Añejo* ('Old Málaga'), from 3 to 5 years.
- *Málaga Trasañejo* ('Very Old Málaga'), over 5 years.

Classification according to the sugar content:

- *Dulce* (sweet)
- *Semidulce* (semi-sweet)
- *Abocado* or *Semiseco* (semi-dry)
- *Seco* (dry)

Classification according to varietal:

- **Pero Ximén** (Pedro Ximénez)
- **Moscatel** (de Alejandría)

Classification according to must:

- *Lágrima* ('Tear'): Made from the first treading (pressing) of grapes, without mechanical extraction.

Classification according to colour:

Wine becomes darker the longer it is aged in the barrel, but also the more *arrope* (concentrated grape syrup) is added.

- *Dorado* or **Golden**: Usually an unfortified naturally sweet wine that has been oak-aged. (Both the Spanish and the English names are recognized by the DOP due to the important historical trade of these wines with the British Isles.)

- *Rojo dorado* or **Rot Gold:** An aged liqueur wine made with less than 5% *arrope* (grape syrup) added by volume. (The German term is recognized by the regulator, again for historical reasons.)

- *Oscuro* or **Brown**: 5–10% *arrope* added by volume.

- *Color:* 10–15% *arrope* added.

- *Negro* or **Dunkel:** ('dark'): More than 15% *arrope* added.

Classification according to style:

- **Dry Pale** or **Pale Dry:** a liqueur wine without *arrope* that contains less than 45 grams of sugar per litre.

- **Pale Cream:** Either a liqueur wine without *arrope*, a wine of natural sweetness, or a naturally sweet wine (unfortified) that contains more than 45 grams of sugar per litre.

- *Pajarete* ('Little bird'): This is an amber fortified liqueur that has a total sugar content of between 45 g and 140 g per litre. It is an oak-aged wine made without any addition of *arrope* (concentrated grape syrup).

- *Dulce Crema* or **Cream:** An amber oak-aged liqueur wine that contains between 100 and 140 grams of sugar per litre.

- **Sweet:** An oak-aged liqueur wine that contains more than 140 grams of sugar per litre. The colour ranges from amber to almost black.

🍾 Sparkling Wine

A number of *bodegas* in the Málaga DO areas produce sparkling wine (*blancos* and *rosados*); mainly sweet or semi-sweet, but with an increasing number of dry styles appearing in recent years. However, although these wines are made in the Málaga region from locally grown grapes, they are not Málaga DO wines because neither Málaga wine DOP authorizes sparkling wines (*vinos espumosos*)… at least not yet.

🍊 Orange Wine

The 'orange wine' that has grown in popularity in the UK in recent years is essentially a version of rosé, but made with white grapes. By contrast, Spanish '*vino naranja*' actually contains orange. The best-known, '*Vino Naranja del Condado de Huelva*', is a fortified sherry-type wine where bitter orange peel is macerated in young wine. The (accidental) dark orange colour is due to the use of sun-dried grapes.

A version of *vino naranja* is made in Málaga, albeit by a different method. Dried bitter orange peel is macerated in grape spirit which is then added to sweet Moscatel wine. Málaga's *vino naranja* is almost clear in appearance, and far lighter on the palate than the version from Huelva.

🍇 Cartojal

Cartojal, a sweet white wine made by Bodegas Málaga Virgen, is the party drink of Málaga, If you are not in the city during the *feria* (the annual fair held in August) then you may not encounter it. If you are in Málaga for the fair, you cannot miss it. It is made from the Moscatel de Alejandría grape, a grape native to Málaga and mainly grown in the Axarquía region. The other grape used to make Cartojal is the Moscatel Morisco grape which is grown in the Montes zone. The harvest of these grapes traditionally takes place at night, to avoid the intense heat of the day.

The name of the wine is taken from the slightly differently spelt Cartaojal, a village located near the vineyard, where the grape dehydration process, or *paseras*, takes place. The grapes are spread out and dried under the sun, in order to increase sugar levels in the fruit, contributing to the wine's unique flavour and aroma.

🛢️ 🍷 Guided Tours and Tastings

The oenotourism (*enoturismo*) scene in Spain has developed considerably over the last couple of decades. Guided tours of wineries in La Rioja have helped draw tourists to the region for many years, and in Catalonia they have become a way of tempting tourists away from the attractions of Barcelona and into the countryside. In the case of the sherry towns — Jerez, El Puerto de Santa María and Sanlúcar de Barrameda — tours of sherry houses are one of the main draws for foreign tourists.

There are only two wineries left in Málaga city, but there are many others scattered throughout the province, producing wines with the *Denominación de Origen* of Málaga and Sierras de Málaga.

Milamores (Ronda)

📍 Calle Guadalcobacin s/n, Ronda
🌐 milamoresronda.com
✉️ info@milamoresronda.com 📱 +34 656 543 343

In addition to being the main agent for booking visits to the Bodega F. Schatz, Milamores, run by the helpful and friendly Antonio Martínez, also organizes tours of other wineries near Ronda, as well as organizing tastings at hotels and in homes. Although you can book via Milamores and they will often conduct the tour and tasting, this does not obviate the need to organize your own transport as they will meet you at the main entrance of the *bodega*. Although the website is in Spanish, tours and tastings can be conducted in English. If you have any questions about Milamores' services, don't hesitate to contact Don Antonio.

White Houses Tours

🌐 whitehousestours.com
✉️ info@whitehousestours.com 📱 +34 634 542 355

This small company, founded by Rodrigo Romojaro and based in Benalmádena, offers tours (including transport) of Bodegas Pérez Hidalgo in Álora with a tasting of 5 wines (3.5 hours). There is also an option to combine this with a visit to the olive oil factory for an olive oil tasting (combined tour: 5 hours). The pick-up point is outside the Tourist Information Office in the Plaza de la Marina in Málaga for a 10 am departure. Tours are limited to a maximum of 7 people, so you can be sure of personal service. They also offer visits (with transport) to a *bodega* in Ronda, a bull-breeding finca, a reserve raising the *ibérico* pig (with *embutidos* tasting), a sherry *bodega*, and more besides.

Rootz Wine Tours

🌐 rootzwinetours.com 📱 +34 644 755 966

If you want to visit a couple of *bodegas* in comfort without worrying about transport, then Rootz Wine Tours could be the answer. Run by Nicky Lloyd (who is originally from the UK), this small company offers several options for winery visits and tastings, covering four of the main five wine-growing areas of the Málaga DOPs: Manilva (Costa Occidental), Serranía de Ronda, Norte (Antequera) and La Axarquía. Nicky is a qualified guide and holds a Level 4 Diploma (DipWSET) from the Wine & Spirit Education Trust.

The tours might seem expensive, but the prices are actually pretty competitive given that the tours are kept small (between 2 and 7 people), last all day, are accompanied by a professional guide, and Rootz Tours will collect you from your accommodation in Málaga (or elsewhere on the Costa del Sol). Most tours take in two or more wineries, and all include lunch.

Oletrips

🌐 oletrips.es 🕐 Consult website for availability
💬 +34 616 598 515

Based in Nerja, this company is run by a young couple (Cipriano and María) and offers a range of tours and 'experiences', mainly in the Axarquía region. There are tours of *pueblos blancos*, visits to avocado and mango plantations, and olive oil tastings as well as a couple of options that offer visits (with tastings) to *bodegas*. Tours are small (no more than 8 people), include lunch, and transport is included. The pick up point can be between Torre del Mar and Nerja (you can take an early bus from Málaga).

El Colmao Wine & Experiences

📍 Calle Real 32, Frigiliana
🌐 elcolmaowineandexperiences.com 🕐 Mon–Fri by prior arrangement

This artisan wine bar and wine merchant in Frigiliana offers three winery tours, as well as winery tours with the optional additions of hiking, horse riding or sailing. Two are in La Axarquía (two wineries, or a winery and a raisin vineyard), and one is in the Serranía de Ronda. The prices drop if you are a group of five or more, but the tours include transport from your accommodation in Málaga (or east of Málaga).

Cerveza (Beer)

Málaga's local brewery, **Cerveza Victoria**, has also enjoyed a spectacular Renaissance in recent years. The Victoria brewery is named after *Santa María de la Victoria* (Our Lady of Victories), co-patroness of the city of Málaga, having been founded on her feast day (8 September) in 1928. The beginning of the tourist boom on the Costa del Sol led to a period of sustained growth. In 1952 they began using the slogan '*Malagueña y Exquisita*' ('From Málaga, and Exquisite'), and in 1958 they began featuring on their advertising posters '*El alemán de la Victoria*' ('the German of Victoria') — a cartoon depiction of a portly German tourist enjoying a glass of Victoria beer while mopping his brow in the summer heat. Both the slogan and the image are still used today.

Having all but disappeared from sale under the anti-free market Franco dictatorship, Victoria reappeared in supermarkets in the 2000s and, in 2007, they returned to bars both on draught and in bottles (*tercios*). On 7 September, 2017, on the eve of the company's 89th anniversary, Victoria inaugurated a vast new factory in the Guadalhorce Industrial Park near the Atlético Malagueño football stadium and not far from the airport.

Victoria Brewery Guided Tour and Tasting

If you are interested in beer and would like to explore what is probably the most modern brewery in Spain (if not Europe) then the Victoria Brewery offers 90-minute guided tours, including tastings of their beers. Tours are conducted in Spanish or English (though there are more dates for Spanish tours available) here: **bit.ly/VictoriaBeerTour**. The brewery is very easy to get to from the city centre: 🚌 **9**, **5** or **10** / 🚇 **L2**. Book as early as possible!

🍺 *Cerveza Artesanal* (Craft Beer)

Whereas 'real ale' and 'craft beer' began to take off in Britain and the United States in the 1980s, the explosion came much later in Spain. In fact, the global financial crisis played a significant role, with people setting up small-scale brewing businesses after finding themselves unable to find work in their former professions.

Some *Malagueño* Craft Breweries

It would be pointless to list the names of individual beers because craft breweries tend to bring new beers to market in quick succession and often brew seasonally. However, the following are some of the main producers:

Cerveza La Axarca is a brewery in Frigiliana which claims to 'have captured the essence of Axarquía' (whatever that is).

Cervezas Gaitanejo is located in Ardales. Gaitanejo has been operating since 2014.

Cervezas Malnombre 'Bad Name Beers' is located in Villanueva del Rosario, in the mountains north of Málaga (Mal Nombre is the name of a famous cave near the town).

Trinidad Cerveza Artesana de Málaga brew their beers in Alhaurín el Grande.

Cerveza Puente Nuevo produce a Blonde and Pale Ale in a very unusual manner: for four months the beer remains submerged at 16 degrees in a secret marine plot near a beach in Estepona.

3Monos — *Tres Monos* or Three Monkeys is a small brewery located in Málaga city itself. Their growing range of beers are highly fermented and neither filtered nor pasteurized. **3monoscraftbeer.com**

BenalHop Beer was born in a brewpub called La Caravana in Benalmádena. They began with three beers — an unfiltered lager, an APA and an IPA.

La Catarina Craft Beer is a microbrewery that emerged in 2012, attached to a bar and restaurant in Estepona and has become one of the best-known craft breweries in Andalusia.

84Brewers have created a beer that is aged for a fortnight in Pedro Ximénez French oak barrels.

Bonvivant Beer is an independent craft brewery located in Málaga city that, in addition to having its own variety of beers, has a lively taproom (♀ Calle Diderot 11 ⊕ bonvivant.beer) with 12 beers on tap and food served — check social media for hours. It's a bit of a trek from *centro* (about 40 minutes: 🚌1), but well worth a visit for beer fans.

 *Vermú*

Vermouth is known as *vermú* (bai**RR**-**moo**) in Spanish. You will often see it spelt (and hear it pronounced) as *vermut* (the Catalan word) because Reus in Catalonia is a major centre of its production. However one spells it, *vermú(t)* is one of the most *castizo* (authentic) fixtures of Spanish *aperitivo* culture, and yet one that few visitors ever bother to try (despite being rather pleased with themselves at how authentically they have embraced '*tapas* culture'). In fact, the drink gives its name to the pre-lunch aperitif, which is known as '*la hora del vermú*' (roughly 1 pm–2 pm) whether or not vermouth is being consumed.

Spaniards drink it neat on ice, sometimes with *sifón* (soda). Because *vermú* is the *aperitivo* par excellence, you will sometimes be given a very modest *tapita* with each glass — usually crisps, olives or a mixture of cornichons and cocktail onions. A common *tapita* is the '*gilda*' — an olive, cocktail onion, anchovy and cornichon threaded onto a cocktail stick to form a tiny kebab. It is named after the character played by Rita Hayworth in the eponymous 1946 film. The reason for the name, it is said, is that like Ms Hayworth, these little cocktail bites are 'spicy' and make a man feel hungry.

Some Good Spots for Vermú in Málaga
Bodega–Bar El Pimpi
Casa Lola
La Odisea Tienda de Vinos
La Tranca
Antigua Casa del Guardia
Bodeguita El Gallo
La Pechá
Más Vermut
Vermutería La Clasica

♥Ginebra (Gin)

The main British gin varieties are all available in Spain; indeed it's the second-largest export market for British gin after the USA. Most popular are Gordon's (which here is export strength, 40%), Beefeater, Bombay Sapphire and Tanqueray. If you order a G&T, you will probably be offered a choice of gins, with the more expensive imported brands being pushed. Ask instead for a *nacional* (nath-yoh-**nall**, *i.e.* Spanish) gin — slightly cheaper and just as good, or better quality. There are over 40 widely available Spanish *marcas* (brands), the most popular of which are originally from Andalucía: **Larios** (once, but no longer, distilled in Málaga) and **Rives** (from El Puerto de Santa María). Their export strength lines are, respectively, **Larios 12** (**la**-ryoss **doh**-THay) and Rives Special (**ree**-bess speTH-**yall**).

Gins produced in the Málaga Province

Simbuya (Cuevas Bajas) The '*morá*' carrot grown on the banks of the Genil has inspired one of the most unusual gins made in the province of Málaga. The company ESALI, has created 'the only gin in the world made with the purple carrot'. There are two versions: **Simbuya Classic** (more classic in style) and **Simbuya Purple** (sweeter on the palate).

Gin Ballix (Vélez-Málaga) is a premium gin that has Osteen mango as an added element, together with juniper, coriander and angelica.

Gin 1895 (Ronda) is made by El Tajo Distilleries, located in Ronda. They also make seasonal and limited edition gins with hints of strawberry, cinnamon, blackberry or mint, as well as **Tagus**, a non-premium (*i.e.* < 40% ABV) London Dry-style gin.

Malaka Gin (Málaga) Carlos Villanueva, owner of the Gin Tonic Bar chain makes 2 gins under the name **Malaka**. One of them is a traditional 'London Dry' for those looking for the most classic flavours. The other has 'a Mediterranean touch with a faint undercurrent of jasmine.'

Oxén Spiritus London Dry Gin (Ojén) The Sierra de las Nieves inspired this gin made in the town of Ojén. The botanicals are coriander, cardamom, and angelica, as well as other plants grown in the Sierra de las Nieves, such as juniper, thyme, rosemary, bitter chamomile and apple mint. A hint of citrus comes from dry lime and tangerine peel. One of the most interesting Málaga gins, to my mind.

Alborán Gin (Almáchar) In addition to a classic gin, where juniper predominates with touches of citrus and some spices, this range also includes 'Orange', 'Lemmon' [*sic*], 'Strawberry' and, more recently, 'Exotic' (with watermelon and melon).

Eating and Drinking

Although Málaga is the fastest-growing tourist destination in Spain, no establishment can survive simply by serving chicken nuggets to unsuspecting foreigners; at least not in the centre where rents are high. The happy result is that there are remarkably few duds.

Regarding the following suggestions, nothing should be read into the order in which they are listed. If you would like to check recent reviews, then have a look on Google (or even TripAdvisor) but, for any establishment, on this list or not, make your own judgement. Look at the menu, take a look inside, observe the other customers, and decide whether it's your sort of place.

🗺 Map

Because the centre of Málaga is fairly compact and walkable, I have listed bars and restaurants only very loosely by location. The companion map will help to show where the places are. Visit **bit.ly/MalagaMap** to consult it (on a mobile device you will need to click on **LEGEND** or the map name at the bottom of the screen to choose which POIs to display).

⚠ *Caveat Lector*

Between writing the first draft of this book and preparing it for publication, six of the establishments I had recommended closed. In 2022, the iconic Café Central closed its doors after 100 years, so nowhere is immune. Málaga is a city on the move and the pace of change is fast. Some of the restaurants and bars listed below may not survive, but others will open in their stead.

Also, opening times are frequently subject to change and can vary seasonally, so the following information is intended to be a rough guide.

✖️ Symbols

Most of the symbols relating to food and drink are intended to give a quick impression of a particular establishment, so are **not comprehensive**. The symbols are intended to denote a speciality.

✖️	restaurant/*comedor*		traditional dishes
🍷	bar	🌍	world/fusion cuisine
	tasting menu ('*menú degustación*')	🥩	steaks or grill
📖	reservations	🥕	vegetarian options
	reserve on www.thefork.co.uk		salads
G	reserve on Google	🐟	fish
	menú del día		seafood
	children's menu		sandwiches/*tostadas*
	tapas		egg dishes
	raciones/medias raciones		cheese
	wine list		soup/stews
	Málaga wine/*vermú*		rice dishes
🍸	cocktails		puddings
	beers		fast food
☕	coffee		breakfast/*almuerzo*
	take away food or drink		sweet bakery/*merienda*
	delivery	🍦	ice cream

🗓 Eating on Monday

Like anywhere else in Europe, Monday is not a good day for fresh fish (*bacalao* is fine because it is dried and salted, ditto '*rosada*' which is mainly frozen). And if fish is on as a 'special' on a Monday then avoid it because it is likely to be 'on the turn' and they are trying to get rid of it.

In fact, Monday is not a great day for eating full stop. Traditionally it is the weekly holiday for the tourism and hospitality sectors. Museums and galleries are mostly closed, and many bars and restaurants preserve the Monday closure '*por descanso del personal*' ('to give the staff a rest'). A few top-drawer restaurants with an eye on Michelin stars, bib gourmands and so forth, will be at the top of their game whenever you visit. Other restaurants that do stay open on a Monday, it's likely to be the Head Chef's day off, so the 'B Team' will be cooking for you. This is often the case on Sunday evening, too — the second quietest night of the week for eating out. Choose a simple *tapas* place instead and leave the sit-down (or more expensive) meals for other days of the week.

💰 Prices

Price categories can be pretty meaningless. One can eat cheaply or expensively in most establishments. For example, at La Taberna de Monroy, a solid 'foodie' place, the cheapest starter and main course (together) might set you back, say, €15, whereas the most expensive choices would come to almost €50. Meanwhile, a bar where no dish costs more than €10 might sound cheap, but if it's a *tapas* bar, then that would put it at the pricier end. I have used a jasmine flower (the symbol of Málaga) to give a rough guide to price/value:

✿	Cheaper than average for its type
✿✿	About average for its type
✿✿✿	Pricier than average, but reflecting superior quality
✿✿✿✿	Top-end, luxury dining, a special treat

🍴 *Restaurantes* (Restaurants)

The following is a list of what I call 'tablecloth restaurants' — establishments with waiter service where you will dine at a table using cutlery from a menu on which dishes are (broadly) categorized by course. However, in choosing somewhere to dine, do not forget that many bars are also effectively restaurants, and vice versa.

Muelles

Cambara ✳✳✳

🍽 MUELLES 📍 Muelle Uno, Local 65 🌐 📖 cambara.es
🕐 Mon–Thu 1200–0100; Fri–Sat 1200–0200
✕ 🍶 🍸 🍤 🦐 🦀 🍵 🍹

This is a luxuriously decorated restaurant and cocktail bar serving 'elevated' Spanish classics. Service can sometimes seem a little slow to foreigners, but it is friendly and attentive.

Amigos Grill Muelle Uno ✳✳

🍽 MUELLES 📍 Muelle Uno, Local 59
🌐 amigosmuelleuno.com 🕐 1200–1800; 2000–2230
✕ 📖 🍴 ♨ 🌍

A somewhat gaudily decorated restaurant that serves Indian, Mexican, Greek and Argentinian food and therefore normally the sort of establishment that I would advise you to run a mile from. However, the food is tasty, the service is warm and there is a lovely family atmosphere.

Gaucho Grill ✳✳

🍽 MUELLES 📍 Muelle Uno, Local 61
🌐 gauchogrillmalaga.com/en 🕐 1200–1800;
2000–2230 ✕ 🌍 🍤

This Argentinian *parrilla* (grill) is owned by the same group as Amigos restaurant (they share a kitchen). The owner, Jaydeep Singh, opened his first restaurant just before the financial crisis of 2008 and now has a chain of seven popular eateries in Málaga and Benalmádena Costa.

Angus ✳✳

🍽 MUELLES 📍 Muelle Uno, Local 55
🌐 📖 angusmuelleuno.com 🕐 1300–0000 ✕ 📖 🌍 🍤
Another Argentinian *parrilla* with good (if somewhat relaxed) service. As far as the quality is concerned, Angus probably just edges it over Gaucho.

❀Restaurante José Carlos García ✳✳✳✳

🍽 MUELLES 📍 Muelle Uno, Plaza de la Capilla
🌐 restaurantejcg.com 🕐 Tue–Sat lunch & dinner
✕ 🌿 📖 🍶

Although Marbella (in the Province of Málaga) has a handful of Michelin-starred restaurants, 'RJCG' was the first restaurant in the city of Málaga to gain a star (it was joined by Kaleja in 2022). The menu is a tasting menu as one might expect. The inclusion of fried food and chilled soups is traditionally *andaluz* and throughout the menu there are constant nods to tradition and showcasing of local products.

Centro Histórico

La Reserva 12 ✿✿✿

🍽 CENTRO HISTÓRICO 📍 Calle Bolsa 12
🌐 lareserva12.com 🕐 1300–2330 🍴 🍢 🥘 🍗 🍲 🍷

La Reserva 12 specializes in typical *andaluz* cuisine. The menu is extensive and fairly pricey, but no more than an equivalent (mid-range) restaurant in London, and average for the area around Larios. It's pretty typical of popular tourist restaurants in the centre of Málaga.

Buenavista Gastrobar ✿✿✿

🍽 LA GOLETA 📍 Calle Gaona 8
🌐 📖 buenavistagastrobar.es 🕐 Thu–Mon 1300–1600, 1930–2330 🍴 📖 🕐 🍢 🌶 🍗 🍲 🌐 🍷

Run by Juan Molina and Marco Silva, both of whom have experience working in Michelin-starred kitchens, with Yolanda Muñoz running front-of-house. They also have a decent choice of vegetarians dishes.

Andino Gastrobar ✿✿

🍽 CENTRO HISTÓRICO 📍 Calle Calderón de la Barca 3
🌐 📖 andinorestaurante.wordpress.com 🕐 1300–0000 🍴 🍷 📖 🍸 🌍

Latin American *tapas* and *raciones* and, unusually for Spain, plenty of vegetarian and even vegan options. Very good cooking.

Vegetariano El Calafate ✿✿

🍽 CENTRO HISTÓRICO 📍 Calle Andrés Pérez 6
🌐 📖 vegetarianoelcalafate.es 🕐 1300–1600, Fri–Sat 2000–2200 🍴 📖 🍲 🌿

El Calafate is considered by many to be Málaga's most interesting and reliable vegetarian restaurant. The price of the *menú del día* is good value with starters of Spanish classics and slightly more exotic main courses.

El Gastronauta ✿✿

🍽 CENTRO HISTÓRICO 📍 Calle Echegaray 3
🌐 elgastronauta.es 🕐 Wed 1900–000, Thu–Mon 1230–1630, 1930–0000 🍴 🍷 📖 🌶 🕐 🍢 🌍 🌿 🍃 🍲 🍲 ⚓

The food at El Gastronauta manages to be traditional and modern. Most of the dishes are traditionally Spanish (even the *paella* is good here) with some interesting flourishes. More 'reimagined' and updated than 'reinvented'. Simple, tasty, well-cooked food and excellent friendly service.

✿ Kaleja ✿✿✿✿

🏛 CENTRO HISTÓRICO 📍 Calle Marquesa de Moya 9
🌐 📖 restaurantekaleja.com 🕐 Tue–Sat Lunch & Dinner 🍴 🦪 📖 🍷

Kaleja — the Ladino (Judaeo-Spanish) word for 'alley' — is the latest venture of the former ElBulli chef Dani Carnero and won him his first Michelin star in 2022. There are 13 and 15-course tasting menus which can be eaten in the 'Living Room' (the traditional dining room) or the 'Kitchen' (next to the open kitchen, a sort of chef's table). Both take 2½ hours to serve. You can opt for a wine pairing or take advantage of the expert advice of the sommelier, Juan Pérez, as you make your way through the 'passes'. Carnero is a fan of legumes, using beans in ways normally associated with pasta, and many of the dishes are slow-cooked. The menus feature a lot of fish and seafood and the meat is often game.

La Cosmopolita Malagueña ✿✿✿

🏛 CENTRO HISTÓRICO 📍 Calle José Denis Belgrano 3
🌐 📖 lacosmopolita.es 🕐 Mon–Sat 1330–1600, 2000–2330 🍴 📖 ① 🍷

La Cosmopolita is Dani Carnero's original Málaga restaurant (it opened in 2010). It calls itself a 'Casa de Comidas' which roughly translates as 'canteen'. The message conveyed by this tongue-in-cheek description, of course, is that this is what Gordon Ramsay would no doubt call 'good, honest food'. It is also a showcase of stellar cooking.

La Cosmo ✿✿✿

🏛 CENTRO HISTÓRICO 📍 Calle Císter 11
🌐 📖 lacosmo.es 🕐 Mon–Sat 1330–1530, 2000–2330 🍴 📖 ① 🍷

La Cosmo is Dani Carnero's latest venture, opening in 2022, and is clearly intended to be a more relaxed version of Kaleja. The décor is bright and the *carta* is concise, running to half a dozen starters, ten mains and three puddings. The cooking is faultless, bearing all the hallmarks of Carnero's signature style with no unnecessary over-complication. The menu changes regularly, reflecting seasonal availability.

Restaurante Mesón Mariano ✿

🏛 CENTRO HISTÓRICO 📍 Calle Granados 2
📘 Mesón-Mariano 🕐 Mon–Sat 1300–1630; Tue–Sat 2000–0000 🍴🍷🍸①🍷🍽🔥🍤🦪🍗🥘🍖🍲🥄🍮🍹

The founder and chef-patron, Mariano Martín recently marked 50 years of professional cooking. He still runs the kitchen, while his daughter Laura runs front-of-house. If you want to experience classical *cocina malagueña* without 'fusion' or fripperies, this is one of the best places to come. And if you like artichokes (*alcachofas*), every day around 50kg of globe artichokes are prepared to be served: fried, grilled, breaded, confited or stewed in Montilla wine. There is also a good *tapas* list.

Restaurante Balausta ✤✤✤✤

CENTRO HISTÓRICO ♀ Calle Granada 57–59
 ⊕ ⌂ **restaurantebalausta.com** ⏰ 1230–0000
 ✕🏛🍂🔖🎫

The food here is undoubtedly *alta cocina* and there is an *à la carte* menu and usually a tasting menu. The restaurant is situated in a restored patio of a renaissance *palacio*.

La Taberna de Monroy ✤✤✤

CENTRO HISTÓRICO ♀ Calle Moreno Monroy 3
 ⊕ **latabernademonroy.com** ⏰ Tue–Sat 1300–1600,
2030–2300 ✕🍷🍴🔖🎫🌐

Owned by head chef Carmen Pozo and her husband Alejandro Fernández, the Taberna de Monroy is a relative newcomer to the *malagueño* dining scene, despite its traditional atmosphere. Carmen and Alejandro are from Córdoba and the food reflects that tradition with *salmorejo* and oxtail in the *cordobés* style always on the menu. Many of the ingredients are carefully sourced from specific local producers

Mesón Antonio ✤✤✤

CENTRO HISTÓRICO ♀ Calle Fernando de Lesseps 7
 ⊕ **mesonantonio.com** ⏰ Mon–Sat 1300–2330
✕🕐🔖🦐🎺🎤🐚

This venerable institution is tucked away down an alley off the Calle Nueva and has been serving classic *cocina malagueña* for over 40 years. Paco Viñolo ran the restaurant for over 20 years and recently handed over the reins to his son Raúl. The service, like the food, is faultless. The large portions make it good value eating so it is a place best visited when hungry.

Terraza de las Flores ✤✤

CENTRO HISTÓRICO ♀ Plaza de las Flores 4
 ⊕ ⌂ **terrazadelasflores.com** ⏰ 1200–1600, 1900–
2300 ✕🍷🏛✂🕐

There are plenty of decent eateries in this square and nearby, but the Terraza de las Flores is always reliable. The prices are fair for the heart of the city centre and the food is tasty and well-prepared.

Restaurante El Jardín 1887 ✹✹

CENTRO HISTÓRICO 📍 Calle Cañón 1
🌐 eljardinmalaga.com 🕐 Mon–Fri 0900–1600, 1900–
0000; Sat 1000–1600, 1900–0000 💬 📖 **+34 635 539 284**

Founded in 1988 by Dolores Gómez de Cisneros and Miguel Trugillo Giménez and occupying a beautiful building designed by the *malagueño* architect Gerónimo Cuervo, this is a cosy and somewhat quirky restaurant overlooking the Cathedral Gardens. It has a small *carta* and specializes in *paella*. It has a moderately priced *menú del día*.

Marisquería Casa Vicente ✹✹

CENTRO HISTÓRICO 📍 Calle Comisario 2 🕐 Wed–
Sun 1230–1540, 2015–2300

This popular fish and seafood restaurant is almost hidden down a narrow side street near the Atarazanas market. The service is good (but can be a little slow when busy) and the food well cooked and reasonably priced (though excellent quality fresh fish is never 'cheap'). Most dishes are offered as *raciones* and *medias raciones*. Come early if you want a seat, because it's a popular place and there is often a queue. As a restaurant serious about fresh fish, it's closed on Monday and Tuesday.

Kortxo ✹✹✹

CENTRO HISTÓRICO 📍 Calle Salinas 3
📘 kortxomalaga 🕐 Tue–Sat 1230–1600, 2000–0000
💬 📖 **+34 951 697 209** 🚶 📖 bit.ly/KortxoFork

A clue to the style of this lovely restaurant is its name, which is the Basque word for 'cork'. The owners Jorge and Lola have recreated a typical San Sebastián bar. *Pintxos* here have intriguing names like '*Delerium*' and '*Kaos*' so you will probably need to ask for clarification from the helpful staff (most of whom speak good English).

El Descorche de Cervantes ✹✹

CENTRO HISTÓRICO 📍 Calle Álamos 8
📷 descorchemalagawinebar 🕐 Tue–Sun 1300–0100
📞 **+34 689 586 795** 🚶 📖 bit.ly/DescorcheFork

Descorche ('uncorking') is a beautiful wine bar-restaurant and a temple to the produce of Málaga, both edible and potable. The food is exquisite, highlighting the very best of the Province's produce, and the wine list is a showcase of local wine. A real treasure.

El Mesón de Cervantes ✿✿

🏨 LA MERCED 📍 Calle Álamos 11
🌐 **elmesondecervantes.com** 🕐 Wed–Mon 1900–0000
✕ 🗺 🎏 ⓘ 🔑 🚆 📞 🎇 👎 🍴 🐾 🍹

The Argentinian restaurateur Gabriel Spatz opened a *tapas* bar (El Tapeo de Cervantes) in 2008, and a few years later, this restaurant. It serves mostly *tapas* and *raciones* that are well executed under the direction of head chef Jesús, and keenly priced. This is a very reliable choice.

Alameda & Soho

Mesón Ibérico ✿✿

🏨 SOHO 📍 Calle San Lorenzo 27
🌐 🗺 **mesoniberico.net** 🕐 Mon–Fri 1300–1700,
2030–0000; Sat 1300–1700 📞 **+34 952 603 290**
✕ 🗺 🔑 🚆 📞 🍴 🐾 🍕 🚚

A very traditional *mesón* serving a huge range of *raciones* as well as *tapas* in the form of '*mini bocadillos*'. Tucked away in a corner of Soho it's slightly off the tourist radar, but is very popular with locals There is often a queue outside before it opens at 8.30 pm. Phone or call in to book ahead.

Restaurante La Marina ✿✿

🏨 ALAMEDA 📍 Alameda Principal 11
🌐 🗺 **lamarinamalaga.com** 🕐 Mon–Fri 0700–2330;
Sat–Sun 0800–2330 📲 🗺 **+34 652 841 336**
✕ 🍷 🗺 🍲 🍴 🚆 📞 👎 🍴

This bar-restaurant is one of the most popular and economical places to eat well on the Alameda Principal. One of the main reasons for its popularity is its two *menús del día*.

La Deriva ✿✿✿

🏨 SOHO 📍 Alameda de Colón 7 🌐 🗺 **laderiva.es**
🕐 Daily 1200–0130 ✕ 🍷 🗺 🎏 ⓘ 🔑 📞 🍴 🚚 🍹

The food here is 'modern Spanish' — well cooked and beautifully presented, making good use of quality ingredients. The main courses are simple, but beautifully cooked with a few carefully measured accompanying flavours chosen to showcase the meat or fish.

Óleo ✿✿✿

🏨 SOHO 📍 Edificio CAC (Centro de Arte Contemporáneo) Calle Alemania
🌐 🗺 **oleorestaurante.es** 🕐 Mon–Sat 1130–1630,
2030–0000 ✕ 🗺 🎏 ⓘ 🔑 🌐 📞 🍴

This '*malagueño*–sushi' fusion restaurant is a triumph that makes perfect sense. Japanese and Asian flavours meet traditional *andaluz* meat dishes while Spain's love for seafood makes sashimi and nigiri obvious choices.

Cávala ✦✦✦✦

🍴 SOHO 📍 Alameda de Colón 5 📞 +34 628 021 363
🕐 Daily 1330–1600, 2000–0000 ✗🦞🍸🍗🍹

This is a fairly new restaurant opened within the Soho Boutique Colón Hotel with Juan José Carmona as head chef. It is not cheap (there is a twelve-stage tasting menu and an *à la carte* menu), but it is excellent, particularly if you enjoy seafood.

La Malagueta

From the city centre, the *barrio* of La Malagueta (between the bullring and the Malagueta beach) is a pleasant 15-minute walk through the Parque de Málaga, so there's no excuse not to explore this part of the city.

Cal y Mar ✦✦

🍴 LA MALAGUETA 📍 Calle Fernando Camino 17
🌐 restaurantecalymar.com 🕐 Tue–Sat 1200–0000;
Sun 1200–1630 ✗🗺🔥🅲🎰🍴🍸⚓🐚🦐🍗🍹🍨

Ecuadorian head chef Jairon Rodríguez delivers consistently excellent food. The dishes cover the traditional bases — seafood, salads, seafood, fish, tartars, steak, pork and so forth — marrying them with more unusual flavours.

Divinno ✦✦

🍴 LA MALAGUETA 📍 Paseo de la Farola 8
📷 divinno.malaga 🕐 Sun–Thu 1200–2300; Fri–Sat
1200–2330 📞 +34 627 142 638 ✗🕐🍸

Divinno is a beautiful restaurant with clean, modern decor, a young and friendly front-of-house team, and a relaxed, local vibe. It is also one of the best restaurants in Málaga, producing perfectly executed Spanish classics albeit in a light and modern style. Most of the 'starters' are available as *raciones*, *medias raciones* and *tapas* and range from light salads and seafood to more hearty staples like *fabada* and *callos* (tripe).

Aire Gastrobar ✦✦✦

🍴 LA MALAGUETA 📍 Avenida de Príes 16
🌐 🗺 airegastrobar.es 🕐 Wed–Sat 2000–2330; Thu–
Sat 1330–1700 ✗🍷🗺🔥🅲🎰🍴🕐🍸🍷⚓

Almost opposite the English Cemetery, Aire Gastrobar is one of Málaga's most innovative small restaurants, with a beautiful, constantly evolving menu and a magnificent wine list. The chef-patron, Pepo Frade, uses local products and plays with traditional dishes, elevating and reimagining them. A reasonably priced tasting menu is available (except on Friday and Saturday evenings) and the *carta* includes a (beautifully prepared gourmet) hamburger option for children.

El Perchel

La Alacena de Francis ✽✽✽

🍴 EL PERCHEL 📍 Calle Montalbán 1
🌐 laalacenadefrancis.com 🕐 Tue–Sat 1300–1600,
1930–2300 🍴 🌶 🍷 🍽 🌍 🍦 🎀 🍸 🍹

I don't know how many Spanish–Russian fusion restaurants there are in Spain. Not many, I suspect. But this one, run by Spaniard Daniel and his Russian wife Natalia is undoubtedly the best. The Russian love of cured and smoked fish fits well with the *malagueño* love of seafood and the resulting 'fusion' is delicious. One of the specialities of the house is the platter of fish smoked by Daniel himself, featuring salmon, trout and bream. It is also one of Málaga's friendliest restaurants.

Beyond Centro

Restaurante Tita Ché ✽✽

🍴 CARRETERA DE CÁDIZ 📍 Calle Francisco de
Salinas 17
📘 titache.restaurante 🕐 Tue–Sat 1330–1600, 2000–
2330; Sun 1330–1700 💬 +34 647 190 496 🍴 🍷 🎀 🕐 🌶 🍽

This restaurant near the Parque del Oeste combines excellent cooking with great service.

Pórtico Puerta del Norte ✽✽

🍴 CARRETERA DE CÁDIZ 📍 Avda de Sor Teresa Prat 76
🌐 porticopuertadelnorte.com 🕐 Mon–Tue &
Thu–Sat 1200–1630, 2000–2330; Sun 1200–1630
📞 +34 952 657 337 🍴 🍽 🌶 🕐 🍶 🍸 🍹

Well-cooked food and friendly service. They offer a very reasonably priced *menú del día*.

Taró ✽✽✽

🍴 HUELIN 📍 Calle Tomás Echeverría 15
🌐 tarorestaurante.com 🕐 Wed–Mon 1300–0000
🍴 📖 🌶 🍽 🍸

The *taró* is the low mist that forms in the Bay of Málaga on the hottest days of the year when the cold waters of the Atlantic meet warm air from Africa. It is a very *malagueño* phenomenon, and Taró is a very *malagueño* restaurant, where local products and dishes dominate the menu. It is a modern restaurant in the *barrio* of Huelin and the cooking is as refreshingly modern as it is reassuringly traditional. The chef patron is the *malagueño* Pachu Barrera who brings an impressive CV of experience in some of Spain's finest restaurants. His local claim to fame is the invention of '*Tartar de salchichón de Málaga*' — a riff on steak tartare made with Málaga's lightly cured local sausage.

Cafetería Vanessa ✹✹

🍴 CARRETERA DE CÁDIZ 📍 Camino de la Térmica 10 👍 bit.ly/CVanessaMLG 🕐 Mon–Fri 0800–1600

✗ 🍷 🍴 ✗ ◑ ☰

This unassuming café-bar near the Parque del Oeste serves an excellent (and very cheap) *menú del día* Monday to Friday as well as doing a roaring trade in the morning for *desayuno* and *almuerzo*.

🍟 *Comida Rápida* (Fast Food)

The following are a few suggestions of 'non-traditional' eateries serving fast food and/or non-Spanish food. These recommendations might be useful to families with children or teenagers.

100 Montaditos ✹

100 Montaditos is always a good bet for a refuelling pit stop when you need something to keep you going, especially on Sundays and Wednesdays when everything on the *carta* is €1. On these 'Euromania' days, you can build quite a filling sandwich lunch, including beer or wine, for a few euros. There are branches at the railway station, the Larios Centre, near the Atarazanas market, the Teatro Romano and on Muelle Uno.

🥟 *Empanadas*

The *empanada* is the Spanish member of that culinary family which also counts the Cornish pasty, samosa, calzone and brik among its members. In Spain, it takes various shapes and forms, but always involves some kind of filled pastry. However, the little shops that have sprung up around Málaga in recent years sell Argentinian *empanadas*, which look like tiny Cornish pasties and tend to have rich fillings involving meat or cheese.

The main outlets are **Malvón (Calle Cisneros 7 & Avenida de las Américas 1, near the Railway Station), Las Muns (Calle Tomás Heredia 4 in**

Soho), El Ombú (Calle Carretería 4 & Calle Victoria 65), and **Panaditas** (Calle Granada 23). All are indicated on the companion Google map.

🍔 *Hamburguesas*

Hamburgers in Spain are generally an excellent, even gourmet, option. Even quite modest bars will produce something somewhere between 'acceptable' and 'excellent'. In short, if an establishment has a grill then they'll make a good burger. However, if you want not only a burger, but a good choice of burgers made from prime cuts of a range of meats, plus a choice of toppings, fillings and sauces as well as onion rings etc., then that means going to an '*hamburguesería*' or burger restaurant. A few notable ones are:

Kanival Burger ✽

🔸 HUELIN 📍 Calle Alfredo Catalani 2
🌐 🗺️ 🚲 **kanivalburger.com** 🕐 Wed–Sun 1300–1600, 2000–0000 🗓️ 🍴 🚲 🍺 🐷 🥗 🍽️

Hands down the best and friendliest burger restaurant in Málaga, but one which will require you to leave the centre to enjoy it (it's situated a few blocks away from the Museo Ruso, in Huelin, though they also deliver). Raúl Retamero and Juan Fernando Duque opened their small but stylish burger joint in the uncertain post-COVID landscape, but it has deservedly gone from strength to strength. Their secret is an absolute commitment to top-quality fresh and local ingredients. Burgers at Kanival tend to be cooked '*en punto*' (medium rare). There are fabulous homemade puddings on the menu, Victoria beer on draught and craft beer from the Gaitanejo brewery in Ardales by the bottle.

Bsmash by Dak Burger ✽✽

🔸 El Perchel 📍 Calle Héroe de Sostoa 14, Local 1
🌐 🗺️ 🚲 **dakburger.es** 🕐 1200–2230 🗓️ 🍴 🚲 🍺 🍽️

Dak Burger is a Málaga burger company based in La Cala de Mijas with a branch in the city centre. It's an excellent choice if you really like meat because the burgers are intensely 'beefy' with lots of umami in the toppings. Anyone used to the insipid offerings of US fast food chains may find their senses overwhelmed!

Gottan Grill Centro ✽✽✽

🔸 LA MERCED 📍 Calle Álamos 12
🌐 🗺️ 🚲 **gottangrill.com** 🕐 1300–1600, 2000–0000
🗓️ 🍴 🍷 🍺 🚲 🐚 🥗 🍽️

Gottan (*i.e.* 'Gotham') Grill offers a children's menu (drink, hamburger/nuggets, fries/potatoes and a fruit yoghurt dessert) but this is only

117

shown on the Spanish menu, so ask for a '*menú infantíl*' (men-**oo** een-fan-**teel**). They also have a branch in Huelin (**Calle Antonio Soler 5**).

Black Label Urban Grill ✽✽✽

🍴 LA MERCED 📍 Calle Álamos 22
🌐 📖 🛵 blacklabelurbangrill.com 🕐 Wed 2000–1200;
Thu–Mon 1300–1630, 2000–0000 📖 🍽 🧊 🛵 🌀 🍴

This is on the same street as Gottan Grill. Their proximity keeps their game up and their prices competitive. The reason for their perfectly cooked, juicy burger is, they say, their prized Josper Grill (a kind of combined charcoal grill and oven developed in Barcelona in the 1960s).

La Calle Burger Málaga Centro ✽✽

🍴 CENTRO HISTÓRICO 📍 Calle Mosquera 3
🌐 📖 🛵 lacalleburger.com 🕐 Mon–Thu 1300–1630,
2000–2330; Fri–Sun 1230–1630, 2000–0030 (Sun 0000)
📖 🧊 🛵 🌀 🍴

'The Street Burger' is an *andaluz* chain with a few franchises in greater Málaga. The city centre branch is on Calle Mosquera, and there are other branches near the Larios shopping centre (**Avenida de las Américas 9**) and the Parque del Oeste (**Calle Diamantino García Acosta 1**). The meat for the burgers comes from the company's own 1,300-hectare farm in the Serranía de Ronda where they raise Angus and Wagyu cattle.

Burguer Parrilla ✽

🍴 SAN FELIPE NERI 📍 Plaza de Montaño 3
🌐 burguerparrilla.eatbu.com 🕐 Mon, Wed–
Fri 1930–0100; Sat–Sun 1300–1700, 1930–0100
🌀 🕐 🧊 🛵 🌀 🍕 🍴 🌙 🍴

Located on the Plaza de Montaño, Burguer Parrilla is a no-frills burger bar a block north of the *centro histórico*. Hugely popular with locals but off the tourist radar, the burgers are homemade and delicious and the chips are hand cut rather than the more usual frozen fries. They also offer a range of homemade salads, *bocadillos* and *platos combinados*. They are also known for their *camperos* (warm sandwiches in an Antequera *mollete*).

Bocatería Los Delfines ✽

🍴 CAPUCHINOS 📍 Alameda de Barceló 16 🕐 Thu–Tue
0800–2300 🧊 🍴 🍴

Bocatería means 'sandwich bar', but not of the egg and cress variety. This bar — 'The Dolphins' — serves hearty *camperos*, *hamburguesas*, *perritos* (hot dogs), *pepitos* (hot pork baguettes), *crestas* (paprika-spiced hamburgers) and their own '*delfipollos*' (hot chicken sandwiches).

🍕 Pizza

La Pizza de María ✿

🍴 SOHO 📍 Calle Alemania 21

🌐 ♿ lapizzademaria.com 🕐 Wed–Mon 1930–2330

📞 +34 651 687 822 🍷 ♿ 🍽️

If you want a freshly made, tasty, reasonably priced and authentic pizza, then Pizza de María ticks every box. It is run by Javier and Bea from Córdoba whose family has been in the pizza business for many years. The toppings are inventive and fun, the quality of the ingredients is exceptional and the pizzas themselves are note-perfect, made with an artisanal sourdough crust. The icing on the cake is the warm and friendly service one receives here.

☕ *Cafeterías* (Cafés)

Solo   Largo   Semi Largo   Solo Corto   Mitad

Entre Corto   Corto   Sombra   Nube   No me lo ponga

Casa Aranda ✿✿

🍴 CENTRO HISTÓRICO 📍 Calle Herrería del Rey 3

🌐 casa-aranda.net 🕐 0800–1230, 1700–2100 🛋️ ☕ 🍷

Founded in 1923 by Antonio Aranda and his sister Lolita, this is one of the best and most popular places in the city centre to eat *churros* (or, rather, *tejeringos*), Casa Aranda is popular for *desayunos*, *almuerzos* and *meriendas*.

Byoko ✿✿

🍴 CENTRO 📍 Calle Strachan 5 🕐 0900–1630

🍴 MERCED 📍 Plaza de La Merced 22 🕐 Sun–Thu 0900–2230; Fri–Sat 0900–2300

🌐 byoko.es 🍴 🛵 🕐 🍷 🍽️ 🌍 🌸 ☕ 🍵 🥤 🍹 🍽️ 🛋️

Lorenzo and Rémi prepare plenty of dishes with fish, poultry, meat and ham, just of the free-range organic variety; and they serve beer and spirits (though, strangely, no wine except Cava), which is unusual for restaurants of Byoko's ilk.

Los Valle Churros ❁

🍴 EL PERCHEL 📍 Calle Cuarteles 54 ⓕ bit.ly/LosValle
🕐 Mon–Fri 0700–1200, 1730–2000; Sat 0700–1700
☕ 🍽 🍵

To my mind, this is the most charming spot for *tejeringos* in Málaga. It's in El Perchel and has an authentic, local feel. It's also *en route* to the railway station so a fine place to fortify yourself for a journey ahead.

Churrería La Malagueña ❁❁

🍴 CENTRO HISTÓRICO 📍 Calle Sebastián Souvirón 6
🌐 tejeringosmalaga.es 🕐 Mon–Sat 0730–1230,
1630–2030 ☕ 🍽 🍵

This is a modern yet traditional café specializing in *tejeringos*, so it's busy for breakfast, *almuerzos* (elevenses) and *merienda*. They serve a good range of *bocadillos* (sandwiches) and *tostadas* with range of fillings/toppings, including *zurrapa* — a spreadable mixture of pulled pork and lard.

La Bella Julieta ❁❁

🍴 CENTRO HISTÓRICO 📍 Calle Puerta del Mar 20
🌐 labellajulieta.com 🕐 Mon–Fri 0800–2100; Sat–Sun
0900–2100 ☕ 🥤 🍵 🍰

Started by Eva Mostazo and Carlos Pérez several years ago, this cafetería has other branches at **Calle Santa Lucía 9** and **Calle Córdoba 5**. La Bella Julieta offers traditional breakfast options as well as pastries, waffles, salads, avocado toast, etc.

Ana La Fantástica ❁❁

🍴 CENTRO HISTÓRICO 📍 Calle Camas 3
🌐 analafantastica.eatbu.com 🕐 Mon–Thu 0815–
1400, 1700–2000; Fri 0815–1400; Sat 0815–2000
☕ 🥤 🍽 🍵 🍰

The Spanish iteration of croissants, although tasty enough, is often a far cry from the *vrai croissant de France*, but here they are the real deal — buttery, light, flaky and perfectly layered. Ana also bakes fantastic bread, including sourdough, Galician olive bread, and walnut bread. She also prepares savoury filled croissants, *tostadas* and other brunch dishes.

La Tetería ❁❁

🍴 CENTRO 📍 Calle San Agustín 9 🌐 la-teteria.com
🕐 0900–2100 (Fri–Sun 2130) ☕ 🍵 🍰

If the cafés above are the place to go for *desayuno* and *almuerzo* then La Tetería (which means 'teapot shop') is the perfect spot for *merienda* (the afternoon snack). It is one of the few places in Málaga where you can find a decent cup of tea, made with just boiled, rather than just hot, water. They serve a wide range of cakes made on the premises.

Café-Bar El Diamante ✤

☷ CENTRO HISTÓRICO 📍 Calle Pozos Dulces 3
f 📖 **bit.ly/CBDiamante** ⏰ Mon–Sat 0730–1230
☕ 🍷 🚮 🐾

A great place for breakfast or morning snack. They serve *tostadas*, *pitufos* and *bocadillos* with a huge choice of fillings. Try the *pitufo de salchichón* (Málaga sausage sandwich). The orange juice is especially good, and an unusual and popular speciality is *leche con fresa* (layered strawberry milk).

Pastelería Ñanduti ✤✤

☷ EL PERCHEL 📍 Calle Canales 3 ⊕ **ñanduti.es**
⏰ Tue–Sat 0900–1400, 1630–2000 ☕ 🏨 🚮 🐾 🧳

Just across the river in El Perchel, this artisanal bakery/café owned by Dora Ortiz is an excellent place for breakfast (and afternoon *merienda*). They also offer some good lunchtime choices, including a '*formula de medio día*' (set lunch menu).

O Melhor Croissant Da Minha Rua ✤✤

☷ CENTRO HISTÓRICO 📍 Calle Atarazanas 13
⊕ **omelhorcroissantdaminharua.com** ⏰ Daily
0900–2030 ☕ 🍵 🚮 🐾 🧳

This Portuguese café serves only croissants, albeit with a huge variety of fillings. There are some good savoury fillings (from the time-honoured ham and cheese to chicken and parsley or salmon and cream cheese) but their popularity rests upon their menu of sweet filled croissants.

La Flor Negra ✤✤

☷ CENTRO HISTÓRICO 📍 Calle Santa Lucía 10
f **flornegravanilla** ⏰ Mon–Sun 0900–2100
☕ 🏨 ⏰ 🍵 🌸 🚮 🐾 🧳

This lovely café has tables inside and out, friendly and attentive staff and a deliciously tempting range of tarts and cakes. They serve a number of options for breakfast, as well as light savoury brunch dishes (eggs, sandwiches, focaccia, *tostadas*, etc.). They also offer a good value *menú del día*.

Desal Café ✤✤

☷ CENTRO HISTÓRICO 📍 Calle Nosquera 2
f **desalcafe** ⏰ Wed–Mon Breakfast & Brunch 📍 Calle
Ollerías 24 ⏰ Thu–Tue Breakfast, Brunch & Lunch
☕ 🏨 🍵 🚮 🐾 🧳

Desal is a portmanteau word formed from **DES**ayuno and **AL**muerzo (breakfast and brunch). The menu is modest but offers classic options like cheese and ham as well as more 'trendy' fillings like avocado and mozzarella as *pitufos*, *tostadas* and *molletes*. The café is run by Violeta Rabasco and her sister Azahara and they pride themselves on using local produce. They recently opened a second branch on Calle Ollerías and began offering a *menú del día* to extend brunch to lunch.

Cafetería Framil ✿✿

🍴 CENTRO HISTÓRICO 📍 Calle Cisneros 1
🌐 bit.ly/Framil 🕐 Mon–Fri 0800–2100; Sat 0830–1500

This simple, modern café serves mainly coffee and soft drinks (though this is Spain, so you can order wine or beer too), a dozen *tapas* and a larger choice of *pitufos* and *molletes*. There is quite a cheap (and basic) *menú del día* served from 1.30 pm Monday to Friday.

Calle de Bruselas ✿✿

🍴 LA MERCED 📍 Plaza de La Merced
16 🔲 bit.ly/CalleBruselas 🕐 1000–0200

This is a place that serves a great '*pitufo mixto*' (grilled ham and cheese roll) for breakfast. The owner, Nacho Valle stresses the importance of good bread, a touch of butter and just enough time under the grill.

Grand Café Gezellig ✿✿

🍴 SOHO 📍 Calle Trinidad Grund 33–35 🌐 gcgezellig.es
🕐 Tue–Thu 1300–0100; Fri 1300–0300; Sat 1600–0300; Sun 1300–2300

Opened quite recently by Dutch expats Naomi Uijlenhoed and Jackie Stor, it aims to recreate a traditional Amsterdam café and it more than succeeds, except that the coffee and food are much better here than in Amsterdam. Most of the menu consists of sandwiches of various kinds, both hot and cold. There are more substantial dishes too.

La Cheesequería ✿✿

🍴 LA GOLETA 📍 Calle Carretería 44
🔲 bit.ly/LaCheesequeria 🕐 Mon 1400–2100; Tue–Sun 0900–2100

This is a fairly new addition to the café scene in central Málaga and its offering is simple and delicious — nice coffee and a huge selection of homemade, delicious cheesecakes and pastries to eat-in or take away.

Taybo Coffee & Bakery ✿

🍴 LA VICTORIA 📍 Calle Victoria 45 ⊕ taybo.es ⏰ Sun 0800–1300; Mon–Tue & Thu–Sat 0800–1300, 1600–1900
☕🍰🥐

Another new addition to the Málaga café scene, opened in 2022, with Gonzo as *barista* and Dani in the kitchen. Like most modern cafés, the coffee is 'natural' rather than *torrefacto*, and the pastries are international (the *alfajores*, for example, are South American-style sandwich biscuits rather than Spanish almond fingers). A really lovely spot for coffee.

🍦 *Heladerías* (Ice Cream Parlours)

There are *heladerías* dotted all over the city centre as well as a branch of the popular frozen yoghurt outlet **llaollao (Calle Granada 23)**. Many of these serve good quality ice cream, but of the kind you can find anywhere in Spain. Outside the city centre, keep your eyes peeled for independent *heladerías* who still make ice cream locally, like **Inma (Calle Moreti 15)** in the western suburbs and **Lauri (Calle Bolivia 117)** in Pedregalejo.

Casa Mira ✿✿

🍴 CENTRO HISTÓRICO 📍 Calle Larios 5
⊕ dimasmiraehijos.es ⏰ from 1030 (Take Away)
📍 Calle Císter 8 ⏰ from 1030 (Eat In & Take Away) 🍦

Not a café, but an *heladería* (ice cream parlour). But what an ice cream parlour! At the end of the 19th century, Severino Mira left Jijona for the the then-booming city of Málaga where he intended to sell his cargo of *turrón* (nougat) transported on the backs of donkeys. After the success of his first trip, he decided to return and established a sales office.

The Mira family settled in Málaga permanently, but the *turrón* only gen-

erated income in the winter season, so, taking advantage of the traditions of the *jijoneco* ice cream makers, he also began the production and sale of ice cream. Casa Mira still makes *turrón* and other sweets, but as an ice cream parlour they are a Málaga institution. Even during the winter, their shops are busy

123

Some of the more unusual flavours include *cuajada con miel* (sheep's curd cheese with honey), *tarta de queso* (cheesecake), *milhojas* (custard *mille-feuille*), *manzana verde* (green apple), *mantecado* (the name refers to a kind of crumbly shortbread biscuit traditionally made by nuns; with subtle flavours of lemon and cinnamon), *crema tostada* (*crème brûlée*), *avellana* (hazelnut) and, not to be missed, *Málaga*. The eponymous ice cream of Málaga is the apotheosis of 'Rum-n-Raisin', flavoured with sweet Málaga wine and studded with fat, Málaga raisins macerated in the same liquor.

In addition to ice cream and sorbet, Casa Mira also serves a range of iced drinks including *granizados* (ice slush in lemon and coffee flavours), *batidos* (milkshakes), *leche fría* (cold milk), *horchata* (tiger nut milk), *granizados ácidos* (ice slushes with a scoop of ice cream), and the hugely popular *blanco y negro* ('black and white' — a coffee ice cream float).

Helados Bico de Xeado Málaga �✿

🍴 CENTRO HISTÓRICO 📍 Calle Méndez Núñez 6
🌐 galimalaga.wixsite.com/misitio 🕐 1100–2300 🍴

For something interesting and artisanal in the city centre, Bico de Xeado is worth a visit. It means 'ice cream kiss' in the *gallego* language and while ice cream is the main business, the shop also stocks a small range of food and drink products from Galicia. The '*requesón y higo caramelizado*' (Spanish ricotta and caramelized fig) ice cream is highly recommended.

Levi Angelo Gelato & Chocolate ✦✿

🍴 SOHO 📍 Calle Tomás Heredia 11 🌐 leviangelo.com
🕐 1200–2300 🍴

Owned by the *chocolatier* Levi Angelo, the ice cream sold here is exceptional, with plenty of vegan and gluten-free options. He also makes artisan chocolates, *turrón* and pralines. Certified kosher.

🍺 *Cervecerías* (Beer & Brew Bars)

Craft beer (*cerveza artesana*) is still fairly new in Spain, but if you want more than Hobson's choice, then here's my list of Málaga's top five craft beer bars (note: most restrict admission to those over the age of 18).

El Rincón del Cervecero ✦✿

🍴 SOHO 📍 Calle Casas de Campos 5
🌐 elrincondelcervecero.com 🕐 Mon–Thu 1900–0000;
Fri–Sat 1300–0000 🍴 🍺

Located in the *barrio* of Soho, this craft beer bar is modern, spacious and bright with a friendly, relaxed atmosphere. Apart from enjoying the draught and bottled beer, customers can also take a variety of brewing workshops and buy materials for home-brew.

La Fábrica ✸✸✸

📍 SOHO ⦿ Calle Trinidad Grund 29
🌐 lafabricadecerveza.com ⏰ Sun–Wed 1230–0100, Thu–Sat 1230–0200 🍴 🏙 🍽 ⚡ ◐ 🍺

Cruzcampo is the main brewery in Seville and its beer is famously... average. However, their microbrewery in Málaga is great, and they serve some really delicious beers of all different kinds — nine resident beers and a couple of guests. The main menu is slightly on the pricey side but the *tapas* menu is pretty good value and quality. Unlike the other *cervecerías* in this section, children are welcome and there is a children's menu.

La Botica de la Cerveza ✸✸

📍 LA VICTORIA ⦿ Calle Victoria 13
📷 laboticadelacerveza ⏰ 1230–1500, 1800–0100 (Fri–Sat until 0200) 🍴 🍺

Like El Rincón, La Botica is first and foremost a beer shop, but it is already starting to resemble a bar, with up to ten beers on draught. The owner, Miguel Arrabal, stocks beers from around the world, but he is especially knowledgeable about the most exciting craft beers from Spain.

Central Beers Craft Beer ✸✸

📍 CENTRO HISTÓRICO ⦿ Calle Cárcer 6
🌐 centralbeers.com ⏰ Mon–Thu 1800–0200; Fri–Sat 1300–0300; Sun 1230–0200 🍷 🏙 ⚡ ◐ 🍺

Probably the best-known beer house in the city. In style, it is modern, industrial and cosmopolitan with warm lighting. It offers up to 15 beers on draught and many more by bottle. The food *carta* is eclectic and international, but the food is tasty and filling.

La Madriguera Bar ✸✸

📍 LA GOLETA ⦿ Calle Carretería 73
🌐 🏙 lamadriguerabar.com ⏰ Mon–Thu 1900–0100; Fri–Sat 1900–0200 🍷 🏙 ⚡ ◐ 🍺

Run by the brothers Manu and Ramón, this small bar (*madriguera* means 'den' or 'lair') is perfectly judged. There are eight beers on draught and almost 70 available by bottle or can. The *carta* of *tapas* and *raciones* may look basic, but Manu has worked in Michelin-starred restaurants and produces really delicious food.

🍷🍴 *Bares de Tapas* (Tapas Bars)

Like every city and town in Spain, Málaga is well served with watering holes. The city of Málaga has well over a thousand bars: 1.84 per 1000 inhabitants. Although this is three times as many per capita than the UK it is quite a modest figure in Spanish terms. However, to put that figure in context, if you wished to visit one bar per day, Tuesday to Sunday, you would have to stay for over three years to sample them all. The following list is, therefore, merely scratching the surface; a handful of suggestions.

Centro Histórico

El Tapeo de Cervantes ✹✹

🍽 LA MERCED 📍 Calle Cárcer 8

🌐 📖 eltapeodecervantes.com 🕐 Tue–Sun 1300–1530, 1930–2330 🍴🍷🦪📖🍴🕐🔔🍽

A very traditional *tapas* bar. The food is even more traditional than the décor, with plenty of seafood, fish and rich meat dishes, though there are some surprises, like their delicious artichoke and goat's cheese quiche.

Cortijo de Pepe ✹✹

🍽 LA MERCED 📍 Plaza de la Merced 2

🌐 📖 cortijodepepe.es 🕐 1300–0000

🍴🍷📖🍴🕐🍽🌐🍷🐚🍴🍶

This is one of many bars in and around the Plaza de La Merced. It's a little place consisting mainly of a large bar with stools to sit on. There is a *terraza* for those who prefer to be outdoors and plenty of room upstairs.

El Pimpi ✹✹

🍽 CENTRO HISTÓRICO 📍 Calle Granada 62

🌐 📖 elpimpi.com 🕐 1200–0000

🍴🍷📖🍽🍴🕐🔔🍶🍷🍷🍽

This *malagueño* institution, set in an 18th-century house, runs through a warren of cavernous rooms before spilling out onto a terrace and garden. The terrace is popular thanks to its stunning views of the Roman Amphitheatre and the Alcazaba.

La Plaza ✿✿

👥 CENTRO HISTÓRICO/LA MERCED

📍 Plaza de La Merced 18 🕐 Sun–Thu 0900–2300 (☀ 0000), Fri–Sat 0900–0000 (☀ 0030)

📍 Calle Alcazabilla 7 🕐 Sun–Thu 0830–2300 (☀ 0000), Fri–Sat 0830–0000 (☀ 0030) ⊕ laplazamalaga.com ✕ 🍷 📖 💈 🕐 🍸 🌍 🍃 🍽

I would normally advise visitors to run a mile from a laminated menu with photographs and 'international dishes', but La Plaza serves reliably good quality food and, as long as you don't choose the more expensive options from the *carta*, it's pretty good value given its prime locations.

Las Merchanas ✿✿

👥 CENTRO HISTÓRICO 📍 Calle Mosquera 5

📷 lasmerchanas 🕐 1200–0000 🍷 💈 🕐 💈 🍽

This bar is dedicated to all things *Semana Santa* (Holy Week), so be prepared for walls covered from top to bottom in religious images, portraits of saints, and *Semana Santa* paraphernalia. Even the background music consists of recordings of Holy Week drum and bugle bands. The *tapas* are classic and well-prepared at a good price. The tiny bar and covered yard on Calle Mosquera is the original, but there are other branches: one just around the corner (**Calle Andrés Pérez 12**), and another in El Perchel near the Carmen market (**Plaza de la Misericordia**).

Restaurante Cofrade Entre Varales ✿

👥 CENTRO HISTÓRICO 📍 Calle Nosquera 15

⊕ entrevaralesmalaga.com 🕐 Tue–Sat 1000~1600, 2000–0000; Sun 1300–1600 ✕ 🍷 📖 🍴 💈 🕐 🍸 🍽 🍃 🍃

Just around the corner from Las Merchanas, this is another bar connected with *Semana Santa* ('*Entre Varales*' means 'between the poles', referring to the poles used to carry the thrones of Holy Week). The bar is owned by Holy Week brotherhoods and is a Formica tables and fluorescent striplight sort of place, but the staff are really friendly, the food is basic but fresh and delicious and, as this is a locals' haunt, the prices are quite a bit cheaper than in the very centre.

Antigua Casa de Guardia ✿✿

👥 CENTRO HISTÓRICO 📍 Alameda Principal 18

⊕ antiguacasadeguardia.com 🕐 Mon–Thu 1030–2200; Fri–Sat 1030–1045; Sun 1100–1500 🍷 💈 🕐 🍸 🍽 🍽

The Antigua Casa de Guardia winery has had a tavern in Málaga since 1840, so this establishment lays claim to the title of the oldest bar in the city. The peeling custard-coloured paintwork, huge wooden barrels (which are not for decoration, but full of wine), black-and-white photographs of local boy Picasso and the all-male *equipo* of bar staff all look fittingly old-school. I have overheard more than one tour guide confidently vouchsafe that the Antigua Casa de Guardia was 'Picasso's favourite bar'. This claim is extremely unlikely to be true, not least because the great painter's family left Málaga when Pablo was 10 years old.

If you want to eat something, the food (all cold) is displayed in a chiller cabinet opposite the bar. Extremely popular are '*encurtidos*' (pickles) — various salty and vinegary morsels threaded onto cocktail sticks to make little savoury kebabs. These are what I recommend your trying here. Have a look at the chilled display cabinets opposite the bar to make your choice, but most are all variations of the '*Gilda*', the little '*banderilla*' (cocktail skewer) combining pickled onions, olives, anchovies, peppers, etc.

You can buy beer as a *caña*, *tubo* or '*quinto*' (200 ml bottle), cider, a basic range of spirits (gin, rum, brandy, Ponche Caballero, *crème de menthe*, *anís seco* from Asturias or Andalucía ['*Machaco*'], and *anís dulce* from Chinchón), soft drinks, mineral water, mixers, and '*mosto*' — unfermented grape juice. Asking for '*un blanco*' or '*un tinto*' will get you an ordinary glass of white or red table wine. Everything else on the menu is a DOP Málaga wine. The alcohol content of almost all the wines on sale is 15% or 16% ABV, so make your choice based on style.

If you want to try a couple of wines first, you can ask for '*una media copa*' (half glass, **oo**-na **may**deeya **koh**-pah). *Vermú* (and any of the wines here) can be served with a dash of *gaseosa* (a slightly sweet soda — add '*con sifón*' — kon see-**fon** — to your order). *Vermú* will come with a cube of ice. You can ask for a double measure by asking for '*un doble*' (oon **doh**-blay).

Traditional Málaga wines are served from the barrels behind the bar and there is a huge range. '**Seco**' is a dry wine (though so rich and fruity it can be difficult to detect the dryness because we associate these flavour profiles with sweet things):

- Seco Málaga (**sek**-oh **mal**-ag-ah)
- Seco Añejo (**sek**-oh an-**yeh**-KHO) 3–5 years in the cask
- Seco Trasañejo (**sek**-oh trass-an-**yeh**-KHO) More than 5 years in the cask

'**Pedro Ximén**' are sweet, fairly dark wines made with the Pedro Ximén

(PX) grape and relatively familiar to non-Spanish drinkers because they are also produced by the Sherry/Jerez DOP and available in British supermarkets. It has dried fruit on the nose — always raisins, but also prunes, figs and light 'toast' in older wines — and in the mouth, generous syrup, dark fruit and a hint of spice.

- Pedro Ximén (**ped**-roh кнее-**men**) 24 months in the cask
- Pajarete (pa-кна-**ray**-tay) 36 months matured

'Lágrima' ('tear') is made from the first pressing of the grapes, so the base wine is very pale but acquires colour in the barrel. It's sweet, but not overly so, with rich caramel notes.

- Lágrima Añejo (**lag**-ree-mah an-**yeh**-кно) 3–5 years in the cask.
- Lágrima Trasañejo (**lag**-ree-mah trass-an-**yeh**-кно) 5+ years in the cask.

'Moscatel' is made mostly from Moscatel de Alejandría with significantly different flavour profiles emerging depending upon age and elaboration (*e.g.* how much *arrope* or concentrated grape syrup has been used or how the wine has been blended).

- Moscatel Dorado (mos-ka-**tell** dor-**ah**-doh) a young, golden moscatel
- Moscatel 2° (mos-ka-**tell** say-**goon**-doh) aka *Moscatel Guardia* (mos-ka-**tell** **gward**-yah) Moscatel de Alejandría (85%) and Pedro Ximén (15%) aged 24 months in American oak barrels. Intense brightness, good balance between sweetness and fine acidity.
- Moscatel 1° (mos-ka-**tell** pRRee-**maiRR**-oh) is essentially the *añejo* version of *Moscatel 2°*. Darker, with more complexity.
- Moscatel Guinda (mos-ka-**tell** **geen**-dah) 'Guinda' means sour cherry, and this dark Moscatel has hints of this fruit, as well as toasted aromas of coffee. Smooth and creamy palate.
- Málaga Quina (**mal**-ag-ah **kee**-nah) A classic, fairly young, Málaga wine with the addition of quinine giving a (very) slight bitter note.
- Solera (soh-**lair**-ah) A blended, semi-seco wine close to a cream sherry in flavour.

When you order your drinks, the barman will chalk your bill on the  wooden counter-top. If you order further drinks, these are added, keeping a running tally (so if you want to move away from the bar and find a quieter corner, you will need to pay first, or tell the barman). Yet another traditional touch is that whenever anyone leaves a tip, they throw it clattering into a metal bucket and ring a bell in celebration.

La Tranca ✿✿

🏛 CENTRO HISTÓRICO 📍 Calle Carretería 93
🌐 latranca.es 🕐 1230–0200 🍺 ✒ 🎶

If you want to enjoy Málaga's traditional wines slightly off the tourist track, then you'd be hard-pressed to do better than La Tranca. You'll probably also be hard-pressed to find space at the bar as it's pretty much a *malagueños*-only joint. It's lively, noisy and popular with a younger crowd, so it's not a place for a quiet drink.

Los Patios de Beatas ✿✿✿

🏛 CENTRO HISTÓRICO 📍 Calle Beatas 43
🌐 🏠 lospatiosdebeatas.com 🕐 1300–1700, 2000–0000 🍴 🍷 ☕ 📖 ✒ ① 🔑 ▤ 🌐 🎏 🔧 🎶 🚗 🍸

This bar-restaurant created from a pair of carefully restored *palacios* could easily have been listed in the restaurants section. The food is excellent, consisting of sensitively 'elevated' classics and there is a beautiful dining room created in the patio of one of the buildings, but I have included it under 'bars' because perhaps the principal reason for its popularity is its excellent wine list of almost 50 *tintos*, *blancos*, *rosados*, *cavas* and *generosos*, all of which are available by the glass and, in the case of still wines, half glass.

Atarazanas Market ✿ ✿

🏛 CENTRO HISTÓRICO 📍 Calle Atarazanas 10

There are several bars in the central market, all specializing in seafood and fish *tapas*, but offering other choices as well.

Gin Tonic ✿✿

🏛 CENTRO HISTÓRICO 📍 Calle Sancha de Lara 5
🌐 gintonicbar.es 🕐 1700–0000 (Thu 0200, Fri–Sat 0300 🍷

This bar offer over 100 gins (and vodkas, rums and whiskies) and 20 tonics plus botanicals for garnish. They also sell their own 'Malaka' gin.

Bodeguita El Gallo ✿✿

🏛 CENTRO HISTÓRICO 📍 Calle San Agustín 19
🌐 bodeguitaelgallomalaga.com 🕐 Thu 2000–0000, Fri–Sat 1300–1700, 2000–0000; Sun 1300–1700
🍴 🍷 ✒ ① 🔑 🎶 ▤ 🍸 🍷

A great *tapas* bar near the Picasso Museum that has a good wine list in addition to specializing in *vermú*. The *tapas* menu is excellent, reasonably priced, and has some unusual dishes that are well worth trying — the *croquetas* for example, where you can choose from among black pudding and pine nuts, *salchichón de Málaga*, Payoyo cheese with raisins and almonds, *Cabrales* cheese with walnuts, ham and sherry, and more.

La Taberna del Pintxo Larios ✸✸

🏛 CENTRO HISTÓRICO 📍 Calle Alarcon Lujan 12
🌐 latabernadelpintxo-malaga.com 🕐 1230–0000
🍷 🗺 ⚔ 🍢 🎴 🌐 🍽 ☕

This is a very popular Basque-style bar serving *pintxos* (small *tapas* on a slices of baguette, impaled with a wooden stick — *pintxo* means 'pierced'). After the Basque fashion, cold *pintxos* are displayed on the bar. Order your drinks at the bar and help yourself to *pintxos*. Wait staff emerge from the kitchen bearing trays of freshly made hot *pintxos*, so help yourself as they pass. When it comes to the bill, they count the skewers (and dishes).

Los Gatos ✸✸

🏛 CENTRO HISTÓRICO 📍 Plaza de Uncibay 9 🕐 1100–0000 🍴 🍷 ⚔ 🕐 🍢 🗂 🎴

This is a traditional bar serving a large range of filling *tapas* (called *canapés* here) and a well-priced selection of *raciones* if you want a more substantial meal. Los Gatos opened in Madrid over 30 years ago ('*los gatos*' — the cats — is a nickname for people from Madrid) and the owner, Miguel, opened this branch in his native Málaga in 2012.

Casa Lola ✸✸

🏛 CENTRO HISTÓRICO 📍 Calle Granada 46 📍 Calle Strachan 11 📍 Plaza de Uncibay 3 📍 Plaza del Siglo 3
📘 casalolamalaga 🕐 1230–0000 🍴 🍷 ⚔ 🕐 🍢 🗂

A modern bar made to look like an old bar, the first Casa Lola opened in 2010, quickly getting a reputation as one of the best *tapas* bars in Málaga. Since then they have opened more bars in Málaga and two branches in Marbella (both called Casa Blanca). The formula — a huge range of *tapas*, cooked with care, good *vermú*, and a fantastic, lively *ambiente* — has proved a hit with locals and tourists alike. They do not accept reservations but they usually operate a walk-up waiting list just before service.

Madeinterranea ✸✸

🏛 CENTRO HISTÓRICO 📍 Plaza de Uncibay 3
🌐 madeinterranea.es 🕐 1200–0200
🍴 🍷 🏮 ⚔ 🕐 🗂 🌐 🌿 🍢 ☕

Another modern *tapas* bar with updated classics. It has consistently good food, carefully executed and beautifully presented, and friendly service. There is often a good value *menú del día* available.

La Casa del Perro ✿

🏛 CENTRO HISTÓRICO ⚲ Calle Hernán Ruiz 7
⊕ lacasadelperro.org ⏱ Wed–Sat 1300–1600,
2000–2300, Sun 1300–1600 ⓦ +34 644 698 270
✕ ☡ 🗺 ⚒ ◔ ⟍ ⊐ 🌐

'The Dog's House' doesn't translate well, but it's a lovely, friendly place presided over by the charming owner, Julia, serving excellent food. The *carta* changes frequently, even daily, and the cooking is some of the best in town. They describe their *tapas* as '*mordiscos y bocados*' (nibbles and bites) so it is a good place to try a selection of different things.

La Barra de Zapata ✿✿✿

🏛 CENTRO HISTÓRICO ⚲ Calle Salina 10
� labarradezapatamalaga ⏱ 1300–1600, 1900–2300
✕ ☡ ⚒ ⊐

A modern bar with clean, cool décor and a list of traditional *tapas* prepared with a modern twist, all beautifully presented. The owner, Rafael, is passionate about his food, the service is friendly, efficient and intimate, and the food is highly 'Instagrammable' (as well as highly edible).

La Farola de Orellana ✿✿

🏛 CENTRO HISTÓRICO ⚲ Calle Moreno Monroy 5
借 La-Farola-de-Orellana ⊘ Mondays ✕ ☡ ⚒ ◔ ⟍ ⊐

La Farola de Orellana is an old bar (1938) that received a facelift/redesign in 2013 and is just as popular as it ever was. With a *carta* of 50 *tapas*, there should be something for everyone. It is also one of the best *tapas* bars in Málaga. It can get very busy, but this is also part of its charm.

Taberna El Carpintero ✿

🏛 CENTRO HISTÓRICO ⚲ Calle Beatas 32
借 ElCarpinteroCasaManzanilla ⏱ Tue–Sat 1300–
1600, 2000–0000 ☡ ⚒ ◔ ⊐

This is another back street bar rarely troubled by tourists. It's a basic sort of place with anaglypta wallpaper and random carpentry tools hanging on the walls, but the welcome is friendly and the *tapas* (most also available as *medias* and *raciones*) are simple, classical and well executed.

Taberna El Harén ✿

🏛 CENTRO HISTÓRICO ⚲ Calle Andrés Pérez 3
借 bit.ly/ElHaren ⏱ Sun–Thu 1300–1600, 2000–0000;
Fri–Sat 1300–0300 ☡ 🗺 ✋ G⚒ ◔ ⚓

This attractive little bar on a quiet back street occupies an old *corralón* with the courtyard transformed into a bar area, and rooms on two levels. This relatively new *taberna* is still finding its feet, and the service can occasionally be slow, but the food is good value and the staff are friendly.

Vermutería La Clasica ✱✱

📍 CENTRO HISTÓRICO 📍 Plaza de Uncibay 1
🌐 vermuterialaclasica.es 🕐 1200–0000

This bar has three *vermús* on tap and another thirteen from the bottle. The service is great whilst the food is traditional and good value given the location, though their website's claim that it is '*cocina en peligro de extinción*' (cuisine in danger of extinction) has more than a touch of the hyperbolic.

Lo Güeno ✱✱

📍 CENTRO HISTÓRICO 📍 Calle Marín García 9
🌐 logueno.es 🕐 1200–0000

Lo Güeno (an idiomatic misspelling of '*Lo Bueno*', i.e. 'The Good One') is another Málaga institution, founded by José Puerto Galveño in 1967 on the Calle Marín García. The founder's daughter, Lidia Puerto, and her husband Mariano, expanded into the next-door lot in 2002, making this the *comedor* and began serving restaurant-style dishes.

Pez Lola ✱✱

📍 CENTRO HISTÓRICO 📍 Calle Granada 42
🌐 pezlolamalaga 🕐 1200–0000

This is the fish and seafood-focused sibling of nearby Casa Lola and, like most bars on the Calle Granada it's popular with tourists. The service is friendly and the *tapas* are of excellent quality. It is also a colourful, bright and modern bar, so if the outside tables are full, don't hesitate to eat indoors and enjoy the surroundings and buzz.

Puerta Oscura ✱✱

📍 CENTRO HISTÓRICO 📍 Calle Molina Lario 5
📘 Puertaoscuramalaga 🕐 1700–0100 (Fri–Sat 0200)

Puerta Oscura ('The Dark Door'), named after one of the entrances to the Alcazaba, is not terribly obvious from the street. Classic cocktails are prepared with skill and care. Background classical music (and occasional live chamber music) plays as you sip your drink and they frequently stage small art exhibitions. Beautiful and stylish, this is very much a cocktail bar for grown ups.

🍸 Other Cocktail Bars

The following is a list of the best (and trendier) cocktail bars in central Málaga (most will close around an hour later on Fridays and Saturdays):

Speakeasy "The Pharmacy" 📍 Calle García Briz 3 🕐 1900–0200

Chester and Punk 📍 Calle Méndez Núñez 4 🕐 1700–0200

Nusa 📍 Paseo de la Farola 6 🕐 1200–0300

Mañana 📍 Calle San Juan de Letrán 7 🕐 1700–0200

Chloe 📍 Calle Correo Viejo, 9 🕐 Tue–Sat 1800–0200

La Vida de la Gente 📍 Calle Carretería 44 🕐 Wed–Mon 1900–0200

La Destilería 📍 Calle Beatas 1 🕐 Thu–Sun 1900–0300

Ghetto 📍 Calle Gómez Pallete 4 🕐 1800–0200

Taberna Uvedoble ✤✤

🍽 CENTRO HISTÓRICO 📍 Calle Alcazabilla 1
🌐 uvedobletaberna.com 🕐 Mon–Sat 1230–0000
📲 +34 951 24 84 78 🍴🍷📖🏍🕐🍶🍸🍶🍽🌍🍹

This very busy *tapas* bar near the *Teatro Romano* will appeal to anyone who loves fish and seafood. The wine list is excellent and the food is some of the best in Málaga. Although the menu is divided into 'starters', 'snacks' and 'mains' etc., it's basically *tapas* dining here with many dishes available as *tapas*, *medias raciones*, and *raciones*.

Bar Jamones ✤✤

🍽 SAN FELIPE NERI 📍 Calle Carretería 87
📘 Jamonesbar 🕐 Mon–Fri 1200–1600, 2000–0000; Fri–Sat 1200–0000 🍷🏍🕐🍶🍴🍽

Great owner, lovely staff, good food. You will sometimes receive a small *tapita* free with your first drink. What more could one want? The food, mostly available as *tapas*, *medias* and *raciones*, is delicious with the accent (as the name suggests) on pork. One of my favourite spots.

Bar Málaga ✤✤

🍽 CENTRO HISTÓRICO 📍 Calle Santa María 4 🕐 1200–0200 🍴🍷🏍🕐🍽

Bar Málaga, on Calle Santa María, dates back to 1852 . Now ably managed by Manuel, you can enjoy classics such as artichokes, octopus with *aioli*, or sirloin in sweet wine. A popular *tapa* is *atún en manteca* (tuna in lard). On the upper floor it has a dining room and a pair of balconies accommodating two highly sought-after tables.

VARO ✿✿

CENTRO HISTÓRICO 📍 Calle Andrés Pérez 20
📷 **varo.1960** 🕐 Tue–Sat 1300–1630, 2000–0000
✕ 🍷 📖 ✂ 🕐 🔖 🍴 ☰ 🍽

The VARO *taberna* is a happy ending to an all-too-familiar story. For decades the Varo family ran a *mercería* (haberdashery) on these premises, but when the owners José Varo and Concepción Fernández retired in 2010 they pulled down the shutters, unable to sell the business as a going concern. More than a dozen years later, their son Eduardo Varo opened this bar preserving many items of furniture, objects and decorations from the original shop. At VARO there is a small menu of *tapas* and *medias raciones*, all using local products. The anchovy dish is accompanied by *pipirrana* of avocados from Axarquía. There are things *para untar* (to spread) — whipped goats cheese and olive oil served with mango jam, *pâté* of Ronda black pudding with fried almonds and apple compote, and *pâté* made from Málaga suckling kid accompanied by fig and date chutney. Filled muffins ('*molletitos*') complete the *tapas* offer.

North and East of the Centro Histórico

As one crosses the Calle Carretería and Calle Álamos that follow the line of the medieval walls bounding the *centro histórico* to the north and east, the bars and restaurants you encounter tend to have fewer tourists and lower prices. *Barrios* like La Goleta, San Felipe Neri, El Molinillo, La Victoria and Capuchinos are really worth exploring. Whilst you're unlikely to find anything listed in the Michelin or Repsol guides, you'll encounter good, traditional cooking, cold beer and decent wine selections.

Palermo Coffee and Drinks ✿✿

LA MERCED 📍 Calle Ramos Marín 2
🌐 **palermocoffeedrinks.com** 🕐 Sun–Thu 0930–0200;
Fri–Sat 0930–0300 🍷 ✂ 🍸 🍽 ☰ 🍽

Specializing in coffee, cocktails and juices, this is one of Málaga's loveliest bars — elegant, comfortable, and relaxed with unfailingly friendly staff — and yet few visitors ever discover it because it is slightly hidden around a corner by the Teatro Cervantes.

La Polivalente ✿

LAGUNILLAS 📍 Calle Lagunillas 53
🌐 **lapolivalente.com** 🕐 Mon–Sat from 1700 🍷 ✂ 🔖 🍸

This friendly local bar serves a small range of *tapas* alongside wine and beer. La Polivalente ('multi-purpose') is a community arts venue and stages live performances of almost anything you can imagine, from very classical flamenco to experimental performance art. Entry to these events usually costs a few euros, though sometimes it's free.

Restaurante Café Bar El Camino ✽

🍴CRISTO DE LA EPIDEMIA 📍Plaza Benigno Santiago Peña 3 🕐 Mon–Fri 0700–1700; Sat 0700–1400
🍷🍵⚥①🍽⛲🐾

A local bar named after a pilgrimage (to Santiago de Compostela). They serve *tostadas* etc. for breakfast and *almuerzo* and there is a very cheap weekday *menú del día* which, although basic, is tasty and filling. Their baked potatoes (a welcome change from the usual chips) are excellent.

Mesón El Picoteo ✽

🍴CRISTO DE LA EPIDEMIA 📍Calle Tejeros 15
📘 mesonelpicoteo 🕐 Mon–Fri 0800–1600 🍷⚥①🍽🐾

A very popular spot for a good breakfast and keenly priced *tapas* and *raciones* for lunch. The food is traditional and prepared from top-quality ingredients fresh from the market, and the owners and staff are friendly and welcoming.

Lorena II ✽

🍴CRISTO DE LA EPIDEMIA 📍Calle Manrique 15
🕐 Mon–Sat 0630–1600 🍷⚥①🍽🐾

There is a chain of family-friendly fast food cafés called Lorena on the Costa del Sol, but this local bar 'Lorena Dos' is not connected. Lorena II is run by Mari, a lovely woman who greets her customers as friends and serves good homemade food.

Victoria Bar ✽✽

🍴CRISTO DE LA EPIDEMIA 📍Calle Zenete 8 🕐 Tue–Sun 1200–0200 🍷⚥①🍽

A modern and spacious bar off the beaten track with a lively and friendly atmosphere. The *tapas* are delicious, reasonably priced and come in generous portions. The owner, Antonio, is an excellent host.

Oliva Tapas ✽

🍴LA MERCED 📍Calle Madre de Dios 39 🕐 Mon–Fri 0800–0000; Sat–Sun 1300–0000 🍴🍷⚥①🍽🐾

The owners of this great *tapas* bar are from Linares in Jaén, and they have introduced another tradition from their home province — that of a free *tapa* with every drink, so if you order a few *cañas* you can eat quite cheaply here. *Tapas* and *raciones* can also be ordered individually.

La Goleta Bar Café ✻

🍴 LA GOLETA 📍 Calle Cruz del Molinillo 5 🕐 Mon–Fri 0700–1630; Sat 0830–1230 🍷 🍲 🖊 ① 🗜 ⚖ ◐ ✌

This friendly neighbourhood bar offers typical Spanish breakfasts, including freshly cooked egg dishes (the scrambled eggs are delicious). At lunchtime the real bargain is the *menú del día*, which is cheap and filling. There is the option to have a one-course half menu.

Mercado de Salamanca ✽

🍴 EL MOLINILLO 📍 Calle San Bartolomé 1 🕐 Mon–Sat: 0900–1400

Since a recent refurbishment, the municipal market in the El Molinillo *barrio* is now surrounded by small street-facing bars.

Molinillo 33 ✽

🍴 SAN FELIPE NERI 📍 Calle Cruz del Molinillo 33 🕐 Mon–Fri 0700–2233; Sat 0800–2230; Sun 0800–1230 🍷 🖊 ① 🗜 🌐 ◐ ✌

This place looks like a very ordinary local bar from the outside, but the speciality here is a mix of Spanish-Mexican-Argentinian dishes, so as well as the expected tortilla and *croquetas*, they also serve fantastic tacos and wonderfully tasty homemade *empanadas*.

La Mona Tapas ✽

🍴 CAPUCHINOS 📍 C/ Eduardo Domínguez de Ávila 2 🕐 Daily 🖊 ① 🗜 🌐 ✌

This is a friendly bar overlooking the Plaza de Capuchinos serving classic well-executed *tapas* and *raciones*. Unusually for a bar outside the main tourist area, they have a very good homemade vegetarian burger on the menu, and interesting dishes like Moroccan-style *pastillas*.

La Malagueta

Casa de vinos La Odisea ✽✽

🍴 GIBRALFARO 📍 Subida Coracha 2
🌐 casadevinoslaodisea.com 🕐 1200–0000
✕ 🍷 📖 🍲 🖊 ① 🗜 🌐 ✌

At the foot of the Monte Gibralfaro, this bar is almost all that is left of the long-demolished slum of La Coracha, and another excellent place to enjoy Málaga wine. It's a friendly bar with a great atmosphere and the food is high quality. There is a mid-price *menú del día* if you're feeling hungry at lunchtime. At very busy times, service can be a little slow, so this is a place for lingering. There is a decent selection of vegetarian and vegan dishes.

Casa Carlos 1936 ✿

🍴 LA MALAGUETA 📍 Calle Keromnes 6
📘 CasaCarlosRestauranteMalaga 🕐 0800–1600
⊘ Sun ✕ 🍷 ✦ 🔆 🍽

Don't be put off by the basic décor — this award-winning bar-restaurant has occupied this site since its foundation by Carlos Cejas Jaén during the Civil War. Mariloli and Carmen run it nowadays. The food is simple and well cooked and very traditionally *malagueña*.

Anyway Wine Bar ✿✿

🍴 LA MALAGUETA 📍 Paseo de la Farola 8
🌐 📖 anywaywinebar.com 🕐 1900–0000
✕ 🍷 📖 ✦ 🔆 🌿 🍽 🪴

Created by David Camino, a *malagueño* who developed a passion for wine while working in hospitality in London, with Daniel Lopez in the kitchen, the focus is on natural, organic and so-called 'biodynamic' wines with over 100 available by the glass. When it comes to food, the specialities of the house are chosen to accompany and enhance the wine offer.

El Ensanche/Soho and Alameda

Bars are opening all the time the El Ensanche/Soho. They are also, just as quickly, closing or changing names. Those listed below are well-established, but have a stroll around and you are sure to discover others.

La Pechá Taberna ✿

🍴 SOHO 📍 Calle San Lorenzo 📘 lapecha2020
🕐 Mon–Sat 0930–0100 🍷 ✦ 🔆 🍽 🌐 🍺

This is a lovely bar in a part of Soho that few visitors explore. It is not an old bar (its owner, Raúl Nieto, opened the doors in 2020), and yet it feels utterly traditional. It is also very *malagueño*, as one can tell from the name ('Pechá' is the *malagueño* rendering of the *castellana* word *pechada*, meaning 'a lot' or 'plenty'). It has a limited but excellent *tapas* list. The *ensaladilla rusa* with fried egg mayo is especially good, as are the small *bocaditos*, black bao buns and *tostitas*.

Bar Atenas ✿

🍴 SOHO 📍 Calle Tomás Heredia 7 🕐 Mon–Sat 0630–1630; Sat 0800–1400 🍷 ✦ 🔆 🍽 🍺 🌐 🍹

This friendly, family-run bar is very popular for breakfast, *almuerzo* and lunchtime *tapas*. Their sandwiches (*pitufos* and *vienas*) are cheap and tasty. The Friday special — *paella* — may not be totally authentic (it contains seafood), but it is very good and always runs out quickly.

La Barra de Doña Inés ✹✹

 ALAMEDA Alameda Principal 15
 bit.ly/LBdDonaM Mon–Sat 1200–0200; Sun 1200–1800 🍴🍷🗺🗡🛈🗝🎫🌐

This bar is run by Antonio Banderas's 'Tercer Acto' Group that also operates three other *restaurantes*. Of the four, La Barra is the one most worth visiting on account of its smart but relaxed *ambiente* and reasonably priced but excellent *tapas* and *raciones*.

West of the Guadalmedina

Más Vermut ✹✹

 EL PERCHEL Pasaje San Fernando 4
 masvermutmalaga Mon, Wed, Thu 1200–1600, 1930–2300; Fri–Sat 1200–1630, 1930–2330; Sun 1200–1700 🍷🗡🛈🗝

This small bar located in an alleyway between Cuarteles and Salitre streets in El Perchel specializes in *vermú*. A small menu of tasty *tapas* dishes is available and, for my money, they serve the best *patatas bravas* in Málaga.

El Añejo Taberna ✹

 LA TRINIDAD Mercado de Bailén, Plaza de Bailén 8, Stall 46 **elanejotaberna** Mon–Sat 0730–1700 🍷🗡🛈🗝🎫

This market bar is one of Málaga's hidden gems. Eduardo and Juan Pablo are friendly and attentive behind the bar, and Marcela prepares delicious *raciones* and *tapas*. This is an excellent place to sample *callos* (tripe slow-cooked with chickpeas, trotters, black pudding, paprika and tomato).

La Reserva ✹

 LA TRINIDAD Calle Francisco Monje 14 Mon–Sat 0800–1800 🍴🍷🗡🛈🗝🎫

It might look like the kind of place that will fall silent the moment a tourist walks in, but it's a very friendly and welcoming place, so do visit if you're in the area. The breakfasts are delicious, with plenty of choice, and there is a bargain *menú del día*.

La Bohemia ✹

 MÁRMOLES Calle Huescar 8 Mon–Fri 0900–1600; Fri 2030–2300; Sat 1230–1600 🍴🍷🗡🛈🗝🎫🍽

The surroundings of boxy commercial offices are far from picturesque, but La Bohemia is one of Málaga's most charming spots to enjoy *tapas* (or breakfast). They offer a huge range of *pitufos* as well *tapas*, *medias* and *raciones* of *ĉhacinas* (*charcuterie*) and cheeses. **In the same commercial complex there are more than a dozen other bars and restaurants nearby, all of which are good quality and deservedly popular with locals.**

La Despensa de Iñaki ✲

📶 EL PERCHEL 📍 Calle Héroe de Sostoa 46
🌐 ladespensadeinaki.com 🕐 1100–2300 (Sun 1600)
✕ 🍷 🛵 🕐 🔖 ᙦ

Located in a gourmet food shop, the name of the owner and the fact they serve *pintxos* (not *tapas*) tells you that this is a Basque bar/shop, though they stock a wide range of products from the Province of Málaga. Iñaki and Ángeles have created a friendly bar in which to enjoy a glass of wine and excellent *tapas* while browsing for local gourmet gifts to take home.

Taberna Los 13 ✲✲

📶 EL PERCHEL 📍 Calle Edison 10
🌐 📖 tabernalos13.com 🕐 Mon–Sun 1300–1630,
2000–2330 🍷 📖 🛵 🕐 ᙦ 🎋 ᙐ 🌀

Run by *gaditanos* (people from Cádiz), this *taberna* serves an extensive *carta* of excellent dishes, many of them typical of Cádiz. This is a great option if you are near the bus or railway stations. If you only want a drink and a snack there is short *carta* of well-chosen and delicious *tapas*.

Base9 ✲✲

📶 EL PERCHEL 📍 Calle Salitre 9
🌐 base9restaurante.com 🕐 Mon–Sat 1330–1600,
2030–2300 🍷 📖 🛵 🕐 ᙦ

Pablo Zamudio and Cristian Fernández describe their gastronomic offer as 'Grandma's cooking for young people' and it doesn't disappoint. Everything is traditional, and yet nothing is. The *garbanzos* (chickpeas) are made into a rich broth and paired not with the expected *ĉhorizo*, but with tiger prawns, while the *tortilla de patatas* is not the usual firm wedge, but almost French-style with a light omelette wrapped around an interior of confit potatoes swathed in a rich, yolky sauce. Stunning cooking.

La Pluma 'El Nido' ✲

📶 EL PERCHEL 📍 Paseo de los Tilos 62
🔗 La-Pluma-El-Nido 🕐 Wed–Sun 1230–1630, 1930–
0000 🍷 🛵 🕐 ᙦ

La Pluma (the feather) 'El Nido' (the nest) is a lovely, local bar, only 5 minutes' walk from the Bus Station. The food is *tapas*-style, with *raciones* and sandwiches too, but freshly cooked from top-quality ingredients. The service, from Antonio, José and Ana, is faultlessly friendly.

🛕 *Azoteas* (Rooftop Bars)

You pay a premium for enjoying a drink on a hotel roof terrace, but the views across the city and the bay make it worth it. Begin your evening with a glass of sherry or even '*un gin-tonic*' a few storeys up before returning to sea level for the rest of the night. The following rooftop terraces are all open to non-guests (though the swimming pools are not).

Gran Hotel Miramar ✱✱✱
📍 Paseo Reding 22

The rooftop bar ('*Terraza* Chill Out') is located on the top floor of Málaga's grandest hotel. It is open to non-residents from Sunday to Thursday between 6 pm and 1 am and on Fridays and Saturdays until 2 am. Booking is advised at weekends: **hotel.miramar@hsantos.es**.

Hotel AC Málaga Palacio ✱✱✱
📍 Calle Cortina del Muelle 1

There are great cathedral views from this large terrace, which was the pioneer in Málaga, and remains one of the best. It's also one of the highest, which means it can get breezy, so take a jacket or shawl if it's windy. This is a popular meeting point during the Málaga Film Festival in March.

OnlyYOU Hotel Lolita Terrace ✱✱✱
📍 Alameda Principal 1

Despite the rather cutesy name of this hotel, it's a stylish place and 'Lolita' is a sophisticated terrace. It is also one of the more expensive, but it offers wonderful views. If you want to enjoy the unrivalled panorama, come up for a glass of wine (about the cheapest beverage option). By the way, 'Lolita' isn't a dodgy Nabokov reference — the hotel's restaurant is called 'Lola' (a diminutive of Dolores) and Lolita is a diminutive of Lola (*i.e.* a double diminutive of Dolores).

Hotel Room Mate Larios ✱✱✱
📍 Calle Marqués de Larios 2

Popular for events and parties, this terrace overlooks the city's most famous shopping street, Calle Larios. Hip monochrome furniture, stone walls, mosaic-tiled bar and night-time entertainment with DJs make it a popular choice.

Hotel Molina Lario ✿✿✿

📍 Calle Molina Lario 22

This seasonal terrace on the eighth floor is more sheltered than the AC Málaga and hosts concerts and other entertainment, mostly in summer.

Room Mate Valeria ✿✿✿

📍 Plaza Poeta Alfonso Canales 5

One of the newer roof terraces in Málaga, this one comes with its own pool (guests only) and great views of the Port and Muelle Dos.

Hotel Sallés Málaga Centro ✿✿✿

📍 Calle Mármoles 6

Just on the other side of the Guadalmedina River, the terrace of the Málaga Centro has a small and cosy atmosphere. Summer nights are lively, as it is full of lights, colours and live music.

La Terraza de San Telmo ✿✿

📍 Calle San Telmo 14

Formerly known as the Oasis attic, this terrace is located near the Thyssen Museum. It has lovely views of the Iglesia de los Mártires.

Hotel Soho Bahia Málaga ✿✿✿

📍 Calle Somera 8

In the heart of the newly-hip Soho *barrio*, famous for its avant-garde graffiti, this new hotel with its bold décor (it has a very colourful façade) has a new terrace featuring a futuristic white bar and shaded tent areas. Probably not for anyone over 35, though.

Hotel Málaga Premium (San Juan) ✿✿✿

📍 Calle San Juan 12

With excellent views of the city skyline and the Cathedral Tower, this is slightly more hidden than the others and therefore often less crowded.

La7 — Hotel Soho Boutique Equitativa ✿✿✿

📍 Alameda Principal 3

Next door to OnlyYOU, this seventh-floor bar-restaurant has a stunning view up the Calle Larios. Although it is primarily a cocktail bar and restaurant, it's also a nice place for a coffee with a view in the late afternoon.

H10 Croma Málaga ✳✳✳

⊙ Calle Prim 4

This hotel is one of Málaga's newest, and most controversial. Located on the east bank of the Guadalmedina, this imposing white cube stands on Hoyo de Esparteros square. The controversy is mainly because to construct the hotel, a building known as 'La Mundial' (by Eduardo Strachan Viana-Cárdenas, the architect of Calle Larios) was demolished. The demolition of a historic building rarely goes ahead without opposition, though I remember La Mundial as a down-at-heel *pensión* and something of an eyesore.

The rooftop bar has fantastic views and a relaxed vibe (though service can be a little slow), but before you go in, have a look at the building behind the hotel. It's a handsome four-storey structure with green shutters, impressive ironwork and gently curving corners — a faithful reconstruction of La Mundial, using the ironwork salvaged from Strachan's original.

Alcazaba Premium Hotel Málaga ✳✳✳

⊙ Calle Alcazabilla 12

This popular terrace overlooks the Alcazaba and the *Teatro Romano*.

Casa Hermandad del Sepulcro ✳

⊙ Calle Alcazabilla 5

A rooftop terrace with a difference: not a hotel, but a bar operated by the Brotherhood of the Sepulchre. When not being used for members' functions and events, they open their roof terrace to the public as a '*terraza benéfica*' ('charity terrace') to help raise funds for the brotherhood's social projects. It's a modern building, so the bar area has something of a '1990s church hall' vibe and the terrace is quite plain (no fountains, sun loungers or DJs), but the view of the theatre and Alcazaba is unimpeded and beautiful. The prices are also very reasonable — just a fraction of what you would pay at a hotel roof terrace and all for a good cause (supporting projects that provide basic household goods and food for poor families in Málaga).

You should plan your visit, however, as it is not a commercial venture and it is often closed for private events. Fridays and Saturdays, when the terrace is open until 1 am, are usually fully booked far ahead. If you would like to visit, send an email to ✉ salonsocial@hermandadsepulcro.org, or use the contact form on the website, specifying 'Salón Social' as the subject: ✉ hermandadsepulcro.org/contacto

🏪 *Mercados* (Markets)

The city's markets are where you can pick up the basics for a picnic — some slices of *jamón*, *chorizo* or other cured meat, some marinated anchovies, a wedge of cheese, fresh bread, olives, tomatoes, a bag of cherries, some peaches (there is always a magnificent range of fresh fruit in season), or maybe some roasted and salted almonds, for example. The market bars tend to stay open for 1-2 hours after the market stalls close.

Mercado Central de Atarazanas

🏪 CENTRO HISTÓRICO 📍 Calle Atarazanas 10 🕐 Mon–Sat 0800–1400

Bars

Bar Central — is confusingly named because it is as far from the centre of the market as it's possible to be, but they have a well-deserved reputation. Their speciality is fried and grilled fish, but there are *tapas* of cheese, ham, *embutidos* and shellfish on offer too. They carry a good selection of Málaga wines, as well as still wines from the region.

Café Bar Mercado Atarazanas — the proprietorial name speaks a truth: this was the first bar in the market and, until fairly recently, the only one. The speciality here is seafood, as well as fried and grilled fish. There is also cold beer and refreshing, chilled Rueda wine. It can get very busy during lunchtime in high season, so don't be scared to sharpen your elbows and approach the bar.

Medina Bar — a third of the market deals in fish and seafood, and the bars reflect this. Medina Bar serves great fish and seafood dishes, but what helps set them apart are their excellent grilled meat dishes and their fantastic *croquetas*. It's popular and sometimes frenetic, but the serving staff are calm and friendly. It has some tables outside. I love all the bars in this market, but if I had to choose a favourite, it would be Medina.

Bar Central No.1 — is a relative newcomer and is currently probably the 'hippest' bar in the market (or so they'd like to think). My advice is to go for the *tapa* portions here so that you can sample a bigger selection. It has some tables outside. Waiters sometimes 'oversell' and with some dishes like jumbo Carabinero prawns costing €25 **each**, make sure you study the menu and order with care and attention!

Marisquería El Yerno — is a seafood bar that has recently expanded into a third *puesto* (stall) so they are clearly thriving. They also have tables outside the market. Their seafood is excellent quality and the service is friendly and professional. It is also the most expensive of the market bars, so again keep a weather eye on the menu/price list.

Mercado de Salamanca

🍴 EL MOLINILLO 📍 Calle San Bartolomé 1 🕐 Mon–Sat: 0900–1400

Mercado de La Merced

🍴 LA MERCED 📍 Calle Merced 4 🕐 Mon–Sat 0900–1400

Mercado de Bailén

🍴 LA TRINIDAD 📍 Plaza de Bailén 8 🕐 Mon–Sat 0800–1430

It only has a couple of bars, but both of them are good. The **Bar Mercado Bailén** is in the centre and an odd sort of building-within-a-building. This is where the market traders come for breakfast, and it's a very traditional sort of place, serving Málaga's own 'Santa Cristina' coffee. The *tapas* and food are all made on the premises by Ana, and many people call in simply to pick up food to take away. The other bar is **Taberna El Añejo** near the Plaza de Bailén entrance. Eduardo and Juan Pablo greet their customers warmly and fortify them with cold beer and good wine while Marcela prepares homemade (and reasonably priced) *tapas* which fly out from the bar with impressive efficiency.

Mercado del Carmen

🍴 EL PERCHEL 📍 Calle la Serna 3 🕐 Mon–Sat: 0800–1430 (bars stay open until 1630)

The bars here are a little cheaper than those in Atarazanas. **Cocedero Victoria** (also known as **Bar Marisquería Desirée y Paola**) serves excellent fish and seafood dishes, both grilled and fried. It has an outside terrace in warm weather. **GastroGrill** attached to the **Carnes de Cholo** butchers shop serves some of the best steak and chips in town. **Bar La Esquinita de Emilio** is a small bar occupying a corner stall and there is always a crowd at its shining stainless steel counter. It's a very popular place for breakfast, and the *tapas* and more substantial dishes start to appear from noon. The meatballs (*albóndigas*) are excellent, as are the *langostino* (tiger prawn) kebabs, but my favourite is *Salchichón de Málaga* on toast.

The final pair of bars — **Bar Mercado del Carmen** and **El Pescaíto del Gran Poder** — are owned by the same people who operate the Atarazanas Market Bar. Both are good and not particularly expensive, but they are bars for people who like fish.

There is also the **Mercado de Huelin** (at the corner of Calle la Hoz and Calle Carpo) which is worth a look if you are walking to the Huelin beach or the Museo Ruso or Automobile Museum. It is just about as 'local' as a Málaga market gets and is largely undiscovered by tourists. It is housed in a spectacularly ugly building but its *puestos* (stalls) sell all the usual goods and the quality is just as high as in other markets. It only has one bar which is well-known on account of its offering the cheapest *menú del día* in the whole of Spain (it was available for an unbelievable €3 until the COVID lockdown though it went up to €5 just after; still an extraordinary bargain).

🍱 Picnics

As mentioned above, Málaga's *mercados* are excellent places to find the basic elements of a picnic. They are, in fact, far better than supermarkets because you can control the portions you buy; for example, just a few slices of ham, rather than a whole packet. Bars and cafés that serve *pitufos*, *molletes* and *camperos* are usually happy to sell them '*para llevar*' (to take away), wrapped in aluminium foil. Other great places to buy sandwiches, cheese, ham, sausage, olives, etc. are the shops known as *ultramarinos* (old-fashioned delicatessens). These are often overlooked by visitors, but are where the locals go.

If you're staying in a hotel, ask to borrow cutlery to use for your picnic. If you're in an *hostal*, or your hotel is uncooperative, you can buy stainless steel cutlery very cheaply in the Eroski supermarket in the Larios centre, or packs of disposable wooden cutlery from Mercadona.

Another good place to pick up the necessary elements of a picnic is an '*asador de pollos*' (roast chicken shop). All of them sell '*menús*' of a full or half roast chicken with fries or some kind of potato plus a drink, and many also sell '*comidas caseras*' or '*comidas para llevar*' (homemade food, or food to go), so you can pick up sides, salads, bread and puddings too, then take your haul to a nearby park or beach to enjoy. Most establishments of this kind will give you disposable (wooden) cutlery.

Parque del Oeste and Playa de la Misericordia:

🍗 Pollos Asados Los Malagueños 📍 Avenida de los Guindos 29
🌐 asadordepolloslosmalaguenos.es

Los Malagueños sell roast chickens, *empanadas*, a huge range of salads (and in summer, chilled soups), and even pastries and puddings. The 100% homemade dishes are prepared with pride by the lovely women who own and run this business in reassuringly spotless premises. As well as chickens, they prepare their own delicious '*patatas de los montes*' (seasoned roast potatoes) and if you're in luck, roast apples.

Parque de Huelin and Playa de Huelin:

🍗 Asador de Pollos Papagallo 📍 Calle Héroe de Sostoa 96

This *asador* is very popular with people living in the neighbourhood, not just for its excellent roast chicken, potatoes and fried peppers, but for a host of other dishes (including *empanadas*, *croquetas*, *albóndigas*, salads and, in the summer, *gazpacho* and *ajoblanco*). The food is great quality, always freshly prepared, and the staff couldn't be more helpful.

Playa Malagueta:

🍗 Asador de Pollos La Cocina de Lola ♀ Calle Fernando Camino 9

🍗 Hoy Cocino Yo! ♀ Calle Fernando Camino 11

Both of these places (on the same street) sell roast chicken and a big range of '*comida casera*'. Both are very good, though, in my opinion, Lola just edges it when it comes to quality and value.

Centro:

🍗 Pollos San Juan ♀ Calle Herrería del Rey 9 ⊕ pollossanjuan.es

This is the best-known *asador* in the *centro histórico*, with a few tables outside. I'm not convinced that all of their 'homemade' dishes are actually made in-house, but for a simple roast chicken and potato *menú*, or a tasty chicken sandwich, it's a great spot. For good quality *comida casera* in the city centre, walk into Soho and pay **Unosiete** a visit:

🍴 Unosiete ♀ Calle Vendeja 9 🔲 unoSieteMalaga

Unosiete ('one seven') is not an *asador de pollos*, but it sells really excellent, super-fresh and genuinely homemade dishes (the menu changes daily), making it an ideal place to shop for picnics (or for meals, should you be staying in a city centre apartment). Mari and Antonio's business has recently expanded into new, larger premises; a development that came as no surprise to their hundreds of faithful customers. The new shop has microwaves for customer use should you need to heat up food to enjoy immediately.

If you are outside Málaga city, use Google to search for an *asador* (bit.ly/AsadorDePollos) nearby if you fancy a juicy roast chicken or ready-made dishes for a picnic — there will be one not too far away!

> *Asdores* are also great places to buy dishes for a meal if you are staying in an apartment. The prices are competitive and the quality of the food is excellent. The UK phenomenon of supermarket 'ready meals' is not mirrored in Spain. If *malagueños* want to enjoy a hassle-free meal, they will go to an *asador* or shop selling '*comida casera*' (homemade dishes) where the food, rather than being mass-produced, will have been freshly made on the premises that day.

Sightseeing

As with restaurants, there isn't much point in giving prices in this section as the information would be out of date almost immediately. Also, how could one compare a small museum with a couple of rooms of exhibits with somewhere like the Alhambra in Granada, arguably one of the cultural wonders of Europe? If they were the same price, the former would be a rip-off or the latter foolishly undersold. Nonetheless, I have used the **ⓢ** symbol as an approximate guide to indicate the price based on admission charges at the time of publication:

ⓢ   free

ⓢ   cheap (or a voluntary or nominal charge)

ⓢⓢ   mid–price

ⓢⓢⓢ more expensive, reflecting popularity/extensiveness

🏛 Historic Sights

Teatro Romano

🍴 CENTRO HISTÓRICO 📍 Calle Cilla 2
🌐 ⊕ bit.ly/TeatroRM 🕐 Tue–Sat 1000–1800, Sun 1000–1600 ⓘ ⊕ bit.ly/TeatroRMinfo **ⓢ**

Probably built during the reign of Octavian Augustus (†14 AD), Málaga's is one of 19 surviving Roman theatres in Spain. It is not as impressive as the one at Mérida (which still has some of its stage columns and statues), much of the stone having been plundered by the Moors to build the Alcazaba (seen towering above it), but it is still remarkably intact. Its location, on the other hand, is stunning. Not only is it (unlike the *teatro* of Mérida) in the heart of the city but the Alcazaba rises dramatically behind and above it. It was only discovered in 1951, having lain (ironically enough) under the buildings of Málaga's then 'Cultural Centre'.

It is unusual in that it is built into a hill, like Greek theatres, while most Roman theatres were constructed on flat ground. It is a 'medium-sized' example of a Roman theatre and most of the *caveae* (seats) are intact.

What makes it especially fascinating is that it was lost for so long. Its

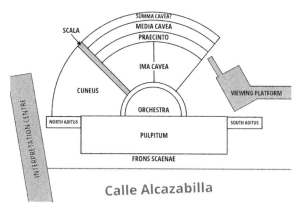

star began to fade in the late third or early fourth century (partly as a consequence of Christian antipathy towards the theatre) and, notwithstanding a short-lived revival under the Byzantines, the area had been given over to the production of garum long before the 8th-century Muslim conquest of the city. The Moors plundered the site for stone when they built the Alcazaba.

The grand civic plan in the early 20th century was to sweep away the unsanitary housing and build a grand 'cultural centre'. This went ahead even though during the construction of that building Roman remains were discovered. But these were different times. Preservation of urban patrimony is a fairly recent concern and plenty of local politicians in the nineteenth century would gladly have demolished the entire Alcazaba in the name of slum clearance and urban regeneration (as they did as late as 1990 with the *barrio* of La Coracha). The excavation of the *teatro* began in the 1950s, but it was not until the final demolition of the *Casa de la Cultura* in 1995 that it became possible to properly open the theatre site.

The Teatro Romano is free to visit, though this fact is not advertised. So if you are passing by, there is no reason not to visit. The information leaflet published by the Junta de Andalucía (link above) that administers the site has lots of information, but the on-site interpretation centre has a great deal more. You can see it from outside of course, but nothing can really compare to venturing inside and adopting the viewpoint of a spectator. To sit on a stone seat that was once occupied by a theatre-goer 2,000 years ago is quite something.

Alcazaba

🏛 CENTRO HISTÓRICO 📍 Calle Alcazabilla 2

🌐 🔗 alcazabaygibralfaro.malaga.eu 🕐 ☀ 0900–1800; ☀ 0900–2000 ⊘ Lift closed on Monday 💶 (♻ Sun from 1400)

Constructed on the ruins of a Punic fortification during the reign of Abd al-Rahman I, the first Emir of Cordoba, around 756−780 AD, the Alcazaba's original purpose was as a defence against pirates, thanks to its commanding position with views over the city, down to the sea and across to Africa. The fortress was rebuilt by the Zirid Sultan of Granada, Badis ibn Habus, between 1057 and 1063 AD, while the fortified double walls that connect the Alcazaba to the neighbouring Castillo de Gibralfaro, over the Coracha ridge, were built by the Nasrid ruler Yusuf I in the 14th century, when most of the inner palace was also refurbished. As a palace, it was home to a number of Moorish rulers.

The Alcazaba has a distinct feel in comparison to its better-known but younger neighbours, the Alcázar of Sevilla and the Alhambra of Granada. It was already three centuries old when the others were built. After the reconquest, it fell into decline, though it was considered fit for a king as late as 1675 when Felipe IV stayed here during a visit to the city. It really began to decay following the 1680 Málaga earthquake. It became, like the now demolished settlements surrounding it, an urban slum with dozens of families living within its walls until restoration work began in 1933; work that continues slowly today. Two of its original three walls remain, as well as over 100 towers and three palaces.

The fortress's entrance area, which is close to the Plaza de Aduana and the Teatro Romano on Calle Alcazabilla, forms part of the city walls. You pass through the Puerta de la Bóveda (Gate of the Vault), a typical Moorish *puerta en recodo* (a defensive castle entrance designed to delay the arrival of attackers — after entering through an arch, they come up against a blank wall, and have to make a sharp turn to gain access to the next part of the fortress). A little higher up, you pass through the Puerta de la Columnas (Gate of the Columns), which was built using Roman marble columns (from the *teatro romano*) to support Moorish horseshoe arches.

You then enter the lower precincts of the Alcazaba, via the second *puerta en recodo* under the Torre del Cristo (Christ's Tower). This was where the first mass was celebrated following the victory over the town by the *Reyes Católicos*, and it continued to be used as a chapel after this date. The lower precinct follows the contours of the hill, and you can stop and rest at the Plaza de Armas, which is now a garden with fountains and a bastion on the south side which once defended the coast.

Follow the little cobbled paths (the Alcazaba is not suitable for wheelchairs or people with mobility problems, although they can use the lift on Calle Guillen Sotelo to visit the palace complex) through the Puerta de los Cuartos de Granada (Gate of the Halls of Granada), which leads into the upper precinct where the pathway passes through attractive landscaped gardens. Inside the Nazari palace, at the top of the fortress, you can explore three courtyards: the Patio de los Surtidores (Courtyard of the Fountains), which features a row of caliphal arches leading to the Torre de la Armadura Mudéjar (*Mudéjar* Armoury Tower) with its 16th-century carved wooden ceiling. The Torre de Maldonado (Maldonado Tower), with its original marble columns and balconies, offers the best views so far. The next two courtyards in the palace are the Patio de los Naranjos (Courtyard of the Orange Trees) and the Patio de la Alberca (Courtyard of the Pool).

The palace is quite extensive with arches, towers, gates, and original marble columns. Some areas, such as the dungeon, the Patio del Aljibe (Courtyard of the Reservoir), and the Torre del Homenaje (Homage Tower), most of the original Moorish dwellings, mosque and baths (accounting for around a third of the buildings in the complex) are still the site of archaeological research and are currently closed to visitors. There is a small archaeological museum, exhibiting fragments of Roman pottery and statues of various sites around the province, including Lacipo (Casares) and Villa de Rio Verde, (Marbella). You can also see Moorish ceramics and other artefacts found on the site. Tickets used to be sold from a temperamental machine, but during COVID this was replaced by a bank of touch-screen terminals. You get the best value by buying a combined ticket to the Alcazaba and Castillo Gibralfaro together. There is an audio guide which you can access via your smartphone, but if you would prefer a human guide, a reliable company is **exploramalaga.com** which runs tours every Tuesday and Saturday afternoon (you pay for your admission and pay the guide whatever you think is fair).

Castillo de Gibralfaro

🏰 GIBRALFARO ⚲ Camino Gibralfaro 11 ⏲ 0900–1800 ⊕ ✎ *alcazabaygibralfaro.malaga.eu* 🌙 0900–1800; ☀ 0900–2000 ⊘ (☾ Sun from 1400)

The castle was built in 929 AD by Abd al-Rahman III, Caliph of Córdoba, on an earlier Phoenician fortification and lighthouse, from which its name was derived. Yusef I, Sultan of Granada, enlarged it at the beginning of the 14th century, also adding the double wall down to the Alcazaba (La Coracha).

The castle was subjected to a three-month siege by the *Reyes Católicos*, Fernando and Isabel, which ended only when hunger forced the Moorish *malagueños* to surrender. Afterwards, Fernando occupied the site, while his queen took up residence in the town. A piece of trivia: this was the first conflict in which gunpowder was used on both sides.

The most visible remains of this historic monument are the solid ramparts which rise majestically from woods of pine and eucalyptus; inside the fortress itself, you will find some buildings and courtyards. The ramparts have been well restored and you can walk all the way around them, providing stunning views in all directions. Come here for the location and the view, and visit the Alcazaba for the architecture. Visit both to get a balance of the two.

The castle is 130 metres above sea level, so it's a fair climb to the top. The easiest way to get there is on the bus (🚌 35), a journey of about 15 minutes. There is only one bus an hour, unhelpfully leaving at irregular times past the hour, so use the Moovit app (or similar) to confirm. The most obvious walking route to the top is via the 'Coracha' — a paved route created in the 1990s after the demolition of the slum of La Coracha (the historic Coracha is not currently usable). But, be warned: it is steep with an average incline of 1:8. A shadier (but longer) route is the Calle Mundo Nuevo on the forested northern side of the mountain, where the average incline is only 1:16. This walking route has been recently upgraded by the *ayuntamiento*: work that included the construction of a children's playground on the way up (or down) and a *mirador* (viewpoint) looking eastwards along the coast. ⚠ Google Maps is pretty useless for calculating walking routes that do not involve major roads, so I recommend you use a different (*i.e.* better) map app like **maps.me** or **osmand.net**.

To return to the city, you have the same three options: the bus, the Coracha (though downhill) and the Calle Mundo Nuevo (slower but shadier). A word of warning about the Coracha route: it is paved with stone that has become quite polished with all the footfall and as a consequence it can get very slippery when wet. Even in dry conditions, you will need shoes with a good grip.

City Walls

🏛 CENTRO HISTÓRICO

🌐 ⓘ ✠ rutasarqueologicas.malaga.eu ⬤

A few small sections of Málaga's city walls (Phoenician, Roman, and Moorish) survive. Some are visible at street level, others are in the basements of museums, hotels, car parks and offices. The archaeology website of the *ayuntamiento* is full of information, in both Spanish and English. A dozen of the most accessible sections (with English descriptions) are included on the companion Google Map (**bit.ly/MalagaMap**). Click '**LEGEND**' then select '**MÁLAGA History**' to display them.

✝ Streets and Squares

Calle Marqués de Larios
🕍 CENTRO HISTÓRICO

This is the main shopping street in Málaga's old town and the main artery of the *centro histórico*, yet it is one of the newer thoroughfares. It runs from the Alameda Principal at its southern end up to the Plaza de la Constitución with its 16th-century fountain to the north. Inaugurated in 1891, the city established a limited company to oversee the street's construction, with the Second Marqués de Larios & Larios buying most of the shares. A fine statue of the great man stands at the end of the street on the Alameda Principal, though he has not always enjoyed a place of honour — the monument was torn down at the beginning of the Civil War and dumped in the sea. Almost all the buildings are the work of a single architect: Eduardo Strachan Viana-Cárdenas, a master of Spanish Belle Époque (one of the cross streets — Calle Strachan — is named for him). The polished marble paving (the street was closed to traffic and restored in 2003) and 19th-century street lamps mean that this street is perhaps even more striking at night than during the day.

More than just a shopping street, the Calle Larios is a promenade and effectively the city's Gran Vía (High Street); a place for an evening stroll to see and be seen. It is one of the main thoroughfares used by the Holy Week processions, it forms the catwalk for the Málaga Fashion Festival and it is where the red carpet is laid for the Film Festival. But it is also used for more pedestrian social interactions. In 2019, a *malagueño* by the name of José Antonio Sánchez saw a couple of French backpackers take out a chess board and begin playing. People gathered to watch, and ever since regular chess games have taken place on Tuesday and Thursday evenings (usually beginning around 5 pm or 6 pm). Dozens of people set up boards on the stone benches along the street, with all ages and nationalities represented.

Calle Larios also has an impressive Christmas light display consisting not of the usual lights strung across the streets at intervals, but often entire edifices constructed from thousands of LED lights. The Christmas lights 'switch on' is a significant event in the annual *malagueño* calendar, with thousands of people gathering to witness it.

Plaza de La Merced
🕍 MERCED

This is another iconic location in Málaga's old town that was extensively remodelled in the 19th century, and before becoming a square for 'leisure and recreation' it was the site of the main market. In late May into early

June, the jacaranda trees blossom, filling the square with a vivid display of pale violet blossom, and for much of the late spring and early summer one is likely to encounter *biznagueros*, Málaga's distinctively garbed jasmine bloom sellers. The *biznaga* has been a favourite adornment of *malagueñas* since before the *reconquista*, and it is made by threading jasmine blooms (collected before sunrise so that they initially remain closed) onto the stems of dried thistles. So emblematic is the *biznaga* that there is a statue of a *biznaguero* in the Pedro Luís Alonso Gardens near City Hall.

Plaza de la Constitución
🏛 CENTRO HISTÓRICO

Under Nasrid Rule, this was the main city square, known as the Plaza de las Cuatro Calles or Plaza Pública. In the 15th and 16th centuries a number of new municipal buildings were constructed, including the Town Hall. At one time the mayor's residence, the court, the jail and a convent of Discalced Augustinian nuns were all found here.

In the 19th century, with the repeated confiscations of ecclesiastical property, it underwent significant changes. Several buildings were demolished, such as the chapel of Santa Lucía and the Public Jail. Influenced by Parisian and London commercial arcades, Manuel Agustín Heredia promoted the Pasaje Heredia for the enjoyment of the Málaga bourgeoisie in 1837, the first commercial arcade in Spain (now sadly a rather soulless cut-through). From the same period dates the Pasaje Chinitas (originally the Pasaje de Álvarez), named after the Chinitas café-theatre, the favourite haunt of Bohemian *malagueños* of the time.

Opened as the Salón Royal in 1857, it was built upon land formerly occupied by the disentailed monastery of Augustinian nuns. The rather grand gateway to the Pasaje Chinitas is all that remains of their convent. The café also operated as a brothel from time to time and was frequently closed due to various scandals and brawls. Nonetheless, for a while it was one of the most popular café-theatres in Spain and an emblem of the city's musical history. It played host to a number of illustrious personalities in the years before the Civil War, including Federico García Lorca, Salvador Dalí, Vicente Aleixandre, and Picasso's cousin Manuel Blasco Alarcón. The café finally closed on the orders of the civil authorities in

1937, but its reputation lives on thanks to Lorca's eponymous poem of 1931, *En el café de Chinitas*.

Most of the city's cultural events are centred on the Plaza de la Constitución. For example, during Holy Week this is where the *tribuna* is located — the place where each brotherhood must officially seek permission to proceed (the '*venia*'). During the Málaga Fair, this is the main centre of the 'day fair', while on New Year's Eve (*Nochevieja*) it is where people gather to eat their 12 symbolic grapes.

Since the 17th century, the Genoa or Charles V fountain has stood in the square. It was carved from marble in the 16th century and brought to Málaga in the 17th. It is assumed to come from the Italian city of Genoa, although there are no documents that corroborate its origin (though there is evidence that it cost the Málaga City Council 1,000 ducats).

Plaza del Obispo
🏛 CENTRO HISTÓRICO

The Plaza del Obispo (Bishop's Square) stands in front of the main façade of the Cathedral of the Incarnation. Its origin possibly dates back to Moorish times, but it acquired its current appearance with the completion of the Cathedral and the episcopal palace in the 18th century.

In the centre of the square is a fountain from 1785, the water for which was once brought via the San Telmo aqueduct (one of the most ambitious hydraulic engineering works of the 18th century bringing water into the city from 10 km north, through 30 aqueducts and over 33 bridges). The fountain is of the same grey marble as the doorway of the Episcopal Palace. Construction of the baroque episcopal palace began in 1762 and took over 30 years. It is no longer the residence of the Bishop of the Málaga and in 2019 it was opened as a 'Cultural Centre' of the Unicaja (Bank) Foundation which announced an 'ambitious programme' of exhibitions of 'top-level artists'. One of the most important events held in this square is the traditional release of a prisoner on Good Friday.

🚶 Statues

Hans Christian Andersen
📍 Calle Ancla

A bronze sculpture by José María Córdoba (2005). It is located in the Plaza de la Marina and is a tribute to the famous Danish writer, commemorating the writer's visit of 1862 recorded in his book *In Spain* (*I Spanien*).

The Cenachero

📍 Plaza de la Marina

A *cenacho* is a round *esparto* (straw) basket that was filled with fish on the beaches and carried by *cenacheros* into the city. The statue is a 1968 bronze sculpture made by the Málaga-born artist Jaime Fernández Pimentel.

The Biznaguero

📍 Jardines de Pedro Luis Alonso

The Statue of the *Biznaguero* is a bronze sculpture from 1963 also by Jaime Fernández Pimentel. The *biznaga* is a characteristic floral corsage of Málaga, consisting of jasmine flowers threaded one by one onto a dried thistle stem. The statue is located in the Pedro Luis Alonso Gardens, next to the Málaga City Hall, and represents the *biznaga* pedlar, dressed in his typical costume, carrying *biznaga*s in his left hand.

The Fiestero

📍 Parque de Málaga

The *fiestero* (*lit.* 'the party man') is the name of a member of a verdiales gang, or '*panda*' (a group of musicians, singers and dancers who perform *verdiales*, the typical musical form from Málaga).

The Marqués de Larios

📍 Alameda Principal

The statue of the Marqués de Larios is a bronze sculpture on a marble pedestal by Mariano Benlliure from 1899. The marquess is flanked by a man with a pick and a hoe, representing work, and a woman presenting an offering to a child, representing charity. The statue was thrown into the sea during the 2nd Republic and recovered after the Civil War.

Pablo Picasso

📍 Plaza de La Merced 📍 Jardines de Picasso

A bronze sculpture by Francisco López Hernández. It shows the painter with a pensive countenance seated on a marble bench with a notebook and a pencil. Showing him with a pencil, rather than a brush and palette, is significant because Pablo lived in Málaga as a child, not as an adult. It is said that his first word was '*piz*' — a child's word for a pencil (*lápiz*).

Parque de Málaga

There are many statues in the Parque de Málaga. Some useful background information about them (including a map) is provided by Simon Needham's excellent personal blog about the park: **bit.ly/MParkStatues**

🏺 🖼 Museums and Galleries

🖼 Centre Pompidou Málaga

🍴 MUELLES   📍 Pasaje del Dr. Carrillo Casaux
🕐 Wed–Mon 0930–2000 ⊘ Tue
🌐 🔖 centrepompidou-malaga.eu €€ (🎫 under 18s
& Sundays from 1600)

This is an outpost of the Centre Georges Pompidou in Paris. It opened its doors in 2015 with a collection of 80 works (and 3 special exhibitions a year) The option to stay in Málaga was renewed in 2020. In the first three months after opening, it received 76,000 visitors. Works in the centre's collection include 20th-century masterpieces such as *The Frame* (self-portrait) by Frida Kahlo, *The Flowered Hat* by Picasso, a self-portrait by Francis Bacon, *The Rape* by René Magritte and *Women in an Interior* by Fernand Léger.

🖼 Museo Picasso Málaga

🍴 CENTRO HISTÓRICO   📍 Palacio de
Buenavista, Calle San Agustín 8 🕐 1000–
1900 🌐 🔖 museopicassomalaga.org €€ (🎫 under
16s and Sundays from 1700)

Although the Pompidou has one Picasso and most of his most famous works are elsewhere, the obvious place to see his work in the town of his birth is the museum entirely devoted to his life and work. It is housed in the 16th-century Palacio Buenavista, formerly the seat of the Condes de Buenavista, which for much of the twentieth century was the Museum of Fine Arts. The museum extends into a number of adjoining buildings that once formed part of the Judería (Jewish Quarter).

The idea of a Picasso collection in Málaga was first seriously discussed in 1953, during the Franco era. Picasso was in touch with Juan Temboury Álvarez, the Provincial Delegate for Fine Arts in Málaga, who asked if Picasso would consider donating two works, and the artist had enthusiastically replied that he would send 'two trucks' instead. The negotiations came to naught, however, because the loathing between Picasso and Franco was mutual and the authorities in Málaga at the time refused to accept any donation for fear if displeasing *El Caudillo*.

Christine Ruiz-Picasso, the widow of the artist's eldest son Paul Ruiz-Picasso, resumed contact with Málaga in 1992 on the occasion of the 'Classic Picasso' exhibition in the city and in 1994 with the 'Picasso, First Look' exhibition. In 1996, she revived the 1953 project, which finally became a reality 50 years later, on October 27, 2003, when the Museo Picasso Málaga was inaugurated in the presence of Their Majesties King Juan Carlos and Queen Sofía.

The museum's collection currently features over 200 works covering 80 years of the painter's work, from 1892 to 1972, ranging from the first academic studies towards cubism to late reinterpretations of the Old Masters. Although the museum is free from 5 pm on Sundays, it is very popular (it's the most-visited museum in Andalucía) and people begin queuing up to three hours ahead of time.

 ## Fundación Picasso Museo de Casa Natal

LA MERCED Plaza de La Merced 15
fundacionpicasso.malaga.eu 0930–2000
(under 18s and Sundays from 1600)

The apartment where Pablo Picasso was born in 1881 has been open to the public for over 25 years, and the displays are as much biographical as artistic, with objects, photographs and letters relating to the Picasso family as well as artworks (there is always a temporary exhibition, too). However, the collection is large (over 3,500 items), and includes less well-known Picasso works such as ceramics, family sketches and book illustrations, as well as works by around 200 contemporaries and other *malagueño* artists. This is not a museum in which to view masterpieces. Instead, it offers something more unusual, and probably of interest to Picasso agnostics as well as Picasso fans: a fascinating glimpse into the childhood and artistic development of one of the twentieth century's artistic geniuses.

 ## Colección del Museo Ruso

EL PERCHEL Edificio de La Tabacalera, Avenida Sor Teresa Prat 15 coleccionmuseoruso.es
Tues–Sun 0930–2000 (under 18s and Sundays from 1600)

Perhaps not top of the list for tourists (who understandably expect to see Spanish art in Spain), the presence of this outpost of the Russian State Museum (St Petersburg) in Málaga is a sign of how seriously the city has gone about the project of establishing itself as a cultural centre. Before the invasion of Ukraine in 2022, the museum mounted three temporary exhibitions each year as well as frequent talks and other events. The future of the Russian Museum was a matter of some debate following the 2022 Russian invasion of Ukraine.

Exhibitions marking the 50th anniversary of the death of Picasso were hastily scheduled for 2023 and further assistance came when Jenny Green, a private British collector of Russian artworks lent almost her entire collection for exhibition. What the future holds for this museum will no doubt be determined by what happens in Russia in the years ahead.

🏛 Museo Carmen Thyssen Málaga

🏛 CENTRO HISTÓRICO 📍 Calle Compañía 10
🌐 ✎ carmenthyssenmalaga.org 🕐 Tues–Sun 1000–2000 💶💶 (💶 under 18s and Sundays from 1600)

The gallery opened in 2011 and occupies the beautiful 16th-century Palacio de Villalón. There is a permanent collection of almost 230 works of Spanish artists from the 13th century onwards — though most are examples of 19th-century Spanish genre paintings and there is a deeply *andaluz* feel to most of them. There are temporary exhibitions throughout the year and in recent years, there have been exhibitions featuring Matisse, Monet, Bruegel, and Gauguin.

La Buenaventura (*c.*1922), Julio Romero de Torres

The works permanently displayed are from the personal collection of Carmen, *la baronesa* Thyssen, widow of the late Baron Hans Heinrich von Thyssen-Bornemisza, whose artworks form the permanent collection of the eponymous museum in Madrid. She was his third wife (and he her third husband) and it was Doña Carmen who first persuaded Hans Heinrich to exhibit his art collection to the public in Madrid, which he did in 1992.

Carmen 'Tita' Thyssen-Bornemisza is a former Miss Spain (1961) and she began collecting art herself only after her late husband's collection went on display in Madrid. The agreement with Málaga city hall is due for renewal in 2025, but *la baronesa*'s statement (in 2022), 'I want this museum to be forever. Forever!' could hardly have been more emphatic. Also, the Thyssen Gallery has helped put Málaga on the cultural map, so it seems vanishingly unlikely that the *ayuntamiento* would allow its continued presence in the city to be put in jeopardy for any reason.

🖼🎭 Museo de Málaga

🍴 ALAMEDA 📍 Plaza de la Aduana
🌐 💻 bit.ly/MdeMalaga 🕐 Tue–Sat 0900–2100; Sun
0900–1500 💶 (💳 EU Passport Holders)

With so many new and unusual museums in Málaga, the municipal museum is often overlooked by visitors, who imagine a dreary collection of dusty artefacts. But they could not be more wrong. In total, the Museum of Málaga has more than 2,000 artworks by artists including Luca Giordano, Bartolomé Esteban Murillo, Antonio del Castillo, Alonso Cano, José de Ribera, Diego Velázquez, Francisco de Goya, Pedro de Mena and Francisco de Zurbarán. As an art gallery, it houses one of the largest collections of 19th-century art in Spain, with works by Joaquín Sorolla, Federico de Madrazo, Antonio María Esquivel, Vicente López and Ramón Casas, as well as several of the most famous members of the so-called Málaga School of painting. It also has an interesting collection of modern art from Málaga and Andalucía up to the 1950s with works by Picasso, Canogar, Barjola, Óscar Domínguez and Guinovart among others.

The other focus of the museum — archaeology — is represented by a magnificent collection. The archaeological collection has more than 15,000 pieces, covering a period from the 8th century BC to the Middle Ages: Egyptian, Phoenician, Greek, Roman, Arab, Visigothic and Byzantine. In recent decades, pieces from excavations carried out by the University of Málaga have been incorporated, as well as various finds from archaeological interventions that have been carried out in the urban area of Málaga, such as those found in the excavation of the Teatro Romano and the Tomb of the Warrior. Also on display is the Mosaic of Venus from the 2nd century AD that was discovered in Cártama in the 1950s.

🏛 Museo del Patrimonio Municipal

🍴 LA MALAGUETA 📍 Paseo de Reding 1
🌐 💻 museodelpatrimoniomunicipal.malaga.eu
🕐 Tue–Sun 1000–2000 (Sep–Jun); Tue–Sun 1000–1400,
1730–2130 (Jul–Aug) 💳

The MUPAM, as it is known, is somewhat out on a limb, near the bullring, and it deserves to be better known and appreciated. Room I is dedicated to pieces from the 15th to the 18th centuries and is divided into several units dealing with the incorporation of Málaga into the Crown of Castilla, festivals and celebration, and the 17th-century painter Alonso Cano. Room II shows 19th-century artworks, mainly by *malagueño* artists. Room III is dedicated to the 20th century, in particular the so-called 'Generation of the 50s' and recent movements. The staff are lovely and will do their best to answer any questions you have about the exhibits.

Centro de Arte Contemporáneo Málaga (CAC)

SOHO · Calle Alemania · Tue–Sun 0900–2100 (☼ 0900–1400, 1700–2130) · Subida Coracha 25 · Tue–Sun 1000–2000 (☼ 1000–1400, 1730–2130) · cacmalaga.eu

Exploring the artistic trends of the 20th century, CAC's permanent collection is particularly strong on international artists from 1950 to the present (think Damian Hirst and Thomas Ruff) and Spanish artists since the 1980s, with a focus on local, Málaga-born talent. The works — which include sculpture and installations — are displayed in futuristic white rooms and are complemented by a full events and educational calendar along with temporary exhibitions promoting Málaga's up-and-coming artists.

The main museum occupies Málaga's modernist former wholesale market, designed by Luis Gutiérrez Soto and dating from the 1940s. The archive and second exhibition space (CAC La Coracha) is at the other end of the Alameda, adjoining MUPAM. Entry to both sites is free, so these are great places to drop into as you're passing

Málaga Arte Urbano Soho (MAUS)

SOHO · mausmalaga.com

This is not a museum but the result of an initiative led by Fernando Francés, the director of the Centro de Arte Contemporáneo (CAC). He worked with the city council to contribute to the regeneration of the Ensanche Heredia (aka 'Soho'). MAUS is a project aimed at promoting street art, or 'curated graffiti'. The website has a map showing the locations of the artworks.

Small and Specialist Museums

Museo Unicaja de Artes & Costumbres Populares

CENTRO HISTÓRICO · Plaza Enrique García-Herrera 1 · museoartespopulares.com · Mon–Fri 1000–1700, Sat 1000–1500 (under 14s and Tuesdays 1300–1700)

This charming museum occupies a 17th-century inn arranged, in the *andaluz* manner, around a shady central patio. The collection consists of artefacts documenting the everyday life of Málaga and Andalucía — equestrian tack, milling, fishing, farming, horticulture, oil pressing, winemaking, bread making, cooking, blacksmithing, dining, costume, children's games and clothes, china and decoration, textiles, popular religion and plenty more besides.

🍷 Málaga Wine Museum

🍴 LA GOLETA 📍 Plaza de los Viñeros 1
🌐 museovinomalaga.com 🕐 Mon–Fri 1000–1700, Sat 1000–1400 💶 🎧

It is fair to say that this museum polarizes opinion. It regularly receives grudging one-star reviews on TripAdvisor and Google, but it also receives plenty of gushing five-star reviews. I am in the latter camp. The display is modest, mostly consisting of wine labels and infographics, but if you are interested in the wines (and raisins) of the Málaga region, then you will find it fascinating. The audio guide is comprehensive and available in several languages (you need a smartphone and headphones to be able to use it). Visits conclude with a tasting of two wines — usually a sweet Málaga wine and a Sierras de Málaga 'table' wine and you can ask to taste an additional wine for a modest surcharge. There is a well-stocked museum shop selling local wines and wine-related souvenirs. The staff are knowledgeable and enthusiastic and go out of their way to be helpful.

🖼 Museo Jorge Rando

🍴 La Goleta 📍 Calle Cruz del Molinillo 12
🌐 museojorgerando.org 🕐 Mon–Fri 1000–1400, 1600–2000 (☀ 1700–2100); Sat 1000–1400 ♻

The Jorge Rando Museum was inaugurated in 2014, occupying a school that was an annex to the Mercederías convent (1893). It is a museum dedicated to the *malagueño* neo-expressionist painter Jorge Rando (b. 1941). The staff are friendly and very happy to give (free) guided tours upon request, either to the whole museum or some room or theme of it.

Rando's painting is characterized by the distortion of the form, an emotional use of colour and the importance of gesture and line. He works mainly by series. Since the late sixties and early seventies, he has highlighted themes such as Prostitution, Maternity, Sorrows, Animals, Landscapes, Africa, etc. Much of his work is marked by religious themes and the scenes of *Semana Santa* have been an important inspiration.

🍷 Museo del Vidrio & Cristal

🍴 SAN FELIPE NERI 📍 Plazuela Santísimo Cristo de la Sangre 2 🌐 museovidrioycristalmalaga.com 🕐 Tue–Sun 1100–1900 ⛺ guided tour only 💶 (♻ children under 6)

The Museum of Glass and Crystal is run by three private collectors. Their combined collection numbers around 3,000 pieces as well as over 60 stained glass windows rescued from all over Europe (though due to limited space only a few of these are on display at any one time). They have Phoenician, Egyptian and Roman pieces on display as well as medieval glassware from Europe and Iran, among other places. The chronological collection then moves through Catalan, Venetian and Bohemian glass of the 16th and 17th centuries, Spanish glass of the 18th, British of the 19th, right up to examples of 20th-century Pop Art.

The only way to visit is by guided tour (offered in 5 languages) of over an hour's duration, and it is the knowledgeable and passionate commentary provided by the guide that brings everything alive; not only describing the pieces on display but explaining glass-making techniques and their contemporary significance.

🖼 Ateneo de Málaga

🕌 CENTRO HISTÓRICO 📍 Calle Compañía 2
🌐 **ateneomalaga.org** 🕐 Mon–Fri 1200–1400, 1730–2100 🏷

Next door to the church of Santo Cristo de la Salud, the Athenaeum of Málaga is a cultural association founded in 1966 and occupies part of the old Jesuit Novitiate College of San Sebastián, built between 1578 and 1599 (the other part of the college is now a primary school). It holds an important collection of contemporary art by Málaga artists and temporary exhibitions are continuously staged featuring a range of artists working in a variety of media, but there is always something to see, and entry is free.

🖼 Museo Automovilístico y de la Moda

🕌 HUELIN 📍 Edificio de La Tabacalera, Avenida Sor Teresa Prat 15 🌐 ⌘ **museoautomovilmalaga.com** 🕐 Mon–Sun 1000–1430, 1600–1900 💶💶

In the same complex as the Museo Ruso, the Automobile and Fashion Museum has 10 rooms with 90+ classic cars from the 19th century to the present day and, curiously, an enormous collection of *haute couture*, hats and handbags (the unifying theme seems to be 'style'). Like the Glass Museum, it is privately owned. Somewhat niche, perhaps, but very popular.

🖼 OXO Museo Videojuego

🕌 CENTRO HISTÓRICO 📍 Plaza del Siglo
🌐 ⌘ **oxomuseo.com** 🕐 Mon–Thu 1100–2100; Fri 1100–2200; Sat 1000–2200; Sun 1000–2100 💶💶💶 (🏷 children under 6) 🎧

The OXO Videogame Museum is 'a unique space in Europe where the past, present and future of the video game industry converge'. Only inaugurated in early 2023, it welcomed over 11,000 visitors in its first month of operation. Over several floors, the permanent exhibition covers the history of video games from the 1950s to the present day, but what is presented is far more than a display of obsolete handsets and controllers. Many of the 'exhibits' are available to play and the visitor experience is intended to be 'immersive'.

Temporary exhibitions feature particular games looking at their design and going, as it were, 'behind the scenes'. Other exhibits focus on the latest trends and developments in the industry. There are audio guides in Spanish and English, with other languages to follow.

Museo Nacional de Aeropuertos y Transporte

AEROPUERTO ♀ Aeropuerto de Málaga (next to 'Aviación General') ⊕ ⓒ aeromuseo.org ⏰ Tue: 1000–2000; Wed–Sat 1000–1400 ◑

Run by the company that operates the airport — AENA–Aeropuerto de Málaga — this is more an 'airport museum' than an 'aeronautical museum'. It covers about 3,000 metres in total and visitors can see historic aeroplanes and items related to the world of aviation collected from airports around Spain. There is also an Aeroplane Observatory located inside the old control tower looking out onto the current runways.

On the way around the exhibition, visitors will be able to see some of the old marketing posters that were used to publicize the airport as well as having the chance to sit inside the cockpit of an Iberian Airlines DC-9. Visits are free and can be guided if desired. The museum can be reached by the ◑ *Cercanías* train to the Airport, or by city buses 10 or 19.

Museo Revello de Toro

CENTRO HISTÓRICO ♀ Calle Afligidos 5 ⊕ museorevellodetoro.net ⏰ Tue–Sat 1000–2000; Sun 1000–1400 ◑ (◑ under 18, over 65 and all day Sunday, with a small charge for audio guide)

The *malagueño* artist Félix Revello de Toro (b. 1926) showed his artistic flair at a young age, and at eight years old he made a stunning sketch of the image of the Cristo de Mena, destroyed a few years earlier. His first exhibition took place in 1938 when he was 12 years old, and at 16 he received his first professional commission from a local brotherhood. The following year he received a scholarship to study at the Royal Academy of San Fernando in Madrid. He was a professor of Fine Art in Barcelona (Escuela de la Lonja) and has been an honorary member of the San Telmo Royal Academy of Fine Arts (Málaga) since 1987.

In 2010, the museum dedicated to him opened with 117 works donated by the painter. The museum is housed in a residential building dating back to the 17th century and which was once the home and workshop of the sculptor Pedro de Mena. It is one of the very few buildings from that century remaining in the city.

Centro Cultural La Malagueta

LA MALAGUETA Plaza de Toros La Malagueta, Paseo de Reding 8

cclamalagueta.com Tue–Sun 1000–1400, 1500–1900

Like many others of its kind in Andalucía, this museum was initially an exhibition of bullfighting memorabilia, offering the visitor a glimpse into the world of Spain's national festival. It included matadors' costumes, photographs, posters and other valuable bullfighting items. However, in 2020, as part of a restoration of the Malagueta bullring, a new cultural centre opened, devoted to exhibitions mostly of art and photography.

Casa Gerald Brenan

CHURRIANA Calle Torremolinos 56

bit.ly/CasaGB Wed–Thu 1600–2100; Fri 1100–1400, 1700–2100

This is probably one for the Hispanists. Opened in 2014, this museum ('cultural centre' might be more accurate) occupies the house lived in by the Anglo-Irish writer Gerald Brenan and his American wife, Gamel Woolsey. It is found in the *barrio* of Churriana, the other side of the airport, though it can be reached fairly easily by bus (10 or C8).

Edward Fitzgerald Brenan was born in Malta in 1894, and dragged by his family through South Africa, England, Ireland, Malta (again), India and Ireland (again), Gerald Brenan was a fundamentally restless man (at 18 he tried to walk to China, though only got as far as Bosnia). He was introduced to the Bloomsbury Circle and had a brief but intense romance with Dora Carrington before breaking it off, frustrated by her doomed love for Lytton Strachey. An inheritance gave him the economic means to travel to Granada, where between 1919 and 1936 he lived for long periods.

In the early 1930s, he conceived the project of writing a biography of San Juan de la Cruz (St John of the Cross) and spent the following years visiting the places associated with the saint. In 1935 he settled in a new house, in the town of Churriana, Málaga, next to what was then a small airfield. He was a perplexed witness to the Spanish Civil War and in 1943 he published *El Laberinto Español* (The Spanish Labyrinth), a study of the social and political background of the 1936–1939 War. The work was banned in Spain but published by Ruedo Ibérico in Paris. In 1946 he wrote his article 'Spanish Scene', as well as several articles on Saint John of the Cross that he published in 1947. In 1949 he went on a tour of Spain and in 1950 published the travel book *La faz de España* (The Face of Spain) where, in its sixth chapter, he revealed his investigations into the murder of Federico García Lorca. In 1953 he returned to Churriana and published *South of Granada* — probably his best-known travel book in English.

He paints a picture of a Spain (and of Andalucía) that is now largely lost (though much is still recognisable) and he does so beautifully. Many of his attitudes will strike the modern reader as benighted, certainly sexist and, for all of his affection for Spain, slightly racist and tinged with remnants of the Black Legend. But I suppose we must remember that he was born a Victorian, and was a veteran of the First World War. He was certainly a more attractive character than the dreadful bluestockings and hypocritical prigs of the Bloomsbury Group with whom he was associated for a time.

The Málaga *Ayuntamiento* spent ten years and over €1 million to create the Casa Gerald Brenan as a centre to foster connections between British and Spanish writers and help promote the culture of Andalucía among the British. Given such an investment, it seems odd that the Casa does not have a dedicated website and relies on Facebook/Meta, but there we are. I love this place, but then I love reading Brenan. For visitors unfamiliar with Brenan and his works, it may feel disappointing, but for anyone with an interest in Spain or travel writing, it should be a fascinating experience.

🔔 Cofradía Museums

Practically every *cofradía* or *hermandad* (religious fraternity) in Málaga has a small museum of some kind, in which the paraphernalia of *Semana Santa* are displayed. This does not mean the statues of Jesus and Mary — they will be in the churches or 'temples' of the fraternity — but everything else: thrones, banners, costumes, candles, incense burners, veils, canopies, lanterns, dalmatics, etc. Most are not routinely open to the public, because each *casa hermandad* is run by volunteers and it would not be economically viable to operate them as public museums.

🔔 Museo del Arte Cofrade–Semana Santa de Málaga

🏛 CENTRO HISTÓRICO 📍 Calle Muro de San Julián 2
🌐 ⓐ agrupaciondecofradias.com 🕐 Mon–Fri 1000–1400, 1700–2100 €

This museum is operated by the grouped Holy Week fraternities. The museum was inaugurated in 2010 in the building that housed the Old Hospital of San Julián, a building from the late 17th century built by the Brotherhood of Santa Caridad de Cristo. Even two years after the relaxation of COVID measures, the museum had not reopened, but presumably it will at some point (and perhaps it already has). Opening times can be unpredictable and sporadic, so to avoid disappointment, check ahead: ✉ museo@agrupaciondecofradias.com 📞 +34 952 210 400

🧍Museo de la Cofradía Estudiantes

🏛 CENTRO HISTÓRICO 📍 Calle Alcazabilla 3
🌐 ⓐ cofradiaestudiantes.es
✉ info@cofradiaestudiantes.es 📞 +34 952 221 264

🧍Museo de la Cofradía del Santo Sepulcro

🏛 CENTRO HISTÓRICO 📍 Calle Alcazabilla 5
🌐 ⓐ hermandadsepulcro.org
✉ secretaria@hermandadsepulcro.org
📞 +34 952 602 150

These two brotherhood houses are next door to one another, just opposite the Teatro Romano. They both have museums, but opening has been sporadic since the COVID lockdowns. If you spend more than a day in Málaga, you are likely to walk past them both a few times, so if you see the door open, call in and ask if the museum is open. Or send an email.

🏺Other Museums

Museo de la Imaginación
Museo Interactivo de la Música

Temporary Exhibitions and Entertainment

🎭🎬 *Teatros & Cines* (Theatres & Cinemas)

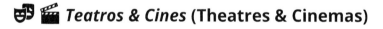

🎭Teatro Cervantes & Teatro Echegaray

🏛 LA MERCED 📍 Calle Ramos Marín
🌐 ✐ teatrocervantes.com

The Teatro Cervantes is Málaga's flagship theatre with a capacity of 1,171, and it is the main venue for opera performances staged by the *Orquesta Filarmónica de Málaga* and the *Coro de Ópera de Málaga* (**corodeoperademalaga.org**). Built in the 19th century, it was initially called the Teatro del Príncipe Alfonso and, later, after the abdication of the Bourbon monarchy, the Teatro de la Libertad. By the 1950s, it was in poor condition and was converted into a cinema. In 1984, the *ayuntamien-*

167

to purchased the building and embarked upon a massive programme of restoration. It reopened on 6 April 1987, in the presence of Her Majesty Queen Sofía, a tireless champion of the arts. The Teatro Cervantes is also the main venue during the Málaga Spanish Film Festival.

🎭 CENTRO HISTÓRICO 📍 Calle Echegaray 6

🌐 ✉ teatroechegaray.es

With only one-third the capacity of the Teatro Cervantes, Teatro Echegaray is another recently restored theatre. In fact, built in 1932, it was originally constructed as a cinema. It was purchased by the *ayuntamiento* in 2001 and completely restored, being remodelled according to a new design that was intended to be faithful to the 1930s 'spirit' of the original.

Both theatres share a website. Choose 'All Programmes' from the menu to see upcoming performances in both theatres, plus screenings of drama and opera at Cine Albéniz.

🎭 Teatro Soho CaixaBank

🎭 SOHO 📍 Calle Córdoba 13

🌐 ✉ teatrodelsoho.com

This is another theatre that began life as a cinema (Cine Pascualini), in 1907. Still privately owned, it is now the Teatro del Soho CaixaBank, operated by an arts company created and promoted by the *malagueño* actor, director, producer, and now philanthropist, Antonio Banderas. It incorporates a performing arts centre and operates as a non-profit. It (re)opened late in 2019 with a première of the musical *A Chorus Line*. Unlike the municipally owned theatres, the Soho CaixaBank stages only two or three productions per month, and they tend to be at the more 'popular' end of things.

🎬 Cine Albéniz

🎭 CENTRO HISTÓRICO 📍 Calle Alcazabilla 4

🌐 ✉ cinealbeniz.com

The Cine Albéniz is a four-screen cinema on Calle Alcazabilla. Since 2008 it has been owned by the *ayuntamiento* and its management is delegated to the arms-length company formed to run the Málaga Film Festival. It is Málaga's main 'art' cinema, so this is a good place to come if you want to see an undubbed film ('VOSE' or *'Versión Original con Subtítulos en Español'*).

🎬 Cine Yelmo

🎭 EL PERCHEL 📍 C.C. Vialia, Explanada de la Estación

🌐 ✉ yelmocines.es

This is a popular 'high street' cinema on the upper level

of the Vialia shopping centre in the María–Zambrano railway station. Though most films are dubbed, there are still a few VOSE screenings. Use the QR code to consult the programme.

🎬📽♂ English Cemetery (Las Noches del Inglés)

🍽 LA MALAGUETA 📍 Avenida de Pries 1
🌐 ✙ **lasnochesdelingles.com**

Beginning in 2023, the English Cemetery stages evening concerts, drama and films between July and September. Tickets are a bargain and entry is free for children 12 and under. There is also a *terraza* bar serving food and drinks.

♂ Museo Jorge Rando

🍽 LA GOLETA 📍 Calle Cruz del Molinillo 12
🌐 **museojorgerando.org**

Before the interruption of COVID, the museum held regular free chamber concerts on Saturday lunchtimes in the chapel of the Mercederías Monastery next door. More recently, however, their concerts have been held in the evenings. Use the QR code to check the website's 'Events' section or keep an eye on their Twitter feed **@museojorgerando**. Concerts are almost always free, but booking (by email) is necessary.

♂ Sala María Cristina

🍽 LA GOLETA 📍 Calle Marqués de Valdecañas 2
🌐 💶 ♂ **fundacionunicaja.com**

The Sala María Cristina is a music auditorium managed by the Unicaja Foundation. It is located in part of what was formerly the Franciscan Convent of San Luis El Real. At the beginning of the 20th century, the Conservatory of Music was transferred to this building, renamed for Queen María Cristina in recognition of her support of the project. In 1975 it was acquired by the *Caja de Ahorros de Ronda* (Ronda Savings Bank), and rehabilitated for use as a cultural venue.

Unfortunately, the Unicaja website is not terribly user-friendly and often it does not even list all upcoming concerts. It is worth checking a general ticket site like **taquilla.com** (use the QR code).

♂🎞🎬🎭🖼 Centro Cultural La Térmica

🍽 CARRETERA DE CÁDIZ 📍 Avenida de los Guindos 48
🌐 💶 ♂ **latermicamalaga.com**

La Térmica is a cultural centre, managed by the *Diputación de Málaga*. As a cultural and social space, there is room for all forms of artistic expression, from the performing arts to fashion, through cinema, plastic arts, and music. Regular (mainly classical) concerts are held in the adjoining Auditorio Edgar Neville. Check **bit.ly/EdgarNev** for tickets to concerts at the Edgar Neville Auditorium.

Centro Cultural MVA

SAN FELIPE NERÍ Calle Ollerías 34

 centroculturalmva.es

The Centro Cultural MVA (María Victoria Atencia — one of Málaga's best-known contemporary poets, born in 1931) is also operated by the *Diputación de Málaga*. It stages a variety of concerts, classical and modern dance, plays, musicals and poetry readings.

Sala Joaquín Eléjar

LAS FLORES Calle San Juan Bosco 79

 maynake.es

The Maynake Cultural Collective is a non-profit association founded in 1981. They stage a variety of shows including theatre, concerts, comedy, etc.

Event Listings

visita.malaga.eu

The official *turismo* website ought to be the most comprehensive event listing of all, but often has just a handful of upcoming events listed. But, switch to the **Spanish** version of the website and that short list of a handful of events suddenly grows to dozens!

mientrada.net

This is the ticket purchase portal operated by the *Diputación* for the venues they operate (Centro Cultural MVA, La Térmica, Sala Joaquín Eléjar and others). It also sells tickets for some events in Marbella, Nerja and other towns.

mmalaga.es

Más Málaga is a great site to find out what's going on and what's coming up in the city of Málaga and surrounding areas. The most helpful section is the '*eventos gratuitos (o casi)*' (free or nearly free events) listing which is a good way to find out about free concerts, exhibitions, and cultural events.

⊕ⓒ⬦ **conciertos.club/malaga**

One of the best websites for music listings, covering all genres from opera and classical to Hip Hop with flamenco. It is especially useful for finding out about bands playing in small venues like pubs and bars. Content in Spanish.

 ⊕ⓒ⬦ **malagadecultura.com**

Málaga de Cultura is a news and reviews website about the Málaga cultural scene, but it carries a very comprehensive listing of upcoming events. Content in Spanish.

♬ Flamenco

Before COVID, Málaga had a settled weekly timetable of flamenco concerts, demonstrations and *tablao* shows, but the venues were hit hard by the restrictions, both those imposed upon licensed premises and upon entertainment (*tablao* is the typical *andaluz* pronunciation of *tablado* and refers to the wooden stage on which flamenco is performed; in this case, it means a floor show in a bar or restaurant). It will no doubt take some time for a new regular pattern to be re-established.

Some will tell you that Málaga is not a place in which to see flamenco, which is of course nonsense. It is certainly a far more obvious place to see authentic flamenco than, say, Madrid or Benidorm. Flamenco is a hugely varied art form with countless influences, patterns of development and expressions. The *palos* (or styles) of flamenco fit into three broad categories: the most serious is known as *cante jondo* (or *cante grande*), while lighter, 'frivolous' forms are called *cante chico*. Forms that do not fit either category are classed as *cante intermedio*. Among these *cantos* there are hundreds of sub-divisions.

Malagueñas are Málaga's contribution. *Fandangos de Málaga* is the name given to a broad array of flamenco forms which, taken together, seem to have little in common. Part of the confusion stems from the fact that the term *fandango* is used across the Spanish-speaking world to refer to a wide range of songs and dances. All of these forms are related to the *verdiales*: traditional folk songs from the mountains around Málaga.

The best places to see top-quality flamenco performances in Málaga are the theatres, like the Cervantes and Echegaray, so check their programmes to see if they have any flamenco coming up. The **Museo Flamenco Peña Juan Breva (Calle Ramón Franquelo 4)** is also a good place. They used to have concerts on Thursday, Friday and Saturday evenings and perhaps these have started again, but information on their rather clunky website (**peñajuanbreva.eu**) is scant. The best thing is to pay them a visit and book in person. **MIMMA (Museo Interactivo de la Música Málaga, Calle Beatas 15 musicaenaccion.com/eventos**) also stages regular flamenco demonstrations in the afternoon — a far more suitable time for families than the late-night shows in bars.

The ⊕ **guiaflama.com** website (in Spanish) is a good source of information about flamenco performances and events in Málaga. They also sell tickets to some *tablaos*. The other options for seeing decent flamenco are the aforementioned *tablaos*. A few of the best-known are:

✗ ⚚ El Gallo Ronco ✿✿

🏛 CENTRO HISTÓRICO ⦿ Plaza de las Flores 1
⊕ elgalloronco.com

This bar (the name of which means 'hoarse rooster') has flamenco shows from Wednesday to Saturday at 1900 and 2100. You can opt for the basic ticket which includes a drink and a *tapita* or you can pay more for a drink and *tapas*. There are two other branches of the bar in town (**Calle Arquitecto Blanco Soler 3** and **Calle Álamos 1**) but these are not bookable online. You will need to pay them a visit and enquire.

✗ ⚚ Restaurante Tablao Alegría ✿✿✿

🏛 MALAGUETA ⦿ Calle Vélez Málaga 6
⊕ ⬦ flamencomalaga.com

This is a flamenco-themed Restaurant near Muelle Uno. It stages shows every day at 1800, 2000 and 2200. The food is good quality if you want to go for the dining option. The duration of the show is approximately 60 minutes and features well-known artists. The basic price is just for the show, but there are set menus and *à la carte* options available. The venue is fully adapted for people with limited mobility.

✗ ⚚ Restaurante Vino Mío ✿✿

🏛 LA MERCED ⦿ Plaza de Jerónimo Cuervo 2
⊕ ⬦ restaurantevinomio.es

Situated in front of the Teatro Cervantes, Vino Mío Restaurant has a flamenco show from Wednesday to Sunday (2000–2130). You make a booking for dinner (you can do this via their website) and pay a supplement for the show. Vino Mío is an excellent choice for children and families because it puts on a show in the early evening (most customers are tourists) and because of its informality.

🍷 ⚚ El Pimpi ✿✿

🏛 CENTRO HISTÓRICO ⦿ Calle Granada 62
⊕ elpimpi.com

On the first Thursday of the month, El Pimpi stages a flamenco *tablao* under the name '*Jaleo en El Palomar*'. Before COVID a dinner reservation was required but recently it has been a post-lunch entertainment. This may change, so check the website for information.

⚱🎗 Kelipé Centro de Arte Flamenco ✿✿

🎪 CENTRO HISTÓRICO 📍 C/ Muro de Puerta Nueva 10
🌐 💬 🎬 kelipe.net

A flamenco school run by the *bailaora* Susan Manzano, the Kelipé Flamenco Art Centre is a good place to see a serious performance of flamenco. With shows every evening between Thursday and Monday, although this is not a restaurant or bar, the entrance price includes a drink (and further drinks may be purchased).

🌐 FlamencoTickets.com

This is a useful website to find out about flamenco performances not only in Málaga city but throughout the Province of Málaga (Torremolinos, Benalmádena, Fuengirola, Ronda, etc.). The website has an English language option.

⛪ Churches

Málaga has a lot of beautiful churches, many of which have been restored in recent years. Most churches in the *centro histórico* are open in the morning (until 1300 or 1330) and then close in the afternoon before reopening in the early evening (around 1700 or 1730) for a couple of hours. (⚠ Donations are necessary to keep these churches open to be enjoyed by other visitors, so please be generous).

Etiquette

If you are not dressed appropriately, you may be refused entry to the Cathedral. In other churches, you might just arouse theatrical 'tuts' from the handful of Spanish *señoras* already in the church. Enforcing minimum standards of dress is more of an issue in the resort towns of the Costa del Sol.

The 'rules', such as they exist, are pretty much the same for men and women: no bare shoulders or thighs. That means that vest tops and 'short' shorts are not acceptable. Men must remove their hats. Be aware of logos (*e.g.* on t-shirts) or tattoos that might be considered offensive or obscene. If you have a pentagram on your t-shirt or a tattoo of a naked woman on your forearm, it will need to be covered up.

As far as I am aware, photography is permitted in all of Málaga's churches, though not with flash. As long as you keep noise to a minimum and talk, if you need to, *sotto voce*, you are free to explore but should not enter the sanctuary (the area around the main altar, reached by steps).

Something you should be aware of is 'adoration'. This is where the Blessed Sacrament is exposed on the altar and people come to pray before it (or, for Catholics, 'Him'). The main church where this takes place every day is Santo Cristo de la Salud, but it happens in other churches too. The signs are that the candles on the altar are lit and that there is a monstrance (a decorative gold stand used to display the Eucharistic host) on the altar. During adoration, do not talk and do not walk between the altar and the people in the pews.

La Manquita (Cathedral of the Incarnation)

🏛 CENTRO HISTÓRICO　◉ Calle Císter
⊕ 🕊 **malagacatedral.com** 🕐 Mon–Fri 1000–1930; Sat 1000–1800; Sun 1400–1800 💶💶 (💷 under 13s, people with disabilities, and Mon–Sat 0830–0900) 🎧

Málaga's Cathedral divides opinion. While some think it one of the jewels of the Spanish Renaissance, Lady Louisa Tenison felt that it could not 'boast of much architectural beauty'. Hans Christian Andersen thought its appeal lay in its sheer size, calling it a 'mountain of marble' (although its tower is only 92 metres high it was — remarkably — the second tallest non-industrial structure in Andalucía until 2012). As far as the height of the nave (the main body) is concerned, it is taller than any British cathedral save Liverpool and around the same height as Notre-Dame in Paris.

Dedicated to the Incarnation, the *Reyes Católicos* ordered the construction of a cathedral on the site of the *aljama* (main) mosque within days of taking Málaga in 1487. Thus, Málaga followed the pattern of practically every other city in Andalucía. Supplanting the 'old religion' by building over it is symbolic because sacred space is important. Almost any significant church in southern Spain is built on the site of a mosque (nowhere quite so clearly as in Córdoba), but dig a little further and you will find that the mosque was itself built over an earlier Visigothic church. Delve deeper and you will probably find pre-Visigothic paleochristian remains, themselves on top of a pagan Roman temple. It seems likely that even those pagan Roman deities will have superseded even earlier Iberian pagan deities. And then when we look at the geographical features of the location, we usually find something nearby to explain the reason for its 'sanctity', such as a hill, cave, crag, well or stream. Sure enough, in the case of Málaga, an underground stream runs beneath the Cathedral.

Construction of the new cathedral began in 1528 according to plans by Enrique Egas of Toledo and Diego de Siloé of Burgos who worked on several cathedrals in both Spain and the New World. The first part of the Cathedral to be constructed was the east end (the rounded part containing the altar), allowing the old mosque to continue to be used during construction. Work stalled for a time, beginning again under the direction of Hernán Ruiz II and Diego de Vergara, continuing until the end of the century. The Cathedral was consecrated on 3 August 1588.

Construction finally ended in 1782, having been funded by the imposition of an export tax on the Port of Málaga. However, as receipts were redirected to other projects, including support for American revolutionaries and a new road to Antquera, the south tower was famously left incomplete. The roof, the main sacristy, the central belfry, and other sculptural ornamentation, were likewise left unfinished.

Málaga's is a Renaissance Cathedral with a baroque façade and significant Gothic elements, which makes it a bit of a muddle, but it is impressive, beautiful and well worth visiting. The audio guide is free. When I last used it, the English narrator was bizarrely unable to pronounce many of the ecclesiastical terms necessary for such a guide, but perhaps it has been updated since then. There is also an audio guide especially created for children, in Spanish, English, French and Italian.

⚠ Something that often confuses visitors is the presence of a number of iron scroll-work structures supporting large stones (a couple are inside the building, the rest outside). These are not obscure liturgical objects but 'artworks' repurposing items left over from the restoration of the Cathedral's 12 bells in 2005. The stones represent 'absent bells', apparently.

Santa María del Sagrario

🏛 CENTRO HISTÓRICO 📍 Calle Císter

'Holy Mary of the Sacristy' is one of four churches constructed by order of the *Reyes Católicos* after the *reconquista*. The whitewashed interior is fairly simple (earthquakes, Napoleon and finally Republican arsonists and, later, artillery destroyed much of the original fabric of Málaga's churches), but there is an impressive plateresque retable — the work of Juan de Balmaseda, from the church of San Pedro de Becerril de Campos (Palencia). The original Gothic doorway dates from 1487 and is the oldest stonework of the cathedral complex. It was cut into the foot of the minaret of the former mosque, probably under the first post-*reconquista* bishop, Pedro Díaz de Toledo y Ovalle. The base of the original minaret is visible in the crypt.

Following the appearance of significant cracks in the walls of the church and an exploratory survey of the foundations, the church was closed in 2020 for both worship and tourist visits 'indefinitely'. Specialist contractors have warned that an earthquake with a magnitude of 4 or more would likely cause the structure to collapse. With Andalucía positioned between the Eurasian and African plates, earthquakes are a real risk with a significant tremor predicted to occur before the end of the century. The work necessary to stabilize the building is likely to take many years.

Basílica de Santa María de La Victoria

🏛 CRISTO DE LA EPIDEMIA

⊕ 🅰 santamariadelavictoria.es ⏱ 0830–1300, 1830–2030 ♻

The current building dates from the late 17th century, but replaced an earlier church which in turn was the expansion of a small chapel. It stands where Fernando II camped during the siege of Málaga. During the long campaign, Fernando was visited by friars of the Order of Minims, who brought him a message from their founder (St Francis de Paola) assuring him of victory. That victory came three days later and in due course, a chapel was erected that later became the first convent of the Minims in Spain. A church and new convent were constructed in the early 16th century, then demolished and rebuilt in the late 17th century. It was raised to the status of minor basilica (that is, a papal church) by Pope Benedict XVI in 2007.

The church houses a number of important images, including that of Our Lady of Victory, patroness of the Diocese and City of Málaga, carved in Germany, a gift to Fernando II from Emperor Maximilian I. It also houses the images of the several *hermandades* that have their headquarters here, including a *dolorosa* carved by Pedro de Mena. There is also an ornate *retablo* (altarpiece) and a highly decorated dome above the crossing.

The highlight, however, is the pantheon crypt* of the Counts of Buenavista; one of the gloomiest in Spain thanks to its sombre decoration featuring skeletons and figures of death in white plaster: a Baroque discourse on death.

*The crypt is currently closed for restoration works** following a devastating ingress of water from the abandoned Doctor Pascual Hospital that caused considerable damage to the plasterwork.

Santos Mártires (San Ciriaco & Santa Paula)

🏛 CENTRO HISTÓRICO 📍 Plaza de los Mártires Ciriaco y Paula ⊕ 🅰 santosmartires.es ⏱ Mon–Sat 0930–1330, 1800–2030; Sun 1100–1400

Another of the foundations of the *Reyes Católicos*, dedicated to Málaga's patron saints, martyred under Diocletian. The earliest extant documentary references to Ciriaco and Paula date only from the ninth century and some historians have suggested that they were martyred in Almería. However, we know that devotion to Ciriaco and Paula was well-established in Málaga very early on. Early editions of the Roman Martyrology record the place of their execution as being beside the river Guadalmedina, a fact commemorated in the name of the *barrio* south of the football stadium: Martiricos.

The church, originally in the Gothic-*mudéjar* style, was rebuilt after the 1755 earthquake. Further works were required after it was struck by a cannonball in 1854, and damaged by another earthquake in 1884. With each rebuilding it became more and more rococo, though it is still relatively plain on the outside. It was badly damaged in 1931 and looted in 1936. The final rebuilding began in 1945 and the most recent restoration was completed in 2022. The fact that it took 90 years to restore the church to its pre-1931 state shows quite how devastating the damage was.

San Juan Bautista

⚐ CENTRO HISTÓRICO ♀ Calle San Juan 3

Saint John the Baptist is another of the foundational parishes erected by the *Reyes Católicos* and was originally a Gothic and *mudéjar* (Moorish style) building, but it was badly damaged in the earthquake of 1680 and was rebuilt in a more baroque style. In 1931 it was attacked by Republicans and many polychrome wooden statues by Alonso Cano and others were destroyed, along with paintings by Murillo. In 1980, another fire destroyed the statues that had been saved in 1931. This church is the headquarters of the *Cofradías Fusionadas* — the eight ancient fraternities that merged in 1980 in order to raise funds for the restoration of the church and its Holy Week processional images. The actor Antonio Banderas is an active member of this fraternity.

The exterior plaster walls of San Juan are painted with geometric patterns. This style became popular in the early 18th century and is known as '*horror vacui*' (horror of emptiness). It was soon extended to secular buildings, adding *trompe-l'œil* elements like columns, sculptures, stone blocks and bricks. During the nineteenth century, these wall paintings disappeared under layers of lime whitewash applied as an anti-epidemic measure, but they have been uncovered again as a result of restoration efforts.

Santiago Apóstol

📍 CENTRO HISTÓRICO ⊙ Calle Granada 78 ⊙ Mon–Sun 0900–1300, 1800–2100

Saint James the Apostle is another foundation of the *Reyes Católicos*. Though it has baroque elements aplenty,it retains clear evidence of the local *mudéjar* architectural style. It was built on the site of a mosque and the *mudéjar* footprint is most clearly seen in the 16th-century bell tower. Initially, the former mosque was used for Christian worship, but construction of the church had begun by 1505 and was complete by 1545. The most famous Holy Week image inside the church is the 'El Rico' Christ and several fraternities are based here. Extensive restoration work has been undertaken recently and the church reopened for worship in July 2017. Picasso was baptized here.

Santo Cristo de la Salud

📍 CENTRO HISTÓRICO ⊙ Calle Compañía 4

This baroque church ('The Holy Christ of Health') was designed by Pedro Sánchez for his own order, the Jesuits (Society of Jesus), and opened in 1630. It is unusual in having a circular floor plan beneath the central dome (no aisles or transepts). The dome is a *trompe-l'œil* rendering of masonry, with portraits of saints, and was completely restored in 2014. In 2016, Santo Cristo was returned to ecclesiastical use. Santo Cristo is the headquarters of the Brotherhood of Students who carry Christ Crowned with Thorns, and Our Lady of Grace and Hope.

⚠ The church is mainly used for Adoration of the Blessed Sacrament, so please visit in silence and keep movement to a minimum so as not to disturb worshippers.

Santo Domingo de Guzmán

📍 MÁRMOLES ⊙ Calle Cerrojo ⊙ Mon–Sat 0900–1300, 1700–2000

St Dominic's is just across the river from the *centro histórico*, in El Perchel, and was originally the chapel of a vast 15th-century Dominican priory. It was the oldest ecclesiastical foundation to be built outside the medieval city walls, and it remains the largest city church after the Cathedral. The church sustained significant damage in the earthquake of 1680 and had to be rebuilt, and its riverside position means that it suffered repeated flood damage. The priory was confiscated in the 19th century, forcing the friars to leave the city, and in 1931, most of the church was destroyed by arson.

It is rather plain on the inside, though this perhaps comes as a relief after the wedding-cake baroque and rococo elsewhere. The chief reason to pay a visit, however, is that Santo Domingo houses the (near life-size) crucifix statue of the *Cristo de la Buena Muerte*, originally carved in 1660 by Pedro de Mena. That image was destroyed by rioters in 1931 and the current image was carved in Málaga in 1941 by Francisco Palma Burgos. During *Semana Santa*, when it is being transferred from the church to the headquarters of the fraternity next door, this image is carried aloft by soldiers of the Spanish Foreign Legion.

San Felipe Neri

🍴 SAN FELIPE NERI ⊙ Calle Cabello 20 ⊙ Thu 1000–1300; Tue–Thu 1800–1900

This church, from the 18th century, is the result of multiple extensions and reforms since the construction of the primitive chapel which was ordered to be built by the Count of Buenavista. Construction began in 1720 and the first chapel opened in 1730. Several religious orders were interested in establishing a house to serve the church but the Count granted it to the Oratorians (founded by Saint Philip Neri) because he had planned to dedicate it to the same saint and he took this to be a premonition. The Oratorian Fathers took possession on 11 November 1738.

The church was set on fire in 1931. On the Calle Parra and Plaza Montaño, bonfires were made with objects taken from the church. Four sculptures by Pedro de Mena and four paintings by Miguel de Manrique were stolen, burned or otherwise destroyed. Since the 1970s, following considerable repairs and further accidental discoveries, a series of paintings has emerged that decorate part of the side of the church. These paintings have been the object of expert restoration carried out by the Ministry of Culture of the *Junta de Andalucía*. Between September 2010 and November 2011, the Church was closed for a thorough restoration, though its Baroque splendour has emerged undimmed.

Nuestra Señora del Carmen

🏛 EL PERCHEL 📍 Calle Plaza de Toros Vieja 23
⊕ ⓔ **elcarmenmalaga.es** 🕐 Mon–Fri 0800–1230, 1730–2030

Our Lady of Mount Carmel is another relatively old (1584) church in the *barrio* of El Perchel constructed as part of the Discalced Carmelite convent of San Andrés. Damaged in the earthquake of 1680, the church was extensively remodelled in the 18th century. The liberal General José María de Torrijos and his 49 companions were brought to the Convent on 10 December 1831 and placed in the chapel, ostensibly so that their confessions could be heard. They were executed by firing squad the next day on the beach of San Andrés.

In 1835 the convent was disentailed and the community expelled the following year. In 1931, almost the entire patrimony of the church was destroyed, including multiple works by Pedro de Mena. Those treasures that remained were destroyed during the Civil War. The Virgen del Carmen (by José Navas Parejo, 1945) is located here and the church is also the *sede canónica* of the images of Jesús Nazareno de la Misericordia (also by José Navas Parejo) and the Virgen del Gran Poder (an image of the 18th century Málaga circle, restored by the *sevillano* sculptor Álvarez Duarte).

San Lázaro

🏛 LA VICTORIA 📍 Plaza de la Victoria 19 🕐 0900–1300, 1800–2000

Founded by the *Reyes Católicos* in 1491, this was initially built as a chapel for the Hospital de San Lázaro, established for the treatment of leprosy. Nowadays only the chapel remains, the hospital having suffered extensive damage during the floods of 1628. After its repair, it played an important role during the plague epidemic of 1637. Since 1706 it has been the headquarters of the Sacramental Brotherhood of *Nuestro Padre Jesús Nazareno de los Pasos del Monte Calvario* which processes with the image of *María Santísima del Rocío*, known in the city as the 'Bride of Málaga' (and the reason that the brotherhood is popularly known as '*El Rocío*'). It is a popular church for the celebration of marriages on account of its beautiful altarpiece and association with the 'Bride of Málaga'.

San Agustín

🏛 CENTRO HISTÓRICO 📍 Calle San Agustín 7 🕐 Sun 0930–1230; Mon–Fri 1730–1930

Until the disentailments and confiscations of the nineteenth century, Málaga was full of friars — Augustinians, Franciscans, Dominicans, Capuchins, Mercedarians, Minims, Trinitarians and Carmelites. Now only the Augustinians still occupy their original location.

Construction of the complex (consisting of a convent, church and former school, with the first two visible from Calle San Agustín, next to the Picasso Museum) began in 1575 following the purchase of land on what was then called the Calle de los Caballeros. In 1843, after Mendizábal 's confiscation, the buildings were seized by the State and ceded to the Málaga *Ayuntamiento*. They were later commandeered to serve as a hospital during the African War of 1863–1865. The buildings were put to various different uses until the friars re-founded a school in 1918. In 1931, it was set on fire during the burning of convents under the Second Spanish Republic.

In 2004 the fabric was significantly restored. In one of its chapels, Saint Rita de Cascia — an Italian Augustinian saint from the 15th century, patroness of marriage and the family and 'advocate of the impossible' — is venerated. On her feast day (22 May) there is a tradition of blessing and distributing thousands of roses.

La Aurora y Divina Providencia

🍴 CENTRO HISTÓRICO 📍 Calle Andrés Pérez 15
🕐 Mon–Sat 1100–1300; Mon–Fri 1700–1900

The Church of Our Lady of The Dawn and Divine Providence was constructed in the 18th century (1787). A married couple, Manuel Francisco de Anaya and Margarita del Villar, bequeathed property to the Dominican nuns provided they were able to build a monastery and chapel within eight years. For the next two hundred years or so, this church was the sisters' chapel. The nuns withdrew from their monastery in 2006 and in 2013 the Diocese of Málaga handed the chapel to the Fraternity of the Vintners to use as their *templo* (canonical seat or church), on the understanding that they would care for the fabric and ensure its upkeep.

Basílica de María Santísima de la Esperanza

🍴 Mármoles 📍 Calle San Jacinto 1 🕐 Mon–Sat 0930
–1300, 1800–2100; Sun 1100–1300

This is another brotherhood temple (The Archconfraternity of *El Paso y La Esperanza*) of recent construction. Built in 1988 and raised to the status of a minor basilica the same year, the single nave is fairly plain, but a richly gilded apse above the high altar forms the *camarín* ('dressing room' or niche) for the images of the brotherhood. These are the Sweet Name of Jesus '*El Paso*' by Mariano Benlliure (1935, replacing a 17th-century image that was destroyed in 1931) and Holy Mary of Hope, a 17th-century carving restored by Luis Álvarez Duarte. The ceiling is decorated with depictions in oils of Marian allegories and portraits of the major prophets by García Ibáñez.

Oratorio de Santa María Reina y Madre

CENTRO HISTÓRICO ♀ Plazuela Virgen de las Penas
🕐 Mon–Sat 1100–1300

This chapel, which is the *sede canónica* of the Holy Week Brotherhood of Sorrows (*Las Penas*) has a fine baroque façade very similar to that of the Episcopal Palace (1762) and one might assume that it is of a similar vintage. This oratory, however, was only built in 2008, making it the newest place of worship in the city. In the view of some it is thus an unimaginative pastiche of the baroque, while others hold it up as an example of a new ecclesiastical building that blends sensitively with its environment and history.

Perhaps the chief reason to visit, though, is to see the extensive murals that cover the entire ceiling of the chapel, some 140 m². These murals represent six years of work by the *malagueño* artist Raúl Berzosa Fernández who completed them in 2014. Raúl, whose secular works are reminiscent of those executed by Joaquín Sorolla, has also completed commissions for other brotherhoods and designed a number of Holy Week posters.

Málaga with Children

Despite its plummeting birthrate, Spain remains a very family-friendly and child-friendly culture. In 2021, the decision of a restaurant in Bilbao to ban children made the national news. There was even talk of challenging the policy in the courts. Children are welcomed in the vast majority of eating (and drinking) establishments in Spain, and Málaga is no different. The obvious exceptions are places which are about 'grown-up drinking' — nightclubs, cocktail bars, rooftop hotel bars, and the like. If you are in any doubt, just have a look around you.

🏃 For Older Children and Teens

Regarding things to do and see, teenagers may be fascinated by the CAC and bored to tears by the Thyssen, or vice versa. If you are planning to take secondary school-age children to Málaga, a good way of involving them in the experience is asking them, tech-savvy as they no doubt are, to help with the planning and booking of the trip: letting them organize the transport links in Málaga, working out which smartphone apps are required, and so forth.

While French just about retains its place as the most widely studied foreign language in UK schools, Spanish is nipping at its heels, having long since displaced German in the number two slot. If your school-age child is studying Spanish, then researching and planning the trip, and taking a lead in communicating in Spanish while in Spain, will help them considerably with the language. There is a world of difference between role-playing ordering breakfast in a classroom, and actually ordering breakfast in a Spanish *cafetería*, from a Spaniard.

⚽ Spectator Sport

The **Málaga CF** soccer team played in the top division but was relegated in 2018, only five years after reaching the Champions League quarter final in 2013. After a long period of decline and a disastrous 2022/23 season, it was relegated again to the Primera Federación (the third tier of the Spanish league system). The **Unicaja Baloncesto Málaga** team plays in the Premiership basketball league. You can check fixtures and buy tickets for football matches here: **malagacf.com**, and, compared to UK tickets, you won't have to take out a mortgage to take the family. Their ground, **Estadio La Rosaleda**, is a 15 minute walk from the centre of Málaga. It is also possible to visit the stadium and see the stands, presidential box, VIP area, pitch, changing rooms, press room and museum. The tour runs daily, Monday to Saturday (match days excluded), in English and Spanish, at 1100, 1300, 1630 and 1800: **malagacf.com/en/museum**. There is no booking form on the website, so contact the club by email or phone to arrange. Tickets for Unicaja basketball games can be purchased here: **venta.unicajabaloncesto.com/en/next-games**. They play at the **Palacio de Deportes José María Martín Carpena** (Ⓜ Line 2 or 🚌 16).

🏃 Physical Activities

An alternative to exploring the streets of Málaga on foot is doing so on a bicycle or Segway®. There are several companies that hire bikes, with **bike2malaga.com** and **biketoursmalaga.com** being two of the best-known. Both will hire out bikes if you want to go off to explore on your own, and Bike Tours Málaga offers 3-hour-long city bike tours twice a day at reasonable rates (with the option to extend the bike hire until the close of business for a few euros extra). Children's bikes are available, and for very young children, they can supply and fit child seats. Booking ahead online is strongly advised, especially with children.

Bike tour companies have agreed their routes with the *ayuntamiento*, but if you hire a bicycle for your own use then you must obey the laws of the road as they apply to cyclists in Spain in general and Málaga in particular. New regulations came into force in February 2021 imposing fines ranging between €60 and €200 for infractions. Ask the bicycle hire staff for advice about where to cycle (and not to cycle). Except on the main road, the speed limit for bicycles is 30 kph (18 mph). Riders under 16 must wear a helmet.

There are few companies offering Segway® tours (which can provide a more relaxed means of getting up to the Gibralfaro Castle). Two well-established agencies are **segwaymalagatours.com** and **topsegway.es**, both of which offer guided tours lasting from just 30 minutes up to 3 hours for adults and children aged nine and above. Booking ahead is also recommended.

And talking of e-scooters, there are currently several companies hiring e-scooters (*patinetes eléctricos*) in Málaga, available to pick up from a number of points in the city after booking using an app. ⚠ Although the Spanish word '*escúter*' sounds like it should mean electric scooter, it is in fact the word for a moped

There are multiple e-scooter hire providers operating in Málaga, so to provide a list here would not be helpful because it would very quickly become out of date. Companies arrive and depart quickly. A fixed unlock fee and then a per-minute tariff seems to be the normal charging structure. Your best bet is to find a rank of e-scooters first (there are several around town) and then download the relevant smartphone app (scooters have a QR code which will open the Google or Apple app store). None of these parking stations are in the historic centre because scooter use is forbidden (except for residents or those making deliveries of medicine). Quite a few stations are positioned along the seafront (both west and east of Málaga) and at the boundaries of the historic centre. The María Zambrano railway station, Soho, Plaza de La Merced and Muelle Uno usually have stations with scooters available.

Scooter Regulations

After spending some time catching up, the *ayuntamiento* brought in new regulations for bicycles and e-scooters in 2021. The rules for e-scooters are similar to those for bicycles, with a few specific additions:

Minimum age: 16 years (18 for some operators). The scooter and driver together must have a minimum height of 1.40 meters.

Maximum capacity: one person.

Lights: must be on at any time of the day for easy visibility.

Use of the helmet and 'hi vis' vest: Is mandatory when using '30 Lanes'.

Civil liability insurance: is mandatory for scooter rental, so you will be covered.

Pedestrian areas: the use of e-scooters on pavements and other areas intended for the exclusive use of pedestrians is prohibited. Most e-scooter hire apps indicate the areas where scooters may not be ridden on a map (basically the historic centre and Muelle Uno/Dos).

Permitted routes: bike lanes, 20 kph zones ('*Zonas 20*'), residential streets or 'single-platform' roads (those with no kerbstones, only bollards, and where pedestrians have priority) at a maximum speed of 20

kph, and in 30 kph zones ('*Zonas 30*'), at a maximum speed of 25 kph. E-scooters may use the road as long as there is no alternative cycle path alongside.

Parking: exclusively in the reserved space indicated for this purpose. Consult the app to find permitted locations.

Other Activities

Kart & Fun

CARRETERA DE CÁDIZ C/ Victoria de los Angeles
kartfun.es 1100–2100

Next to the 'Plaza Mayor' out-of-town shopping centre, 'Kart & Fun' operate two floodlit go-kart tracks, with circuits supervised by qualified staff. 'Extreme Kart' is for drivers over 15 years old (and over 1.60 metres tall) in 270 cc karts, and 'Junior Kart' allows 10 to 14-year-olds (1.45 to 1.60 metres tall) to race 160 cc karts. 5 to 10-year-olds (1.20 to 1.45 metres in height) can race 35 cc karts on the children's track. Two-seater karts allow kids under 5 (or under 1.20 metres) to race with an adult. You can either take the ⊘ *Cercanías* (local) train to the Plaza Mayor stop just after the airport or the No. 5 bus from the centre.

Skate Park

BAILÉN–MIRAFLORES Calle Camino Cuarto
skateparkmalaga.info Daily

In the suburb of Camino Cuarto, north-west of the centre, near the University Hospital, the Rubén Alcántara Skatepark has a number of installations (bowl, mini-ramp, halfpipe, street zone and dirt track) for BMX, skateboarders, skaters and scooter users. The courses were designed by the twice-world-champion BMX star Rubén Alcántara, who is from Málaga. The park is easily reached by bus from the centre (C1 923 Magistrado Salvador Barberá). However, although the skatepark's website has a link marked '*Alquila tu material*' (rent your equipment), it does not seem to lead anywhere. Plans to offer equipment hire were delayed and complicated by the COVID pandemic, but it may be a service offered in the future.

Museums

If the more traditional art galleries and museums fail to elicit much enthusiasm from your adolescents, there are still a few unusual exhibition spaces and collections that may pique their interest.

Museo de la Imaginación

SOHO Calle Martínez Campos 13
museoimaginacion.com Wednesdays

This is one of Málaga's newer museums/exhibitions, having opened in 2018. It is also one of the most popular, attracting 5,000 visitors in its first four months of operation. The 'Museum of the Imagination' is small (only three large rooms), but there is plenty to see and experience. Essentially an exhibition of optical illusions, this is far more than a collection of curios. There is a wealth of information (in Spanish and English) which explains how the toys and exhibits challenge reason and visual perception.

Though clearly the sort of museum that would be of particular interest to inquisitive children and teens, I defy anyone not to be fascinated and captivated by this place. This is not a 'children's museum', but it is most certainly a place where even the most jaded adults can feel like children.

Principia Centro de Ciencia

🚇 LA ROSALEDA 📍 Avenida de Luis Buñuel 6
(near the La Rosaleda Football Stadium)
🌐 principia-malaga.com 🕐 Mon–Sat 1700–2000

This is undoubtedly one of the best science museums anywhere, though it is mainly about labs, workshops and demonstrations as opposed to static exhibits. Situated near the home ground of Málaga FC, it was founded by local science teachers and school groups make up the majority of visitors. However, they are open for visits by the general public of all ages, both on green days (school days) and blue days (non-school days). Helpful staff will do their best to answer any queries you have by email.

See also the **National Airports Museum**

🤸 For Younger Children

🏛 Museums and Exhibitions

One of the museums that seems particularly to appeal to primary school-aged children is the **Artes y Costumbres** because its collection is of everyday objects from typical homes — things that any child can recognize and compare to their modern (or British) equivalents. The **Centre Pompidou** goes out of its way to welcome children and there is almost always an exhibition curated with younger visitors in mind. In July (the first full month of the school summer holidays) the **Centre Pompidou** and **Museo Casa Natal Picasso** often organize activities and workshops aimed at children. The **Museo Casa Natal Picasso** has events for families with children aged 3–12 almost every Saturday. In recent years, some of these sessions have been conducted in English. Check the websites for details.

The **Museo de la Imaginación** has plenty to interest primary school age children. Also not to be missed is '**MIMMA**' — the Museo Interactivo de la Música Málaga, or Interactive Málaga Museum of Music:

Museo Interactivo de la Música

CENTRO HISTÓRICO Calle Beatas 15
musicaenaccion.com Mon 1030–1600, Tue–Sun 1030–1930 €

This fascinating and highly enjoyable museum first opened in 2002 but was little known thanks to its poor location. But in 2013 it moved to the Palacio del Conde de las Navas in the historic centre. The museum itself has a collection of some 1,000 musical instruments, of which around 400 are on display at any given time. The entire museum is designed with younger visitors in mind and perhaps what will appeal most to children is the museum's motto, '*Se ruega tocar*' — 'Please play'.

The museum also stages frequent flamenco concerts, which are ideal for families with children. They are reasonably priced (you will not be required to spend money on drinks and dinner), last 45 minutes (so will not put too much strain on a child's attention span), and usually take place at family-friendly times in the afternoon. Consult the website to see what's coming up and buy tickets from the ticket office at the museum.

The English Cemetery

MALAGUETA Avenida de Pries 1
cementerioinglesmalaga.org Tue–Sun 0900–1400 € (if attending church services or visiting a family grave)

A family 'fun day' in a cemetery? As strange as it may seem, yes. Family visits take place on Saturdays throughout the year. There is an email booking form on the website (click on 'VISITS') and the entrance fee is payable upon arrival. Choose your arrival time (between 10.30 am and 1.30 pm, though remember that the cemetery closes at 2 pm). The cemetery provides you with the materials you need to take part in the self-guided activities — maps, quizzes and games, in English and Spanish — which help children learn about the history of the cemetery itself, discover the stories of some of the people interred there and find out about the history of Málaga in the 19th and 20th centuries.

The Alcazaba and Castillo Gibralfaro

Children who may be too young to appreciate the history or Moorish architecture of these monuments will still enjoy exploring their battlements and nooks and crannies. Keep a close eye on them, though — the Spanish attitude to 'Health and Safety' is somewhat more relaxed than that in the UK, so you cannot assume that there will always be a safety railing to prevent a small adventurer from climbing over the top.

ℛ Beaches

Málaga's beaches are likely to be a draw for most children, as are boat trips. During the 'beach season' (roughly from Easter until mid-September), beach-side kiosks sell bucket and spade sets, beach games, cold drinks and ice creams. During the same period, both of the city's 'blue flag' **Malagueta** and **Misericordia** beaches have lifeguards. The safest places for children to swim are either at the far end of the Misericordia Beach near the spit ('Espigón de La Térmica'), or in the sheltered bays along the **Pedregalejo** Beach, but keep an eye on the flags on any beach. Green means safe to bathe, yellow advises caution (for strong swimmers, and keep close to the shore), and red indicates danger. Both beaches are journeys of around 20 minutes from the city centre by bus.

⅄ Play Parks

The play parks in the centre are more suited to younger children or toddlers, so if it's big slides and zip-wires you are looking for, then head to the beach or to a park. You can find abundant play parks in both directions — going east of the city to the Malagueta, Caleta and Pedregalejo beaches, and west to the Huelin and Misericordia beaches.

Of the two options, I would recommend travelling west. This takes you into the working-class Carretera de Cádiz *barrio*, a taste of real, 'local' Málaga. As these are the areas where *malagueña* families actually live, you will find plenty of parks and attractions for children. You can take the bus (e.g. 🚌 **3 or 7**) from the city centre, or with plenty of stops for playing, eating and enjoying the beach, it's a pleasant walk from María Zambrano Railway Station.

If you choose to walk (you can always hop on a bus if you get tired), then there is a shady promenade all the way from the Port to the Guadalhorce Nature Reserve. En route, you will pass the Parque de Huelin, which has a children's play park. On your walk along the promenade, you will come across three chimneys, standing like obelisks on the seafront. The first, by Burger King at the end of Huelin Beach, is the smallest of the three, and the last is the chimney of the La Misericordia thermal power plant, known as 'La Térmica'. The tallest and most iconic chimney, however, is the one in the middle, level with the San Andrés beach. This is the **Los Guindos** Chimney, also known as the 'Mónica Tower'. Built in 1923 it was once the tallest structure in Spain and though the lead works closed in 1979, the chimney remains as a reminder of Málaga's industrial past.

If you turn right (*i.e.* north) at the chimney you will find the large Parque del Oeste, with play parks, lakes, and modern sculptures (and lots of cafés nearby). Further west is the Misericordia beach, which has a play park (with zip-wire) at its eastern end and good swimming for children at the sheltered west end next to the spit (Espigón de La Térmica). Beyond the spit is the small Sacaba Beach, and just inland from here is one of the best play parks in town — Parque Litoral, which has play parks for younger children and, as its centrepiece, an artificial mound with three precipitous slides and rope webbing to grapple your way back to the top. You are in a residential district, so there is no shortage of family-friendly restaurants if you want to have some lunch and make a day of it.

A bus ride away from the centre in the Teatinos neighbourhood is the Parque del Cine (Cinema Park) — a 10,000 m² landscaped space inspired by the world of cinema, and where you can also find corners dedicated to the universe of books. It has a fun zip line, swings in the shape of a whale and a rhinoceros, a trampoline, a climbing structure, revolving games and a ping-pong table.

🌴 *Chiringuitos*

Eating at the beach is always fun, so have lunch at a *Chiringuito*. If a skewer of delicious sardines (heads and all) is a step too far, most *Chiringuitos* have non-fish options, even if they are not terribly exciting. French fries are pretty ubiquitous, and a few places even offer burgers and pizzas.

Along the almost two-mile stretch of the Huelin, Misericordia and Sacaba beaches, there is a wealth of places to eat and drink. You will find more than a dozen *Chiringuitos* serving barbecued fish and seafood, most with seating indoors and outdoors, at least in the warmer months. Litoral Pacífico and Gutierrez Playa, both at the west end of San Andrés Beach, are very well known and reliable, but with so many competing outlets in such a compact area, you should be able to dine pretty well wherever you go. Find one that you like the look of; preferably one with plenty of customers eating, rather than twiddling their thumbs as they wait for food from an overwhelmed kitchen. If grilled sardines do not appeal, then there are plenty of other seafront options — pizza, burgers, *tapas*, and fast food (KFC and Burger King), including a branch of **100 Montaditos** (next to the Torre Mónica). There is also a handful of ice cream shacks and, between the Litoral Pacífico and Gutierrez Playa *Chiringuitos*, '**Mums**

Cafetería' — a friendly, relaxed spot for breakfasts, coffee, ice creams and the filling sandwiches known in Málaga as *camperos*.

🏖 Beaches (City Centre and East)

The city centre beach, on the other side of Muelle Uno is the Malagueta Beach which extends as far as the 'Espigón de la T' spit, where it becomes the Caleta Beach. There is a small children's playground between the two beaches and plenty of bars and *chiringuitos* for refreshments. A little further east are the beaches of Pedregalejo and El Palo which have their own distinctive characters. The Playa de Pedregalejo is only half an hour's walk from the centre of Málaga, but you can preserve your energy for a morning or afternoon at the beach by taking a bus (🚌 3 or 8, towards El Palo) from the city centre. Get off at **Baños del Carmen** (Ⓑ1111).

The **Baños del Carmen** ('Carmen Baths') were constructed in 1918 as a state-of-the-art bathing station for well-heeled visitors. After beach-going tourists migrated westwards it fell into near ruin but is nowadays the site of a bar and restaurant, 'El Balneario' ('The Spa' **elbalneariomalaga.com**). The prices are fairly reasonable given the prime location and the service is first class.

A little farther on from the Baños del Carmen are the **Astilleros Nereo** (Nereus Shipyards **astillerosnereo.com**), a working boatyard making, repairing and restoring wooden boats. They have a small but fascinating museum and offer guided tours of their workshops for groups of 4 or more. Contact them to book: ✉ **info@astillerosnereo.com** ☎ **+34 952 291 198**

Continuing to walk eastwards, you'll follow the promenade to the four sheltered bays of Pedregalejo Beach, where there are a number of smart *chiringuitos* that seem to be busy all year round. Leaving the Pedregalejo beach, the esplanade crosses the Arroyo Jaboneras ('Soapmakers' Stream') and you come to the district of El Palo, which has a real 'seaside' feel to it. You are only 3 km from the centre of Málaga, but it feels further away. There are very few, if any, tourists here (though it is a popular spot for city-dwelling *malagueños* at weekends) but it is well-served by bars and restaurants. There are *chiringuitos* on the beach itself, another strip of restaurants and bars along the promenade (Calle Quitapenas and Calle Banda del Mar), and even more options as you venture into 'town' from the beach (north of the Avenida Salvador Allende). The dining options here are a bit more rough-and-ready than those in Pedregalejo, but the food is just as good and the bill will be much less. To take the bus directly to El Palo, get off at Avenida Juan Sebastián Elcano–Iglesia (Ⓑ 1131).

Out of Town

Bioparc Fuengirola

Bioparc Fuengirola is a compact urban zoo (it's even smaller than London Zoo). Run by committed, friendly staff. Take the *Cercanías* train from Málaga to Fuengirola.

Sealife

Sealife is an impressive aquarium in nearby Benalmádena — just under an hour by bus (🚌 **M-110**) from the Muelle Heredia, or take the local train (🚉**C1 to El Pinillo**).

👪 Toddlers

As much as Málaga might be about bars, restaurants and museums, it is still a welcoming place for families with very small children. Save for the most exclusive locations, most bars and restaurants will be used to (well-behaved) children of all ages. There is a decent play park in the historic centre in the **Plaza Enrique García-Herrera**, and lots of smaller playgrounds dotted about. The main bike hire shops will hire bikes with children's seats (best to give them a bit of notice to be sure of availability).

The play parks west of Málaga should appeal, as should the **Parque del Oeste** with the added attractions of a resident wallaby, emus and terrapins. In the centre, the **Parque de Málaga** is fun for small children to explore and can seem deceptively expansive despite being sandwiched between two busy roads. Lots of trees and pathways provide opportunities for playing *el escondite* (hide and seek). There is a small play park near the auditorium. Parallel to the park is **Muelle Dos**, which is a wide, open promenade where children can safely run around. The glass barrier prevents them from falling into the water and there are play parks to enjoy.

The **Gibralfaro Castle** and the **Alcazaba** both have lots of interesting corners to explore, though you will need to keep a watchful eye on very young children. The Spanish approach to 'Health and Safety' is not quite as belt-and-braces as that followed in the UK. Generally speaking, the expectation is that parents will see to their children's safety rather than a multiplicity of railings, barriers and striped hazard tape. If you go up to the Gibralfaro Castle on foot, take the **Calle Mundo Nuevo** route, which is not only shadier but has playgrounds to break up the walk.

Some of the attractions listed in the sections above should be sufficient to entertain younger children, particularly the beaches, Fuengirola **Bioparc** and Benalmádena **Aquarium** (which is free for children under 3). The 'hands-on' section of the **Music Museum** would be fun, too.

The Great Outdoors

🌳 Parks and Gardens

Jardín Botánico de la Concepción

📍 Camino del Jardín Botánico 3

🌐 laconcepcion.malaga.eu 🕐 Tue–Sun 0930–1930 💶

Continually rated as one of the best botanical gardens in Europe, La Concepción is a subtropical paradise that features formal gardens adjoining lush green forest. Created in the mid-19th century by an aristocratic couple, Jorge Loring Oyarzábal and his wife Amalia Heredia Livermore, the gardens fell into decline in the 20th century but have been restored to their former glory by the *ayuntamiento*. Following the basic route takes around an hour and a half, but you could easily spend all day there. There is a *cafetería* and seven picnic areas if you want to bring your own food. It has a route designed for wheelchair users and those with limited mobility. They also stage frequent art exhibitions and lay on fantastic family activities around Christmas time.

The gardens are on the northern edge of Málaga — too far to walk, but one can take a local bus.

How to get there:

(A) The Number 91 Tourist Bus (5–7 buses per day) from the *centro histórico*, direct.

(B) The Number 2 bus (every 12–15 mins) from the *centro histórico*, plus a 15-minute walk.

Bus No. 91

The departure stop closest to the *centro histórico* is **Pasillo de Santa Isabel** (🚏 202), though you can also catch it from in front of the María Zambrano railway station. 🚌 91 is operated not by the EMT Málaga bus company, but by the same firm that runs the open-top tourist buses. Thus, the '*bonobús*' card is not valid, but there is a special return fare. The timetable changes seasonally, like the opening hours of the gardens. Search for *linea* (line) 91 on the EMT app (QR code above) and you will be directed to a link showing a special timetable. This link is blocked for IP addresses outside Spain but should work locally. As the information on the website/app is not always up-to-date, I advise you to check with the *turismo*, or at the EMT office (**Alameda Principal 47, Mon–Fri 0900–1330, 1700–1900; July–August: Mon–Fri 0830–1430**).

Bus No. 2

The departure bus stop is called **Pasillo de Santa Isabel (Ⓑ 202)** which is behind the Museum of Popular Arts and Customs, that is, facing the river. Get off at the final stop, which is called **San José (Ⓑ 251)**, and then walk to the garden entrance.

To take the bus back towards the city, retrace your steps and catch the 🚌 2 from the same stop at which you got off (Ⓑ **San José: 251**). The bus route takes you on the west side of the river, past El Corte Inglés, and then turns east along the Alameda. The final stop is near the Atarazanas market.

Parque de Málaga

At the eastern end of the Alameda Principal, south of the Cathedral and Alcazaba, this park is a cool oasis in the centre of the city. In 1876, the engineer Rafael Yagüe oversaw a project to reclaim land from the sea in order to extend the Alameda Principal (and thus creating Muelle Dos as it is today). The project had been the brainchild of the *malagueño* Antonio Cánovas del Castillo who, between 1875 and 1897, served six non-consecutive terms as Prime Minister of Spain. Rubble from demolished slum housing surrounding the Alcazaba and from dredging the Guadalmedina river bed was used for infill, and thousands of tonnes of rocks from quarries near El Palo arrived by barge.

Planting began in 1899, though it would take another 20 years to achieve anything like its current appearance. Since then, the park has undergone several renovations, most recently in 2007, when its biodiversity was expanded to 300 species.

 The Parque de Málaga is not large (1.5 hectares) and occupies a seventy-metre-wide space between two busy roads (the Paseo del Parque and the Paseo de los Curas), but the plentiful vegetation and mature trees shield visitors from the noise of the city to create a '*rus in urbe*'. The 'main' park is known as the '*banda exterior*', but across the Paseo del Parque, in the shadow of the Museo de Málaga, is a small triangular section known as the '*banda interior*'. The hundreds of mature trees in the park come from six continents and include many tropical and subtropical species making it one of the most important subtropical flora gardens in Europe. The website of the *ayuntamiento* has a wealth of information about some of the most interesting arboreal species, but only in Spanish: **bit.ly/parquedemalagaspecies**.

The Parque de Málaga is also home to many works of sculpture, mainly in the form of monuments topped with busts of illustrious men (and they are all men) — poets, composers, politicians and soldiers — associated with Málaga. There are also more 'cultural' and poetic representations, like the *Ninfa del Cántaro* (Pitcher Nymph) and *Ninfa de la Caracola* (Conch Shell Nymph) fountains, and the *Burrito Platero* (Little Silver Donkey). This latter work celebrates a character in the lyrical poem *Platero y yo* (subtitled *An Andalusian Elegy*) by the Nobel Prize winner Juan Ramón Jiménez, and you will find it in the children's play area in the centre of the park next to the amphitheatre. You can find information about a lot of the sculpture and flora of the park (in English) on the British horticulturist Simon Needham's excellent personal blog: **parquedemalaga.wordpress.com**.

Cemeteries

Málaga has two 19th-century cemeteries worth exploring. The more famous among visitors is the Anglican Cemetery near the bullring. The English Cemetery in Málaga is the oldest non-Catholic cemetery in Spain, having been established in 1831 to provide a decent burial place for British subjects who died in Málaga. Previously, Protestants were buried on the beach, at night, in an upright position. When the cemetery opened, the locals, who had only a vague grasp of Reform Christianity, were surprised to see a cross at the entrance, having been unaware that 'these Jews' [*sic*] worshipped under the same symbol that Catholics did.

The new cemetery began to fill up towards the end of the 19th century because by then Málaga had become popular as a winter destination for recuperating invalids. By the end of the 20th century, with no source of stable funding, it was in a sad and run-down state, but since 2006 it has been operated as a charitable foundation, so while the admission price may seem a bit steep to visit a small, albeit peaceful and beautiful, grave-yard, entrance fees are a vital source of revenue that go towards the cem-etery's restoration and upkeep.

There is also the city's Catholic cemetery north of the city, about half an hour's walk from the centre, or a fifteen-minute bus ride (🚌 1, 2 or C2) from the Alameda or Plaza de La Merced. The **San Miguel Cemetery** is of interest due to the numerous mausoleums that the 19th-century bour-geoisie had built there.

 The San Miguel Cemetery was consecrated in 1810, at a time when the city was occupied by Napoleon's troops. Nevertheless, it would be a couple of decades before it took on its current aspect. The wall around it was not built until 1827 and it would be another two years before it was con-sidered completed, a fact that is commemorated in the inscription on the triangular plaque above the entrance arch.

Parque del Oeste

 The 'Eastern Park' is a relative newcomer among Málaga's green spaces, only inaugurated in 1992. It is the largest park in the suburbs, in the *barrio* of Carretera de Cádiz. If you are visiting Málaga as a family with children, then the Parque del Oeste should be on your list of places to visit, but even *sans enfants*, it is a pleasant and diverting place. If you are taking a walk along the beaches south-west of the city then take a detour, or if you take a bus from the centre (🚌 16) then alight at **Luis Barahona Soto/ Parque del Oeste** (Ⓑ 1523).

This park packs in a great deal with over 800 trees, areas for basketball and football, an open-air gym, a lake with an impressive fountain, doz-ens of modern sculptures (by the German sculptor Stefan von Reiswitz, an adopted son of Málaga), a couple of children's play parks, wildfowl and other animals including a wallaby, emus, a tortoise and a chameleon. There are even two examples of that rarest of features — a public lavatory.

🦅 Birding

 David Lindo (aka **@urbanbirder**), known from UK TV programmes like Springwatch and Countryfile recom-mends Málaga as one of the best urban birding locations. Even in the city centre, you will see birds that are rarely seen in urban spaces in Britain. There are the squawking escaped parakeets, of course, but also starlings and sparrows in abundance. You will also see Lesser Kestrels, and even Peregrine Falcons, flitting around the towers of the Cathedral and other churches, as well as Black Wheatears and Blue Rock Thrushes around the *Teatro Romano* and Alcazaba. The prime spot for birdwatching, however, is the Parque del Guadalhorce (Guadalhorce Natural Park) near the airport

For more information about this and other birding sites throughout the province, consult the excellent website of the *Diputación* (Provincial Government) **birdingmalaga.es** and also **wildandalucia.com/bird-watching-in-malaga**.

🚶 Walking and Hiking

The possibilities for walking and hiking in the city and province of Málaga are extensive. You are limited only by your energy, time and shoe leather. Walks around urban areas are one thing, but in the countryside and mountains, then you need to make adequate preparations. The terrain can be tough, particularly in the summer heat, but if you are an experienced hiker, there are lots of possibilities.

To find suitable routes outside Málaga city, begin with the website of the local *turismo* as many of them will have a section about walking and hiking routes, as well as maps. Most tourist offices are good at responding to queries. Other good places to find tried and tested routes are **komoot.com**, **alltrails.com**, **hiiker.app**, and **wikiloc.com** (the site/app that the *Diputación de Málaga* has chosen to partner with). It is also worth searching online more generally, and you may find that using Spanish delivers more relevant results (*ruta* = route, *camino* = path, *senderismo* = hiking, *a pie* = on foot).

Gran Senda

This is the official hiking route through the Province of Málaga — 650 km and 35 stages of the *Gran Senda* (Great Route) *de Málaga* covers 9 regions and 50 towns going through, or around, 13 protected natural areas: **gransendademalaga.es**. A number of PDF guides (to trees, birdlife and more) are available to download, though most are in Spanish. However, there are a couple of guides in English that you can download for free:

 Sierra de las Nieves Path

 The Great Málaga Path

If the links are broken, consult the main page at: **malaga.es/en/laprovincia/publicaciones**

Senda Litoral

The *Senda Litoral* is the coastal path of the Province of Málaga, a project of the *Diputación de Málaga* in cooperation with the coastal municipalities. Although unfinished, the eventual aim is to allow a person (on foot, on a bicycle or in a wheelchair) to travel from Nerja in the east to Manilva in the west, some 160 km to 180 km, depending upon the final route.

The path has the reference GR92. 'GR' footpaths are a network of long-distance walking trails in Europe, mostly in France, Belgium, the Netherlands and Spain, where the network is called '*Sendero de Gran Recorrido*'. The *Senda Litoral* will form a stage in the long coastal route from Catalonia to Tarifa. There is a website with information at **sendalitoral.es** and Chris Chaplow at **andalucia.com** is maintaining a very useful map

 showing the current state of play vis-à-vis the progress of construction (GREEN — complete; ORANGE — port or marina; BLUE — beach with no boardwalk; RED — you need to make a diversion to reach the next section). Use the QR code to view the map, or go to: **bit.ly/SendaLit**

⛱ Beaches

The 'bathing season' is reckoned to be between 15 June and 15 September (with July and August the peak), so although the beaches are open and accessible from mid-September to mid-June, the showers, bathrooms and some of the beach bars won't, there will be no lifeguards and you will not be able to hire deckchairs or parasols. Consult the following websites for the most up-to-date information, including occupancy and flag status:

 bit.ly/MalagaCityBeaches — use the 'map' view

 playas.malaga.eu — the official town hall site (in *castellano*)

 aforocostadelsol.es/aforo — live information about beaches in the Province of Málaga (in *castellano* and only updated during the June-September bathing season)

Beach Rules

Foreign visitors are often caught out by local laws regarding the use of the beaches in the Málaga municipality. A sensible approach is not to do anything that you don't see others doing. For example, smoking is prohibited on some beaches', and on any beach the disposal of cigarette butts anywhere other than refuse bins could attract a large fine (of up to €3,000). The use of soap or shampoo in the showers is also prohibited.

Nudity is forbidden on any beach that is not a '*playa nudiſta*', though topless bathing is generally permitted. On the other hand, beachwear is for the beach, not the town. Other prohibited activities include playing music that might annoy others, leaving litter, camping, lighting fires and cleaning anything other than your own body in the showers.

🚤 Boat Trips

A popular sightseeing option in Málaga is to take a boat trip around the bay. The basic trip lasts an hour and the rates are standardized between the three operators. Children aged 14 and over count as adults. The standard trip takes you out into the open sea — just — but you get a different, and beautiful, view of the city of Málaga. All three operators embark at the intersection of Muelle Uno and Muelle Dos.

CitySightseeing Spain Boat Tour

This is operated by the 'CitySightseeing' tour bus franchise based in Sevilla whose open-top buses you see in almost every city in Europe. The boat uses the same gaudy red livery, so is easy to spot. Booking online is advised.

Fly Blue

With this company, which appears to be the most popular, you have a choice between the standard 1 hour excursion or, for a higher ticket price, a 90-minute sailing at sunset.

Catamarán Mundo Marino

This company offers the most choices. You can choose the standard 1-hour cruise or the 90-minute sunset cruise as above, but other options include a sunset cruise with music, a 90-minute trip including half an hour's swim, a 3-hour excursion further along the coast, etc.

Outside Málaga

Costa Sol Cruceros operate a regular cruise launch between Benalmádena and Fuengirola (an hour each way), as well as a separate 2-hour dolphin-spotting trip.

♨ Hammams

In Moorish times there would have been dozens of bath houses in the Medina of Málaga, as there were all over Andalucía. For some time now there has been a modern hammam in the Plaza de los Mártires, where a pair of narrow doors open into a 1,300 square metre facility, that opened in 2013. It's not original, of course, but hammams are popular in Andalucía and the same company operates in Madrid, Granada and Córdoba. More recently, another hammam has opened near the Cathedral.

Hammam Al-Andalus Málaga

🏛 CENTRO HISTÓRICO 📍 Plaza de los Mártires Ciriaco & Paula 5 🌐 malaga.hammamalandalus.com
🕐 Mon–Sun 1000–0000

Hammam Open Space and Spa

🏛 CENTRO HISTÓRICO 📍 Calle Tomás de Cózar 13
🌐 elhammamspa.com 🕐 Mon–Sun 1100–2200

🚻 Lavatories

Visitors to Spain often remark upon how few public lavatories there are. Spending most of the day out of your hotel or accommodation, it's worth engaging in some forward planning regarding 'comfort breaks'. Try to use the loo before setting out for the day, whenever you visit a museum, and every time you stop to eat or drink. As in English, the *castellano* words for the loo are all euphemisms: *baños* (bathrooms), *servicios* (services), *aseos* (washrooms), etc. If you need to ask for directions ask, '*Dónde están los servicios*' (**don**-day ess-**tan** los sair-**beeth**-yoss).

Bars, restaurants and *cafeterías* all have lavatories for the use of customers but some establishments won't object to your using their facilities if you ask politely (*¿Puedo usar el baño?* **pway**-doh oo-**sar** el **ban**-yoh), though those near the tourist hot spots can understandably be less accommodating. Of course if buy a drink, you have every right to use their facilities. Facilities in bars can range from modern and immaculate to somewhat basic. When you switch on the light, remember where it is! Most lights are on timers and you may find yourself suddenly plunged into darkness.

Lavatory paper and paper towels (or a working hand dryer) are also something of a lottery, so make sure you are prepared and keep a few sheets of loo paper in your bag or pocket. The supermarket Mercadona (branches in the main railway station and on Paseo de Reding) sells biodegradable moist wipes, including in a pocket size (15 wipes).

Also, if there is a bin next to the pan, this is where you **must** deposit your lavatory paper. Although this mode of disposal is far less common than in the past, there are still areas where it is necessary due to ancient plumbing.

You can find public lavatories at the following locations:

Beaches — there are basic facilities at most of Málaga's beaches (during the bathing season)

Parque del Oeste — rather unusually, this urban park has two sets of public conveniences

María Zambrano Railway Station — there are two sets of free facilities in the Vialia shopping centre, one on the ground floor and one upstairs next to the cinema. Both are fully accessible, modern and clean.

Málaga Bus Station — two very basic, but free, facilities at either end of the main vestibule.

Shopping Centres — in Málaga city this means the **Centro Comercial Larios**, near the bus station. The facilities are clean and accessible. There are also basic loos in the **Mercado Atarazanas** and other markets.

Muelle Uno — there are public lavatories on Muelle Uno which are very clean and fully accessible.

Turismo — the main office at Plaza de la Marina has a single-cubicle loo.

Department Stores — in other words, El Corte Inglés on the El Perchel side of the river. There are facilities on every floor.

CAC — the toilets in the **Centro de Arte Comtemporáneo de Málaga** are for the use of patrons, but they are accessible (go through the main entrance and they are downstairs on the right) and admission to the gallery is free in any case.

Car Parks — walking around Málaga, you may wonder where all the multi-storey car parks are. The answer is that they are largely underground. There are lavatories in the subterranean car parks at Muelle Uno, Plaza de la Marina, Alcazaba and Calle Salitre, generally situated near the pedestrian access point and ticket machines.

Municipal Automatic Cubicles — the *ayuntamiento* is spending almost €760,000 installing five free, automatic and self-cleaning public conveniences in different areas of the city. The first appeared in the Plaza de la Marina in October 2022, and others are planned. All are (or will be) fully accessible.

Portaloos — during *Semana Santa* and the *feria*, portaloos are provided by the *ayuntamiento*.

Shopping

Most of the big-name Spanish stores (Mango, Massimo Dutti, Bimba & Lola and Zara) are on, or near, **Calle Larios**. **Calle Nueva** (the parallel street to the west) is also a busy shopping street. The **Calle San Juan** has a number of local, independent stores, and **Calle Especería** (running west from the Plaza de la Constitución towards the river) is the street for typically Spanish clothing — flamenco dresses, shawls, and *sombreros* (hats).

🛒 *Supermercados* (Supermarkets)

For everyday items, there are a few 'express' type supermarkets around the *centro histórico*:

🛒 **Carrefour Express** ♀ Calle Atarazanas s/n ⏱ Mon–Sat 0830–2200

🛒 **Preba** ♀ Calle Fernán González 4 ⏱ 0900–1430, 1700–2100

🛒 **Carrefour Express** ♀ Calle Tejón y Rodríguez 1 ♀ Calle Especería 7 ⏱ 0900–2130

🛒 **Día** ♀ Calle Carretería 105 ⏱ 0900–1500, 1700–2100

Outside these times, or for basics and/or emergencies, there are plenty of small corner shops in the centre, mostly run by Chinese families and known colloquially as '*chinos*'. Like corner shops in the UK, they sell snack foods, milk, soft drinks, alcohol etc., and like UK corner shops, you pay over the odds for convenience. Most are open from mid-morning until late (usually midnight or even later).

Although fairly small, the best-stocked supermarket in the city centre is **Maskom** (**Calle Gómez Pallete 2**) which occupies space in the **Mercado de La Merced**, just off the plaza of the same name. Open from 0900–2130 daily and 0930–2100 on Sundays and holidays.

A lot of the small Spanish supermarkets are being taken over by **Carrefour**, so some on the list and on the companion map may have changed! For more choice and lower prices, take a 20-minute walk or bus ride from the centre to **El Corte Inglés**, **Eroski** (Larios Shopping Centre) or **Mercadona** (María Zambrano railway station).

El Corte Inglés

🍴 Mármoles 📍 Avenida de Andalucía 4–6 🕐 Mon–Sat 1000–2200

El Corte Inglés is the Selfridges of Spain. Food in the basement supermarket is reasonably priced by UK standards (the most expensive lines are stocked in '**Gourmet Experience**' on the top floor) with a huge range of products. For other goods, it has the advantage of stocking almost anything you need all under one roof. It's useful to know that there is a branch of **Mister Minit** here. This is the continental equivalent of Timpsons and useful if you need your shoes or watch repaired.

🛍️ *Centros comerciales* (Shopping Centres)

Centro Comercial Larios

🍴 EL PERCHEL 📍 Avenida de la Aurora 25 🕐 1000–2200

In Spain, a *centro comercial* is a shopping centre in the UK sense, a mall in the US sense — *viz.* chain stores and a few basic eateries. Larios Centro is the nearest such shopping centre to the *centro histórico* and while it is never going to feature on any visitor's sightseeing itinerary, it is handy to know where it is should you need it. In the basement, there is a very large, low-cost but good quality supermarket called Eroski. It is also where Málaga's branch of Primark is located. It's barely a 5-minute walk from the rail and bus stations.

Centro Comercial Vialia

🍴 El Perchel 📍 Explanada de la Estación 🕐 1000–2200

If you happen to be passing through (or near) the railway station (María Zambrano) then remember that there is a good supermarket on the upper level (Mercadona) that not only carries a wide selection of groceries but also a good range of toiletries. Picking up some essentials here when you arrive in Málaga could save you from having to make a special journey later on.

Plaza Mayor

🍴 CARRETERA DE CÁDIZ 📍 Calle Alfonso Ponce de León 🕐 1000–0100

Plaza Mayor is a large, out-of-town shopping centre just past the airport. It can be reached in 10 minutes by the 🚆 *Cercanías* train. It has 79 stores, a **Mercadona** supermarket, 33 eateries, all the major Spanish brands and plenty of international ones, including designer boutiques.

👜 Independent shops

Corcel (Handbags)

🏛 MÁRMOLES ⊙ Calle Hilera 6 🕐 Mon–Sat 1000–1400, 1730–2030

A very small shop opposite El Corte Inglés (on the north side).

Zerimar-Málaga (Handbags and leather goods)

🏛 CENTRO HISTÓRICO ⊙ Calle Granada 12 🕐 Mon–Sat 1000–2030; Sun 1100–1900

The Málaga store of a company based in Campillos (between Málaga and Córdoba). The shop is 50 metres north-east of the Plaza de la Constitución. They have branches in Torremolinos, Benalmádena and Fuengirola

Misako (Fashion Bags)

🏛 CENTRO HISTÓRICO ⊙ Calle Nueva 29 🕐 Mon–Sat 1000–2130

Misako is a very popular brand of handbags (they also make bags for men, backpacks and purses) based in Barcelona. They are faux leather, but good quality and sold at amazingly low prices.

Souvenirs

Temporánea Concept Shop

🏛 CENTRO HISTÓRICO ⊙ Calle Santos 4 🕐 1030–1330, 1700–2100

If you want to avoid the usual mass-produced tat then this little shop selling tasteful and high-quality products is a good start. Also worth looking out for is anything made by malagapatterns.com and lamalagamoderna.com though currently both stores are online only.

🔔🚚⛴ *Ultramarinos* (Delicatessens)

An *ultramarinos* is a traditional Spanish grocer's shop. The name was originally due to their stocking of 'exotic' products that have come 'across the seas', but nowadays they are valued more for selling local delicacies. They have an old-fashioned set-up with a shopkeeper behind a counter, rather than supermarket-style self-service. They are excellent places to buy local products as gifts and souvenirs. Do support them!

Zoilo

🗺 CENTRO HISTÓRICO 📍 Calle Granada 65 (near Plaza de La Merced) 🕐 0900–1430, 1630–2100; Sat 0930–1430; ⊘ Sun

Founded in 1956, Zoilo carries a huge range of products, many of them from the Province of Málaga. It also sells a small range of *empanadas* and delicious, freshly made *pitufos* (small sandwiches). The staff are very friendly and good at making helpful recommendations.

Zoilo sells all the usual staples and delicacies: Málaga *salchichón*, Ronda *chorizo*, local cheese, sweet and table wines, ham, *borrachuelos*, carob and almond cakes, homemade jams, raisins, fig bread, olive oil, vinegar, cane honey, olives and the rest. It is probably most famous, though, for its sandwiches (fillings include jamón, cheese, *tortilla*, pork belly, *salchichón* and turkey).

Juan de Dios Barba

🗺 CENTRO HISTÓRICO 📍 Calle Martínez 10 🕐 Mon–Fri 0930–1400, 1700–2030; Sat 0930–1400; ⊘ Sun

This traditional shop is known for its excellent quality *bacalao* (dried salt cod), great rolls of which fill the window, but it stocks a huge range of gourmet products from salted Málaga almonds to La Torre olive oil, acorn-fed *jamón* and local cheeses. It is now run by Javier and Carlos Crespillo, great-grandsons of the founder.

El Almacén del Indiano

🗺 CENTRO HISTÓRICO 📍 Calle Cisneros 7 🕐 Mon–Sat 1130–1500, 1800–2100; ⊘ Sun

Although it is not particularly old, this is a typical *ultramarinos* where you can taste and buy an exquisite selection of wines, craft beers, hams, cured meats, cheeses, oils and pickles from Andalucía and other parts of Spain. It's primarily a shop, but the 'tasting' element means that it's also an intimate *tapas* bar. A good plan (for two or more people) is to order a glass (or a bottle) of the excellent house wine and the '*surtido malagueño*' — a selection of cured local meats and cheeses.

La Princesa Pastelería

🗺 La Merced 📍 Calle Granada 84 🕐 1000–1430, 1700–2100

Strictly speaking a *pastelería* (confectioners or patisserie) rather than an *ultramarinos*, but it is one of the most traditional shops in Málaga having chalked more than 80 years of serving customers. María Ángeles Guerrero, daughter of the founder, is to be found behind the counter and she does a good trade in traditional sweets and biscuits from the region. Doña María's meringues are much loved by *malagueños*.

 ## La Mallorquina

📍 **CENTRO HISTÓRICO** 📍 Plaza de Félix Sáenz 7
🕐 Mon–Sat 0900–1400, 1730–2030, Half Day Sat)

Founded in 1943, La Mallorquina was acquired by José Palma Aguilar in 1982. Now run by José's son, José Palma Medina, its range of interesting jams is especially noteworthy and includes plenty of unusual (and local) varieties like chestnut or Pedro Ximénez. Don José has recently moved into online commerce with an excellent website, but in the shop the service is as kind and professional as it ever was.

La Despensa de Iñaki (see the listing under **bars**)

 ## Crespillo Innova

📍 **MALAGUETA** 📍 Calle Cervantes 10 🕐 Mon–Fri 0930–1400, 1730–2100; Sat 0930–1400

Only established in 2004, this is an Aladdin's cave of gourmet delights behind the bullring, selling the finest products from all over Spain — wine, oil, vinegar, ham, chocolates, *conservas* (tinned seafood) and preserves, Málaga honey, etc. It is run by the Crespillo brothers who also own Juan de Dios Barba.

 ## Manzana de Oro (Golden Apple)

📍 **MALAGUETA** 📍 Paseo Reding, 16 🕐 0900–1400, 1700–2100

The shelves of this charming *ultramarinos* are meticulously stocked with great attention to detail. At Manzana de Oro, you will find a huge range of local products from Málaga and the surrounding region; among them some of the highest-quality wines in the province. Friendly, knowledgeable staff.

 Books

 ## Mapas y Compañía

📍 **CENTRO HISTÓRICO** 📍 Calle Compañía 33 🕐 Mon–Fri 1000–1330, 1700–2000; Sat 1000–1400

This is a lovely bookshop with a focus on travel. The English section isn't huge, but it is well worth a visit just for the experience. This is the closest that Málaga has to Daunt or Stanfords bookshops in London. A delightful place with really helpful staff.

Librería Luces

🏛 ALAMEDA 📍 Alameda Principal 37 🕐 Mon–Sat 0930–2030

This much-loved independent bookshop is an important cultural landmark in Málaga (they organize the regular chess tournaments for children on the Alameda Principal). They stock a modest range of books in English.

Librería Rayuela

🏛 CENTRO HISTÓRICO 📍 Calle Cárcer 1 🕐 Mon–Fri 1000–2000; Sat 1000–1400)

Another independent bookshop with a decent range of books in English.

🛍 Others

Tea and Coffee: Golden Tips

🏛 CENTRO HISTÓRICO 📍 Calle Especería 26 🕐 Mon–Sat 1000–1400, 1700–2030

A lovely boutique shop specializing in teas, coffees, chocolates and all related accessories.

Accessories: Ten to Nine

CENTRO HISTÓRICO 📍 Plaza Constitución 7 🕐 Mon–Sat 1000–1400, 1700–2030

This small independent shop sells goods made in Málaga. The clothes are marketed under the 'Smach' brand and the accessories under the 'Boho' brand.

Jewellery: Calamita

🏛 CENTRO HISTÓRICO 📍 Calle Cárcer 1 🕐 Tue–Sat 1100–1400, 1730–2030

This jewellery shop was started by Nora Zurita (with her partner Ale) and specializes in simple items made with silver, crystal and leather. For handmade artisan pieces, the prices are reasonable.

Ceramics: Alfajar Cerámica Artesanal

🏛 CENTRO HISTÓRICO 📍 Calle Císter 1 🕐 Tue–Sun 1000–1330, 1600–1830; Mon 1000–2030

Run by husband and wife team José Ángel Ruiz and Lola Díaz, this store sells pottery and ceramics with vaguely 'cubist' designs.

Records: Discos Candilejas

CENTRO HISTÓRICO Calle Sta. Lucía 9 Mon–Sat 1030–1330, 1730–2030

Some families go to Discos Candilejas on Saturdays to teach their children what music is 'really' about. They introduce them to the world of CDs, vinyl and tapes, while the kids watch in wonder (and perhaps disbelief).

Wine

The better supermarkets carry a decent selection of wine. But if you want to buy a bottle of local wine to enjoy during your stay, or want to take a bottle or two home while avoiding the airport offerings, try an *ultramarinos* or the following:

Málaga Wine Museum

La Goleta Plaza de los Viñeros 1 Mon–Fri 1000–1700, Sat 1000–1400

The museum's shop carries a good selection of the best wines from the region, with knowledgeable staff to tell you about the wine, its region and *bodega*.

El Templo de Vino

CENTRO HISTÓRICO Calle Sebastián Souvirón 11 1030–1400, 1800–2130

The aptly named El Templo de Vino is one of the newer wine shops in Málaga, having opened its doors in 2011. Many of the wines on sale are available to try by the glass. The passionate, knowledgeable staff speak Spanish, English, French, Italian and German.

Dulces de Convento

One of the more unusual purchases one can make in Spain is confectionery made by local nuns, sold from the convent door. This is one of those times when visitors need to take a deep breath and go for it. Ring the bell and wait for the voice behind the wooden *torno* (a kind of enclosed lazy susan) to say, '*Ave María purísima!*' ('Hail, purest Mary!') to which you respond, '*Sin pecado concebida!*' ('Conceived without sin!' sin peh-**kah**-doh con-thay-**bee**-dah) and give your order. Next to the *torno* will be a list of products, all with extraordinary and ancient names: *roscos de vino, mantecadas, borrachuelos, roscos de vanilla, pastitas de almendras, clarinas, pujaldrinas, hortolanas, hugolinas, yemas*, and many more. Place your money into the lazy susan and after it turns back and forth, retrieve a box of sweet biscuits, wrapped in tissue paper.

Contemplative nuns support themselves by making sweets and it is also one way in which they can share their secluded life with 'the world'. As the Mother Superior of the Minim Nuns in Archidona puts it, 'What we intend with these sweets is that they provide the flavour of heaven, that when tasting the sweets you will experience the sweetness of God.'

La Trinidad 📍 Plaza Zumaya 5 🕐 Mon–Sat 1030–1330, 1600–1830; Sun 1200–1330, 1600–1830

In Málaga, sweets are made and sold by the Poor Claire Sisters at the **Monasterio de Nuestra Señora de la Paz y Santísima Trinidad** (Monastery of Our Lady of Peace and the Holy Trinity). Each sweet biscuit is sold in boxes of 250 g, 500 g or 1 kg, and you can also buy selection (*surtido*) boxes in the same weights.

In the city centre, one can also buy sweets and biscuits made by nuns from the Province of Málaga (Málaga, Antequera, Ronda, Coín, Archidona, etc.) in most *ultramarinos*.

🎁 Gift Ideas from Málaga

The best places to find the food and drink items in this section are the *ultramarinos* listed above, any of the city *mercados* (markets) or larger supermarkets (El Corte Inglés has the most choice and a better selection of premium and gourmet products).

Goat's Cheese

Málaga is famous for its goat's cheese. Most goats from Málaga are descended from two ancient goat breeds: the Pyrenean mountain goat from the north of the Peninsula, and the Maltese goat, originally from North Africa. The cheese produced is exceptionally buttery and creamy. To take home with you, the best kinds are *curado* (mature) or *semi-curado* (medium mature). Look out for *Crema* (or *Pâté*) *de Queso* — goats cheese whipped with olive oil to make a very grown-up cheese spread. It is sold in jars.

Jamón Ibérico y de Castaña

Some slices of good ham (*jamón ibérico* is the best) is an obvious food to take home with you. Supermarkets sell a huge range, all the way from the basic (but still very good) *serrano* right up to the eye-wateringly expensive top brands. If you want to try before you buy, quite a few market traders will now vacuum pack your purchase (such as **Charcutería Delgado** in the Atarazanas market).

A unique local product is *jamón de castaña* (chestnut ham). The main difference between this and traditional *ibérico* ham is that the pigs have been fed with chestnuts, alongside acorns and cereals. The final cured ham has its own distinct flavour profile and is rich and soft in texture. The main producer is '**Melgar**' from Arriate, near Ronda, but it is on sale in Málaga in their own shop (Calle Martínez 2). As well as *jamón de castaña*, the shop sells their own range of cured pork products (varieties of ham, cured shoulder, sausages, salami, black pudding, etc.) plus a huge range of gourmet products from the Ronda area (wine, cheese, jam, honey, etc.). The shop also sells delicious ham rolls to take away.

Embutidos (Charcuterie)

If you have visited a few bars and enjoyed some *tapas*, you will likely have tasted a variety of local *embutidos* already — *chorizo*, *salchicha*, *salchichón*, *morcilla*, *morcón*, etc. ('*embutido*' means 'something that is stuffed'). Most emblematic of all is the *Salchichón de Málaga*, a very soft, lightly cured (and fermented) sausage that is soft enough to be spread on toast. Supermarkets will stock all the typical Spanish *embutidos*, but if you want to take something locally produced, then go to an *ultramarinos* or a market stall like **Charcutería Delgado** or **Carnicería Jesús** in the Atarazanas market.

Alcohol

If you have checked-in bags on your return journey, then you have lots of options. It seems a waste to carry home a bottle of Rioja or a bottle of Bombay Sapphire when both are available at home (admittedly at higher prices). Take some DOP Málaga or DOP Sierras de Málaga wine, some Resoli or Mistela, or even some local (or at least Spanish) gin.

Olive Oil

Another delicious bottled liquid that is worth taking home is extra-virgin olive oil. Spain is the world's biggest producer of olives and olive oil and produces some gourmet varieties of stunning quality. If you buy a bottle of excellent AOVE (Extra Virgin Olive Oil) to take home, then please look after it. Olive oil does not improve with age but begins to deteriorate from the moment it is pressed. Store it in a dark cupboard in the coolest part of your kitchen.

Dried Fruit

Málaga is world-famous for its Moscatel raisins (*pasas de Málaga*). These are sold either **con** (with) or **sin** (without) *semillas* (seeds). Markets and *ultramarinos* are the best places to buy (and try) these. Alongside the raisins will be the almonds (*almendras*); another typically *malagueño* product. You can buy them plain, roasted, fried, salted, caramelized and even spiced. However, beware — those you buy in a Málaga market are a natural product without preservatives, so their shelf-life is short. If you take a bag home with you, consume them within a couple of weeks at most. To keep for a special recipe (like Christmas Pudding), you should freeze them.

Also in the 'dried fruit and nuts' (*frutas secas/frutos secos*) category is the fig. The province is a significant producer of figs and because the season for fresh figs is short (August to October), most of the crop is dried and available all year round. A typical product is *pan de higo* or 'fig bread'. It is not bread (it contains no flour) but rather a pressed cake of dried figs, sometimes with nuts and other fruit, and it is a delicious accompaniment to cheese. The best-known kind is from Coín.

Another fig-based treat is the *rabito* ('little tail'). *Rabitos* are figs soaked in liqueur, stuffed with praline truffle, and dipped in chocolate. They are fairly expensive but utterly delicious.

Turrón

In the last few years, a number of touristy, faux-olde-worlde shops selling *turrón* (nougat) have sprung up throughout Málaga. *Turrón* is originally from the Valencia region, but has been made in Málaga for so long that it can now be considered 'local'. It comes in two kinds: hard (*duro* from Alicante), or soft (*blando* from Jijona/Xixona). The hard kind can be tooth-shatteringly hard, and the soft kind can be very chewy. If you like it, then fill your boots and buy great ingots of the stuff. But if you're more of a mind that it's an interesting local sweet and an unusual gift, then go for a selection box or chocolate coated *turrón*. As always, try to buy it from an *ultramarinos* or from Casa Mira and not one of the new chain stores.

Paprika and Saffron

Neither paprika (*pimentón*) nor saffron (*azafrán*) are cultivated in the Province of Málaga, but both make good gifts to bring home from Spain. Saffron is mainly produced in La Mancha and will be slightly cheaper (and certainly fresher) than what you can buy in the UK. Paprika — *pimentón* — comes in two kinds and three intensities. It is produced in two geographical 'denominations of origin'. *Pimentón de Murcia* is unsmoked, and *Pimentón de la Vera* (from Extremadura) is smoked. There are also three grades of heat (though no one who has eaten at an Indian restaurant in the UK would consider any of them especially 'hot') — *dulce* (sweet), *agridulce* (medium), and *picante* (hot). One of the reasons why *pimentón* makes a lovely gift or souvenir is that it is often packaged in a beautifully decorated tin.

Other Products from Málaga

The Diputación has created the '*Sabor a Málaga*' (Taste of Málaga) brand to bring together local producers in order to showcase and promote their products. Have a look at their website to discover the full range (the translation link for English is in the top right-hand corner). *Sabor a Málaga* also organises food fairs all over the Province, including a huge event in the Paseo del Parque in Málaga city during December (**saboramalaga.es/categoria/ferias**).

Religion
♟ Catholicism

Spain is culturally, though not officially or constitutionally, a Catholic country. There are hundreds of Catholic masses celebrated in Málaga city every Sunday, and dozens every day. Anyone is welcome to attend Mass in a Catholic church (although only baptized Catholics are able to receive communion), so if you'd like to experience a Spanish liturgy, you certainly can, whatever your personal religious beliefs (or lack thereof). Most churches have a morning or lunchtime mass, and an evening mass, but please check locally. Mass times change seasonally so it would not be helpful to try to provide a timetable here, but the 🌐 misas.org website may be useful (if you access this site on a mobile device, it will use GPS).

The busiest city-centre church is also the least beautiful — Stella Maris on the Alameda Principal — a huge brick-built box served by the Carmelite Friars. There are five daily masses and seven Sunday masses 🌐 stellamarismalaga.es.

Mass is celebrated in the extraordinary form (*aka* the Tridentine Rite) at the **Iglesia Conventual de San Agustín** (Augustinian Canons) at 10 am every Sunday. For other masses, check the Una Voce blog: **bit.ly/UVMalaga**

Mass is celebrated in the ordinary form (*missa normativa*) in Latin in the Cathedral on Sundays at 10 am.

Mass is celebrated in English at the **Parroquia de Cristo Rey** (Avenida Santiago Ramón y Cajal 5) at 11.30 am on Sundays. For information about masses (and confessions) in the greater Málaga area, it's best to search online for up-to-date information: **bit.ly/MisasMalaga**

✝ Other Christian Denominations

St George's Anglican Church (in the English Cemetery) has a sung Eucharist each Sunday at 11 am: **stgeorgeschurchmalaga.org**

There are many Baptist and Evangelical churches in Málaga, which a Google search will quickly uncover. A rough rule of thumb is that when the name (and website) is in Spanish (*e.g.* '*Iglesia evangélica la puerta Málaga*') then services will be in Spanish with a mostly Latino congregation, and when in English (*e.g.* 'The Worship Place') then the congregation will be almost entirely composed of ex-pats.

There is a Romanian Orthodox Church in Mijas (Costa), and there is a small Moscow Patriarchate congregation in Málaga city (**Русская Православная Церковь в Малаге** 🅕 **russkayapravoslavnayatserkov**). They use rented office space but hold regular liturgies and seem to have a resident priest. Consult the Facebook/Meta page for details. The largest orthodox community is in Marbella.

✡ Judaism

Spain, like most of Europe, has a rather shameful record with respect to Jews. The period of Moorish rule is often held up as a time of tolerance and even flourishing for *sefardíes* (Sephardi or Hispanic Jews), yet in this period there were pogroms, expulsions and even crucifixions. After the *reconquista*, Jews fared no better and, arguably, much worse, in part due to their reputation for having 'collaborated' with the Moorish 'enemy'. Worse was to come, with the edict of expulsion in 1492.

And yet Spain's connection to Judaism runs deep. Much of what we take to be 'Spanish cuisine', and even that often assumed to be 'Arab', is almost certainly

A service in a Spanish synagogue, from the *Sister Haggadah* (c. 1350)

Jewish in origin. Ironically perhaps, the food now most associated with Lent, Easter and Christmas (*torrijas, tortas de aceite, buñuelos, bizcochos,* etc.) has a clearly Jewish origin.

The Jewish quarter of Málaga is the sector of the historic centre where the Jewish *aljama* lived during the Middle Ages (*viz.* even in the so-called

'Golden Age' they were concentrated in ghettos to keep them under surveillance and control). It is known that, at the time of the *reconquista* of Málaga, there were some 450 Jews in the city and any who refused to convert were deported in October 1487. Following that came the practical disappearance of everything that could preserve the memory of a once significant and vibrant Jewish presence in the city.

Since 2004, works have been carried out for the recovery and rehabilitation of the Jewish quarter. The so-called 'Plan of the Jewish Quarter' of the *ayuntamiento* has seen the restoration of a *mudéjar* tower (the Centro Ben Gabirol) which houses on the ground floor a tourist information office with, on the top floor, a kind of covered terrace and small exhibition space. It stands in the former Plaza de la Nieve, recently renamed the 'Plaza de la Judería'.

On the Calle Alcazabilla, facing the Teatro Romano, there is a rather beautiful, yet sad-looking, statue of Solomon Ibn Gabirol, the Jewish poet and philosopher born in Málaga around 1021. Gabirol's gaze might well be downcast and his countenance sorrowful, for so was his life, afflicted with some unknown malady which left him unable to work and caused him great pain. His parents had moved to Málaga after falling out with the Moorish ruler of Córdoba and then had to move again, to Zaragoza, taking the young Solomon with them. He lost his father in his teens and his mother a few years later and his poetry, although beautiful, tends towards the elegiac and maudlin. His philosophy was, as far as we can tell, entirely ignored by Muslim thinkers, and mostly ignored by Jewish ones, but to the  medieval Christian world he was known as Avicebron and his writings were assumed (by William of Auvergne at least) to be the work of an Arab Christian.

The **Comunidad Judía de Málaga** is currently situated in the Soho district (⊙ **Calle Duquesa de Parcent 8** ⊕ **cjmalaga.org**) and occupies an unremarkable office block. There is a shul (and mikvah) but many visitors complain that they have been unable to find it. Sadly, in common with many Jewish places of worship around the world, security is necessarily tight and the community does not advertise its presence, so if you want to worship during your visit to Málaga, I suggest you get in touch by email first: ✉ **rabinocjma@gmail.com**, ✉ **info@cjmalaga.org**.

There is a kosher fast food restaurant in Málaga city (**La Kaña Kosher, Calle Alemania 17**), and a kosher supermarket in Huelin (**La Makolet, Calle Góngora 20**). Where Jewish visitors wanting to keep kosher will have to be careful is in dealing with the Spanish obsession with 'garnishing' all kinds of dishes with *jamón* or *chorizo*, and also understanding the distinction between '*pescados*' (fish) and '*mariscos*' (seafood), with the latter often finding its way into dishes that appear to contain only the former. Apart from clams and prawns, most of the best-loved local dishes are fish (not seafood) based, but the phrase '*¿lleva mariscos?*' ('Does it contain seafood?' – **yay**-bah ma-**riss**-koss) may be useful. Remember that even a chickpea stew is almost certainly going to be cooked in meat stock. The easiest way forward is probably to be a 'vegetarian' for the duration of your visit. For other links and information about the Costa del Sol more generally, use the QR code link or visit: **totallyjewishtravel.com**

☪ Islam

Despite the ubiquity and prominence of alcohol and pork in Spanish gastronomy, Muslim visitors to Málaga should not encounter too many difficulties. The Province of Málaga is home to over 50,000 Muslims, mostly of Moroccan descent. As far as eating is concerned, it is far easier to avoid meat than fish which makes it relatively easy to eat halal in most bars and restaurants. Muslim visitors should remember that biscuits and pastries in Spain are often made with lard (pork fat) and that some traditional stews and soups, while apparently 'vegetarian', will be made with meat stock.

The large Moroccan population means that it is also relatively easy to find fully halal restaurants in which to eat (quite a few are found around the railway and bus stations near the Larios Shopping Centre).

The city's largest mosque, and the closest to the *centro histórico*, is part of the Saudi-funded **Centro Cultural Andalusí de Málaga (♀Calle Ingeniero de la Torre Acosta 3 ⊕ ccandalusi.org)**, and there are numerous smaller mosques in the western part of Málaga. **HalalTrip** has produced a free guide to Málaga for Muslim travellers: ❶ **bit.ly/HalalMLG**

The main mosque has a most interesting and sensitive design. In the wake of a *reconquista*, the *mudéjar* (neo-Moorish) architectural style became hugely popular, incorporating horse-shoe and multi-lobed arches, brickwork, carved wood, glazed ceramic tiles, stucco work, etc. The Málaga mosque, on the other hand, owes something to typical Spanish ecclesiastical architecture.

Málaga Through the Year
📅 National and Local Holidays

When you look at the '*horarios*' (timetable) for a bar or museum in Spain you are likely to see different opening times for '*laborales*' (weekdays), '*fines de semana*' (weekends), '*domingos*' (Sundays), etc. as well as for '*festivos*', which can occur on various days of the week and are public religious or civic holidays. In Málaga, these are as follows:

1 January:	**New Year's Day**
6 January:	**Epiphany**
*28 February:	**Andalusia Day (*Día de Andalucía*)**
March/April:	**Holy Thursday (Thursday before the moveable feast of Easter)**
March/April:	**Good Friday (Friday before the moveable feast of Easter)**
1 May:	**Labour Day**
15 August:	**The Assumption of the Blessed Virgin Mary**
*19 August:	**Incorporation of Málaga to the Crown of Castilla**
*8 September:	**Feast of Our Lady of the Victory (*La Virgen de la Victoria*)**
12 October:	**National Day of Spain (*Fiesta Nacional de España*)**
1 November:	**All Saints Day**
6 December:	**Constitution Day**
8 December:	**The Solemnity of the Immaculate Conception**
25 December:	**Christmas Day (Navidad)**

If any of these dates falls on a Sunday, then the public holiday is transferred to the Monday in the same way that people in the UK get a holiday on 2 January when New Year's Day falls on a Sunday. *All of the dates above are holidays throughout Spain save three: 28 February, 19 August, and 8 September.

🎴 A Floral Calendar

 The Mediterranean climate and mild winters of Málaga mean that there are flowers in bloom all year round. The best places to see these displays of colour are the Parque de Málaga, the Jardines de Pedro Luis Alonso and Puerta Oscura opposite, and around the Alcazaba and Cathedral. But for the biggest variety, the Botanical Gardens cannot be beaten. Use the QR code link for a calendar of trees and shrubs in bloom and/or fruit (in Spanish with Latin botanical names).

All Year Round: Bougainvillea (Jardines de Pedro Luis Alonso, English Cemetery)

February to April: Seville Orange blossom (Paseo del Parque, Jardines de Pedro Luis Alonso, Cathedral); Judas Tree (*Cercis siliquastrum* — Avenida de Andalucía)

May to June: Jacaranda (Jardines de Puerta Oscura, Plaza de La Merced); Jasmine

Spring to Autumn: Roses (Jardines de Pedro Luis Alonso); Hibiscus (Cathedral, Alcazaba, Paseo del Parque); Jasmine

November to December: Silk Floss Tree (*Chorisia speciosa* — Cortina del Muelle, Parque de Málaga, Plaza del Poeta Alfonso Canales, Avenida Andalucía)

December: Seville Orange fruit (Paseo del Parque, Jardines de Pedro Luis Alonso, Cathedral); Poinsettia (Ayuntamiento, Plaza del General Torrijos); Crane Flower (*Strelitzia Reginae* — Paseo del Parque, Cathedral)

January

🍇 *Nochevieja* (31 December–1 January)

In Spanish, New Year is called *Nochevieja*, which means 'old night' (*i.e.* the last night of the old year). In Málaga the celebrations get going in the Plaza de la Constitución around 10 pm, with live music from 11 pm.

If you are lucky enough to find room in the square, you may find that someone hands you one or more little paper bags. These bags contain either 12 grapes or a handful of confetti. The event organizers distribute around 3,000 of each. Don't throw the confetti (yet) because it is for midnight. The grapes too. When the hush descends just before the stroke of midnight, have your grapes ready. With each chime of the clock bell, you are supposed to eat a grape — one grape for each month of the year to come. When the chimes stop and you've eaten your grapes, you throw the confetti and hug and kiss your neighbours. The music then begins again and continues until 2 am.

ᵗᵗᵗ *Los Reyes Magos* (6 January)

The Feast of the Epiphany, known as *Los Reyes Magos* (The Magi Kings), is the major celebration connected with the birth of Jesus in Spain. For all that Spanish cities have Christmas trees and lights, and even Santas and reindeer in shop windows, Christmas Day itself is not the main celebration of the season. The big day, especially for children, is *Los Reyes Magos*, mainly because they are the bringers of gifts. Spanish children write their letters full of wishes not to Santa Claus, but to 'The Kings'.

The Eve is when the public celebrations take place, including a lavish parade. If you happen to be in Málaga for 'The Kings', search on the web to find the exact programme, because the precise timings sometimes change. (Searching for '*cabalgata de Reyes de Málaga*' **bit.ly/3KingsMLG** should come up with the information from a newspaper website).

The Kings are gift-givers, and the parade is no exception. In 2023, the floats distributed 1.44 tonnes of *mantecados* (very crumbly shortbread biscuits often eaten around Christmas), and almost 20 tonnes of jelly babies and assorted sweets.

February/March

 *Carnaval*

The events leading up to and during *Carnaval* are coordinated (with the *ayuntamiento*) by the *Fundación Ciudadana Carnaval de Málaga* (Citizens' Foundation for the Málaga *Carnaval*). Preliminary events (*La Previa*) begin in mid-January, four weekends before Shrove Tuesday. These consist of gastronomic and musical celebrations held in different *barrios* of the city. A full week before, *murgas* (street musicians) and *comparsas* (*Carnaval* troupes) perform as part of a singing competition, the final of which is held in the Teatro Cervantes. Tickets go on sale at **malagaentradas.com** around the end of December. To see the full programme, consult the FCCM website (Spanish only): **carnavaldemalaga.es**

March

 Festival de Málaga (Málaga Film Festival)

 The Málaga film festival focuses on Spanish and Spanish language cinema. The red carpet is laid out along Calle Larios and all the events, celebrity arrivals and awarding of prizes can be viewed on huge screens erected in the Plaza de la Constitución. The lavish closing gala takes place at the Teatro de Cervantes.

Hundreds of films are shown during the festival at multiple locations, including all the main theatres and cinemas in the city centre. These range from full-length feature films to shorts and documentaries. Tickets can be purchased from the relevant box office(s), including online. Consult the festival website for the programme and to buy tickets: **festivaldemalaga.com** (Spanish only).

'VinomaScope'

 Running alongside the Film Festival, the *Consejo Regulador Denominaciones de Origen* (the Málaga DOP wine and raisin regulator) arranges a *tapas* and wine route around the city centre. Dozens of bars and restaurants participate in VinomaScope, offering *maridajes* (pairings) of a signature *tapa* with an especially selected Málaga or Sierras de Málaga wine for a few euros. You can find the details here: **vinomascope.es**.

March/April

Semana Santa in Málaga is a huge affair, and it involves so many processions and public acts of worship that it lasts more than a week, with smaller processions known as 'translations' beginning before Palm Sunday. It takes over the city centre to such an extent that if public religious observance is not your cup of tea, it would probably be best to avoid Málaga during Holy Week. But if it interests you — culturally, artistically or religiously — then there are few more beautiful and fascinating places in Spain in which to spend this week. (A detailed, 100-page guide to *Semana Santa* is provided in *Málaga: A Comprehensive Guide to Spain's Most Hospitable City*.)

You can download the itinerary for the upcoming *Semana Santa*. It should be available a month or more before Palm Sunday (which is a moveable feast occurring between 15 March at the earliest and 18 April at the latest). The official itinerary can be downloaded from the website of the Association of

Brotherhoods: **agrupaciondecofradias.com/horarios-e-itinerarios**.

Their website also features a map that shows the location of the brotherhood houses **agrupaciondecofradias.com/hermandades** (click the drop-down menu at the top of the map to choose the day).

The **El Penitente app,** which covers Sevilla and Málaga, is excellent and contains all the information you might need, including route maps for each brotherhood, though it is only available in Spanish. In 2023, the Málaga brotherhoods adopted El Penitente as their official app.

  Android   iOS

May/June

   Noche en Blanco

 The 'White Night', loosely tied to midsummer, is usually celebrated in late May. *Noche en Blanco* has been marked in Málaga since 2008 and each year there is a different theme, chosen by popular vote since 2016. Beginning around 7 pm, it is probably the most concentrated cultural festival anywhere in Europe, with almost 200 events taking place within five or six hours. Almost every cultural and municipal institution in Málaga takes part. The vast majority of the programme is free, or at nominal cost (to secure a place) if not. Comprehensive programmes are available from the turismo, but these are only in Spanish. **lanocheenblancomalaga.com**

Corpus Christi

The Feast of Corpus Christi (The Solemnity of the Most Holy Body and Blood of Christ) is celebrated 60 days after Easter (the Thursday after Trinity Sunday), so it is a moveable feast, occurring in the last week of May or the first half of June. It is a feast that celebrates and promotes the Catholic belief in the real presence of Jesus Christ in the Eucharist or Blessed Sacrament (the transformation of bread and wine).

In Málaga, there is a public procession on the Sunday morning. The previous evening, there is a Vigil Mass (usually around 6.30 pm) followed by Vespers (evening prayer) and then a concert in the Plaza del Obispo. The procession begins from the Cathedral at 10 am on Sunday (it seems to vary between 10 and 11 every few years).

Semana Popular de los Corralones

 At the end of May and/or the beginning of June dozens of *corralones* (a traditional form of housing arranged around a shared patio) in La Trinidad and El Perchel are opened to the public. Some patios in Capuchinos, Cruz Verde–Lagunillas and Ollerías also participate.

San Juan

San Juan is usually celebrated on the night of 23 June, which is the Eve of the Feast of the Nativity of St John the Baptist (on 24 June). Although the name is religious, it is nowadays pretty much a secular celebration, more linked to Midsummer (21 June). Although celebrated all over Spain, it is primarily a beach festival, so very popular along the Málaga coast. Traditionally, huge bonfires (*hogueras*) are lit on the beach and the party continues into the small hours. In Málaga city, the party centres around La Malagueta, where there are usually concerts, a huge bonfire, and fireworks. Parallel celebrations take place on the La Misericordia and El Palo beaches.

June-August

Cine Abierto (Open Cinema)

An extension of the (Film) *Festival de Málaga*, this is a programme of (mostly free) film screenings in different locations around the city. **festivaldemalaga.com/cineabierto**

July

Virgen del Carmen

The *Virgen del Carmen* or *Nuestra Señora del Carmen* is how *Santa María del Monte Carmelo* (Our Lady of Mount Carmel) is known in Spain, one of the various invocations of the Virgin Mary. Her title comes from veneration of her on Mount Carmel (in the Holy Land) by the friars who came to be known as Carmelites. Spain is one of the countries where this dedication is most deeply rooted and she is the patron saint of sailors and fishermen.

Practically all Spanish coastal towns and cities celebrate the feast of the Virgen del Carmen on July 16 and Málaga is no exception. The processions that take place are real demonstrations of community devotion — less solemn or tightly choreographed than those of *Semana Santa*, but just as moving. People carry the image of the Virgin on a small litter, surrounded with flowers and candles, from the church to the sea. Not just the seashore, but the sea, carrying the throne into the water.

Where to watch a procession

⚠ Please check the timings of these celebrations online (you will probably see posters around town) as they do not always take place on the feast itself (16 July) but a day earlier or later, or are transferred to a weekend.

One of Málaga's largest *Virgen del Carmen* processions, and perhaps the most famous, is held in **El Palo** district. The district is decorated for the festivities with the image leaving **Nuestra Señora de las Angustias** church (**Calle Villafuerte 1**) around 5.30 pm and carried along **El Chanquete** beach.

Beginning around 6 pm, the streets and waters of **Pedregalejo** hold their *Virgen del Carmen* procession. The image sets off from **Corpus Christi** parish church (**Calle Ventura de la Vega 8**) and is then placed aboard a fishing boat moored at the mouth of the Pilones River.

In **Huelin**, the *Virgen del Carmen* procession usually starts at 5 pm from **San Patricio** church (**Calle Abogado Federico Orellana Toledano 2**).

There is an earlier start for the procession from **El Perchel**, which includes a blessing of the waters and a commemoration of all those who have perished at sea. The image of the *Virgen del Carmen Coronada del Perchel* leaves the parish church in El Perchel (**Plaza de Toros Vieja 23**) at 8 am and is taken in procession to Muelle Dos. At 10 am, the image embarks on a two-hour boat journey from the port to the **Playa La Malagueta**, after which it moves to the **Cathedral** for an afternoon mass, before returning to El Perchel in the evening.

August
 The *Feria*

The Málaga *feria* (Annual Fair) runs for seven full days, from Saturday to Saturday, with the anniversary of the *reconquista* of Málaga (18 August) occurring during the festivities (*i.e.* it can start as early as 12 August, or as late as 18 August. The first event of the *feria* is the fireworks display and beach concert that takes place at midnight on Friday night.

 The *ayuntamiento* usually publishes a map of the *recinto fe-rial* and the programme for the *feria* a few weeks ahead: **malaga.eu/feria-de-malaga**. These are PDF documents in Spanish, so if you need a translation, try searching for '*Feria de Málaga*' and '*programa*' to find a newspaper listing that you can run through Google Translate (**bit.ly/MLGFeriaInfo**).

 From about 1 pm, the *Feria del Centro* gets going. There is live music (everything from Europop to R&B, Rock to Merengue) in the Plaza de la Constitución, Plaza de las Flores, Plaza del Obispo and Plaza de San Pedro Alcántara. From midday until 3.30 pm in the Plaza de La Merced there are events for families and children — theatre, workshops, parades, magic shows, etc. The Calle Marqués de Larios is where to find more traditional folk music, with different *Verdiales* '*pandas*' (gangs) performing each day, as well as folk choirs from around the city and province.

The *recinto* (fairground) gets going each day at noon with processions of carriage rides. Flamenco is performed from 2 pm, and there are equestrian displays at 4 pm and 10 pm daily. In the children's *caseta* there are films, theatre performances and other entertainment each evening from 9.30 pm. To reach the *recinto*, although you could take the ⊙ *Cercanías* train from the centre to Victoria Kent, by far the easiest way is to take the special bus (🚌 F) from the centre (Alameda Principal). This bus runs 24 hours a day during the *feria*, while a number of services covering the suburbs operate an extended service. The *bonobús* isn't valid on the special *feria* service, but you can use a contactless card to pay the fare.

⚠ If you need help or advice, visit the '*Información Feria*' caseta.

🐂 The Bulls

Running concurrently with the August Fair is the *feria taurina* (bull fair) when *corridas* (often called 'bullfights' in English) are held each evening at the Malagueta bullring (*plaza de toros*). The history of 'taurine spectacles' (events involving wild bulls) have been a feature of life in Spain for centuries, almost certainly stretching back into antiquity, although the modern *corrida* (bullfight) is the result of developments that took place in the 18th century. The birthplace of the *corrida* as we know it was Ronda, in the Province of Málaga.

The *corrida de toros*, generally speaking, has either captivated travellers in Spain (Orson Welles, Ernest Hemingway and Ava Gardner, for example), or appalled them. Some hispanophiles, like Hans Christian Andersen, found themselves simultaneously captivated and appalled.

As an art form it is not universally popular in Spain either, though the notion that it only survives thanks to tourists is nonsense (if anything, the opposite is true). Despite the regular assurances from Britain's most devoutly anti-bullfighting newspaper, *The Daily Mail*, that *corridas* are in their death throes, they continue to draw huge audiences and contribute billions to Spain's GDP.

Despite the ubiquity of bullfighting imagery found in bars, on postcards and on numerous advertisement hoardings, few foreign visitors to Málaga will probably have much interest in going to watch a *corrida*. For the curious, however, there are few better places to experience this most Spanish of spectacles. Málaga's is a first class ring, meaning that the quality of both *toros* (bulls) and *toreros* (bullfighters) is high. But the *corrida* is not a sport and it can be very hard to make sense of for the first-time spectator. For a more detailed explanation of the *corrida* and a step-by-step guide to watching one in Málaga, see the unabridged version of this book: *Málaga: A Comprehensive Guide to Spain's Most Hospitable City*.

September

Málaga Fashion Week

 Also known as '*Pasarela Larios*', Málaga's annual fashion show takes place in the first half of September. The trade event lasts almost a week, but the catwalk shows happen on the Friday and Saturday evenings. In recent years the first show has been as early as 2 September or as late as 17 September. There is an exhibition area set up in the Plaza de la Constitución and the Calle Marqués de Larios is transformed into a 300-metre catwalk (*pasarela*) with the addition of a turquoise carpet — a nod to Málaga's maritime position and heritage. The shows begin at 8 pm. There are no tickets on sale and most of the chairs are set aside for buyers, journalists and fashionista hangers-on. However, if you can find a spot, the event is free to watch.

Virgen de la Victoria (8 September)

Our Lady of the Victory is the Co-Patron of the Diocese and City of Málaga (along with the Cristo de la Salud and Saints Ciriaco and Paula). Her feast day is a public holiday in the Málaga municipal area.

On the Saturday afternoon before 30 August, the image (statue) of Santa María de la Victoria is lowered from her place above the high altar to the transfer throne. Early on Sunday morning, the image is transferred from the Basilica of La Victoria (Plaza Santuario) to the Cathedral Basilica. In the Cathedral, between 30 August and 7 September nine days (a 'novena') of prayer are celebrated. On September 8, after Mass, an offering of flowers by the people of Málaga is made in the atrium of the Main Gate in the Plaza del Obispo, organized by 'La Coracha', an association dedicated to the preservation of *malagueña* culture and heritage. While the floral offering is made, people dance *malagueñas*.

In the evening, beginning around 7.30 pm, the triumphal procession takes place, from the Cathedral to the Basilica and Royal Sanctuary. The image is carried on a throne carried by one hundred and fifty members of the Brotherhood of Our Lady of the Victory, and adorned with the flowers from the various offerings. This brotherhood (**santamariadelavictoria.es**) is an example of an important and popular Málaga brotherhood that does not take part in the ceremonies of *Semana Santa*. They are a brotherhood '*De Gloria*' — committed to the promotion of devotion to a cult or saint, in this case, the Virgin of Victory.

October

 *Fiesta Nacional de España* (National Day of Spain)

October 12 is a national holiday and most shops are closed. It is also traditionally and commonly referred to as the *Día de la Hispanidad* ('Spanishness Day'), commemorating Spain's legacy worldwide, especially in Hispanic America. Events are usually held in which the Latin American communities resident in Málaga share their culture, traditions, gastronomy and handicraft products. There are events for children such as plays or contests, as well as parades, Latin dance classes and many more activities. These activities have been held for years in **Parque de Huelin (Calle Orfila)**, a ten-minute walk from María Zambrano railway station starting around noon and continuing into the evening.

🎃 Halloween (31 October)

The fact that this celebration is called 'Halloween' and not '*Noche de Brujas*', '*Víspera de Difuntos*', '*Víspera de Todos los Santos*', '*Noche de los Muertos*', or '*Noche de Difuntos*' tells you all you need to know about this recent addition to Málaga's cultural agenda. Indeed, one listing of events in Málaga rather sniffily explains that it takes place due to '*contagio cultural*' from the '*angloesfera*' ('cultural contagion from the Anglosphere')!

Events are held at the Botanical Gardens (treasure hunts for children in the day and a scary tour for adults in the evening) and the English Cemetery (in Spanish). Booking is essential for both, so check websites for times and information. Between 5 and 9 pm, events for children are organized in the Soho district (around the pedestrianized portion of Calle Tomás Heredia) and on Muelle Uno, both featuring fancy dress competitions, face painting, music, dancing, sweet treasure hunts and games.

November

✝ *Todos Los Santos* (All Saints)

The feast of *Todos Los Santos* (often shortened as '*Tosantos*') on 1 November is a public holiday in Spain, but most of the 'celebrations' are private and observed within families. The reason is that the following day, *La Conmemoración de Todos los Fieles Difuntos* (The Commemoration of the Faithful Departed, or All Souls) is the day when people pray for their dead loved ones.

As for any Spanish feast day, certain sweets are associated with this day. We are well into the season for roasted chestnuts by this point, and street vendors will be busy. Other typical treats eaten today are *buñuelos*, *borraĉhuelos* and '*huesos de santo*'. The deep-fried fritters or doughnuts called *buñuelos* are a popular snack at the time of any feast or celebration (especially *Semana Santa* and the *feria*). *Borraĉhuelos* (which means 'drunken ones') originate in Málaga (probably) and are closely related to *peŝtiños*. Made from dough enriched with wine, brandy (or anisette), orange, cloves and aniseed (known as '*matalahuga*' in Andalucía), they are stuffed with '*cabello de ángel*' (a sweet jam made from a kind of pumpkin), deep fried then dusted in sugar or rolled in honey. *Huesos de Santo* are only made and eaten at this time of year — the name means 'bones of a saint'. They are tubes of marzipan filled with a rich egg yolk custard (or *cabello de ángel*, jam, chocolate, or other filling). The marzipan is the 'bone', and the custard, or jam, is the 'marrow'. Like many limited edition Spanish '*dulces*' (sweets), they are very, very sweet.

🎷 Málaga International Jazz Festival

This festival has been running for over 30 years and usually takes place in the first or second week of November. The main concerts are held at the Teatro Cervantes, so consult their website for the programme (⊕ teatrocervantes.com), which includes details of other performances mounted in other venues.

Luces de Navidad (Christmas Lights)

The switch-on of the Christmas lights in Málaga usually takes place on the last (or penultimate) Saturday in November. Search for '*¿Cuándo se encienden las luces de Navidad en Málaga?*' (⊕ bit.ly/46DYABQ) to find the schedule. The precise dates are often not fixed until October or even early November. Christmas lights begin to appear in the streets of Málaga during October, but the big displays are in the Plaza de la Constitución, the Plaza de la Marina and, par excellence, along the Calle Marqués de Larios.

December
🏃 Maratón de Málaga

The Málaga Marathon (and Half-Marathon) takes place in December, usually on the first or second Sunday. Registrations close about a week before the race takes place. To find out more, search online for '*maratón de Málaga*' (🌐 **bit.ly/3O7sGGM** — there is no point giving a website link because the address changes each time there is a change of sponsor).

🕯 La Inmaculada Concepción
(The Immaculate Conception 8 December)

The winter holiday season kicks off in Spain in early December with two national holidays falling only a day apart: *Día de la Constitución* (Spanish Constitution Day) on 6 December and *La Inmaculada Concepción* (The Immaculate Conception, also known as *La Purísima*) on 8 December. While you will not see public celebrations of either, these days are eagerly anticipated by many for the opportunity to plan a long, much-needed (hopefully) weekend getaway.

On this day, a lot is going on in Málaga, but not on the streets. There is no obvious partying today. Nonetheless, all the Holy Week brotherhoods, and many others, observe the feast in their canonical seats, or temples. The images of the Virgins are usually enthroned on the eve of the feast (7 December) and a solemn Mass celebrated on the feast day itself (8 December). Try an internet search for '*la Inmaculada*' and '*Málaga*' to find this year's programme.

Besamanos (18 December)

18 December is the Feast of the 'Expectation of the Blessed Virgin Mary' (*Nuestra Señora de la Expectación*), primarily celebrated in Spain, Portugal, and parts of Italy and Poland. The 'expectation' is the expectation of a child, and the feast is closely linked with the virtue of Hope, and thus the *Virgen de la Esperanza* — a popular image in Málaga.

On the feast, and over the day or two beforehand, there is a tradition of visiting these images to 'kiss the hand' (*besamanos*). Many of those who make this small pilgrimage are mothers, expectant mothers and families with very young children. In recent years around 30 of the Málaga brotherhoods have used this feast as an opportunity to collect food, household products and money to assist poor families in the city. Volunteers from the *cofradías* (brotherhoods) volunteer in supermarkets during the week leading up to the feast, inviting donations of food and, although the many concerts and recitals over the '*triduum*' (three days of celebration) are technically free, the 'entrance price' is a donation of food or a child's toy. To find the programme of events, search online for '*festividad de la Esperanza*' and '*besamanos*' in the days before 18 December.

Navidad (Christmas)

Christmas Day is largely a day enjoyed at home by families, so there are no big events in Málaga on this day, and no grand religious processions or street parties. However, Christmas is an increasingly popular time to visit Málaga due to the pleasant weather. The average daytime temperature is 17° or 18° Celsius (rarely dropping below 14°C) and night-time lows are around 8°C, which is basically as cold as Málaga gets. More importantly, the weather is often sunny, so if you find a nice spot it can feel significantly warmer than the temperature in the shade.

During the run-up to Christmas, though, there is plenty going on:

Ice Skating

A modestly sized rink (35m x 15m) has for a number of years been set up on Avenida de Andalucía, next to the entrance to El Corte Inglés, which offers children the opportunity to enjoy ice skating during the Christmas holidays (from the end of November until 6 January).

The MIMA children's fair (**f mimamalaga**) takes place every year at the Palacio de Congresos, near the fairground (**Avenida de José Ortega y Gasset 201**). It runs from 26 until 30 December and then from 2 to 4 January. Covering an area of 1,850 m², there are more than 60 activities and rides for children, and some years there has been an ice rink.

Belénes (Nativity Scenes)

The Crib or Nativity Scene celebrated its eight hundredth anniversary in 2023, having first appeared in 1223, designed by St Francis of Assisi (though he used only animals rather than figurines of people).

In the city centre, some of the most impressive Nativity scenes in Málaga are the one showcased at Málaga City Hall, outside the Cathedral, and those created by the brotherhoods (naturally, they all claim to have the most impressive *Belén* in Málaga). There is an official nativity scene route with a 'passport' showing the location of all the main ones in the city — ask for a copy at the tourist office, or try this search: ⊕ **bit.ly/RutaBelenesMLG** — the programme usually hits the press around the beginning of December).

Christmas Markets

Like more or less any large city in Europe, Málaga has a Christmas Market, usually opening at the end of November and continuing until Christmas. Some stalls are found at the Plaza de la Marina end of the *Paseo* del Parque, and another collection pops up on Muelle Uno. Similar markets operate in Torremolinos, Benalmádena and Fuengirola.

Botanical Gardens Light Installation

From the end of November until the first week of January, the Jardín Botánico Histórico–La Concepción is illuminated with dozens of beautifully curated light installations covering a 2.2km route, each year taking as a theme elements of the Christmas story such as 'Bethlehem', 'Persia of the Kings' or 'The Star'. There are food and drink stalls and admission is between 6.30 pm and 9 pm (with buses running later than usual). It is a stunning and extremely popular display attracting over 100,000 visitors.

La Misa del Gallo (Midnight Mass)

Midnight Mass, once a mainstay of Catholic worship, is becoming a rarer occurrence in Europe, and Málaga is no exception. The following list shows the usual times of 'Midnight Mass' in Málaga *centro*, though as always, please check before making plans to attend.

Santa Iglesia Catedral Basílica de la Encarnación: Advertised as 23.55 for 00.00, preceded by an organ concert starting at 23.20. This is a combined celebration for the Cathedral and the city centre parishes of Santos Mártires (Ciriaco and Paula), San Juan, San Felipe Neri, and Santiago Apóstol.

Nuestra Señora del Carmen (El Perchel): 00.00

San Carlos y Santo Domingo de Guzmán (Perchel Norte): 19.00

La Divina Pastora y Santa Teresa de Jesús (Capuchinos): 00.00

Santa María de la Amargura (Mármoles): 19.00

Santa María de la Victoria (Victoria): 00.00

Stella Maris (Alameda): 00.00

Día de los Santos Inocentes (Holy Innocents – 28 December)

The Feast of the Holy Innocents (the commemoration of the slaughter of children under two years of age born in Bethlehem, ordered by King Herod the Great) is the Spanish equivalent of April Fools' Day. People play tricks on one another and the media report on fantastical (and invented) stories. There are no special municipal celebrations on this day, but if you watch the Spanish news or buy a newspaper, don't believe anything you hear or read!

🎸 *Fiesta Mayor de Verdiales* (Verdiales Festival)

This is the big annual competition of *verdiales* '*pandas*' and it has been held on the Feast of Holy Innocents for more than 60 years. It brings together more than a dozen *pandas* (troupes) representing the three traditional styles: Montes, Almogía and Comares. The members of *verdiales* troupes are called *fiesteros* (party men) or *tontos* (fools), hence the link with the Feast of Holy Innocents. It takes place in the **Parque de Andrés Jiménez Díaz** in the Puerto de la Torre district of north-west Málaga starting around 1 pm. It's a 30-minute journey taking the bus (🚌 21) from the Alameda Principal — get off at the **Lope de Rueda - Correos** stop (🚏 2108).

If you want to see genuine, local folk music performed to the highest standard, then this event is not to be missed. The atmosphere is joyful and friendly, and there is a busy bar serving drinks. There is plenty of food in the form of *paella* (or a *malagueña* approximation of it), so if you're not a rice and/or seafood fan, take a sandwich with you or have an early lunch before leaving the city centre.

Day Trips

This book is primarily a guide to the city of Málaga and anyone spending a few days in Málaga will find plenty to occupy themselves in the city. One could easily spend a week gently exploring the walkable centre of Málaga, with maybe a bus journey to the Botanical Gardens or a trip to a nearby beach for an *espeto*. However, if you are staying for longer, there are plenty of interesting places that can easily be visited in a day using public transport. The following pages provide a few suggestions but constitute a far from comprehensive guide.

For a more detailed guide to these and more destinations, including travel advice, please see the unabridged 630 page version of this guide: *Málaga: A Comprehensive Guide to Spain's Most Hospitable City*.

🎟️ Buying Train Tickets

The Train in Spain

Although RENFE is still the major carrier, at the time of publication two other companies operate intercity trains in Spain: **Ouigo** and **Iryo**, both of which offer far cheaper tickets, albeit across a more limited range of journeys.

Buying Tickets

Tickets for most RENFE (and Ouigo and Iryo) services can be booked via UK websites such as **omio.co.uk**, **raileurope.com** or **thetrainline.com**. However, not all routes or trains are always available on these sites, so it is worth consulting the operators' own websites. The **thetrainline.com** website has improved a great deal recently and sometimes gives a wider choice of journeys than the RENFE site, so it is always worth checking. For RENFE tickets, it is almost always cheaper to buy via their own website: **renfe.com/es/en**. There is also a RENFE smartphone app for iOS (**apple.co/3EMRbEg**), Android (**bit.ly/AndroidRENFE**) and Huawei (**bit.ly/HuaweiRENFE**) which saves you the trouble of printing out your tickets (keep a separate record of the ticket booking references so that you can print your tickets at a railway station if you lose or break your phone). You can also use the smartphone app to book and pay for tickets

Rail tickets in Spain are dynamically priced, so generally speaking, the earlier you buy your ticket, the cheaper it will be. Tickets for most journeys go on sale 60 days before travel and are available in three classes: *Básico*, *Elige* and *Prémium* ('*elige*' means to choose).

Básico is, as the name suggests, the basic option. The cheapest fare with automatic seat allocation.

Elige offers a choice of seat, including a 'comfort' seat, usually in a carriage with rows of 2 seats on one side of the aisle and 1 seat on the other (like UK first class).

Prémium is the nearest RENFE has to First Class. It allows you to choose your seat, block the seat next to you and change your booking even when you miss your train.

🚌 Buses

A useful website worth checking is **movelia.es/en**. Many of the journeys can also be found (and purchased) using **thetrainline.com**. However, both sites only search the large transport providers (**RENFE**, **Avanza**, **ALSA**, etc.). For smaller and local bus companies, you'll need to consult their own websites or visit a ticket office at the bus station.

The Málaga Bus Station website has a lot of useful information, though access to some sections is (unhelpfully) blocked for IP addresses outside Spain: **estabus.malaga.eu**

ⓘ The *turismo* is your friend...

Whilst we might prefer to think of ourselves as 'travellers' not 'tourists', there are excellent reasons to pop into the *turismo*. The first is that your visit helps to secure future funding — a *turismo* that no one visits will have its funding cut. But a more immediate benefit to you as a tourist (sorry, 'traveller') is that the *turismo* has the latest information — a *ruta de tapas* that's taking place today, a free exhibition at the *Ayuntamiento*, a historic building that's only open this weekend, a free lunchtime concert, or a craft or gourmet food market. Such occasional events won't be listed in a book like this one and can be hard to find out about even online, but they can often turn out to be the highlight of a day trip.

If you want to take a day trip and can't decide where, then try consulting the calendar of events (called '*Agenda*' in Spanish) on the websites of a few *turismos*. An interesting temporary exhibition, or an annual asparagus or *chorizo* festival should not be missed!

West of Málaga
(Costa del Sol Occidental)

Torremolinos

🌐 **turismotorremolinos.es** ❶ Calle Cuesta del Tajo 1 ❶ Plaza de las Comunidades Autónomas (Bajondillo-Playamar) ❶ Plaza del Remo (La Carihuela) 🕘 Mon–Fri 0900–1400 ☎ **+34 608 208 871**

Torremolinos is Málaga's nearest neighbour and the main tourist 'resort', especially popular with Irish holidaymakers. The main reason for visitors to Málaga to visit 'Torroles' is for the club scene, especially the lively LGBT scene.

Benalmádena

🌐 **disfruta.benalmadena.es/en** ❶ Castillo de Bil-Bil, Avenida Antonio Machado 78, Benalmádena Costa 🕘 Mon–Fri 0900–1800; Sat 0900–1500

Benalmádena is the next resort along, travelling west. Also known for its sandy beaches and plentiful hotels, it never shared the slightly louche reputation of Torremolinos, being known instead for wholesome 'family tourism'. Indeed, many of the attractions of interest to children are located in Benalmádena, so if your children want a break from Málaga's museums and monuments, then it's a great nearby destination.

Some popular attractions include:

🐟 **The Sea Life Aquarium** is located in the Puerto Deportivo de Benalmádena (the Marina) and is a shark conservation and protection centre that opened in 1995.

🐬 **The Selwo Marina Dolphinarium and Penguinarium** is a marine fauna park that houses the only dolphinarium (*delfinario*) and ice penguinarium (*pingüinario*) in Andalucía.

 🚠 **The Teleférico (Cable Car)** connects the centre of Arroyo de la Miel with the summit of Mount Cálamorro, 771 metres above sea level. From the summit, you can see the Rock of Gibraltar (and even Africa) on clear days.

 🦋 **The Mariposario (Butterfly Garden)** is the largest in Europe and is located just beyond Benalmádena Pueblo (🚌**121 from Benalmádena, or** 🚌**112 from Málaga**). It has around 1,500 butterflies drawn from over 150 species.

 🚢 **Two ferries** leave the port of Benalmádena daily during high season. One is a two-hour 'dolphin spotting' cruise, and the other is a coastal ferry to Fuengirola (and back).

Mijas

🌐 **turismo.mijas.es/en** ℹ️ Plaza Virgen de la Peña 2, Mijas Pueblo ℹ️ Bulevar de La Cala de Mijas, La Cala de Mijas

Mijas, like Benalmádena, is a single municipality comprising three non-contiguous urban centres. Mijas Pueblo, located on the slopes of the Sierra de Mijas, is the oldest of the three, and of the most interest. The journey from Málaga takes between 80 and 90 minutes, either by bus or a mixture of 🔵 *Cercanías* train and bus. From Arroyo de La Miel railway station, the 🚌 M-121 takes you to Mijas Pueblo, or from Fuengirola station, it is the 🚌 M-122. Check routes on Moovit or on the provincial transport consortium website: **bit.ly/ctmamalaga**

Fuengirola

🌐 **turismo.fuengirola.es/en** ℹ️ Paseo Marítimo 32, Plaza Teresa Zabell ℹ️ Paseo Jesús Santos Rein 6 🕐 Mon–Fri 0930–1800; Sat–Sun 1000–1400

Fuengirola, yet another 'former fishing village' grown wealthy as a result of 20th and 21st-century tourism is at the end of the line (for now) on the 🔵 *Cercanías* railway line from Málaga.

Marbella

🌐 **turismo.marbella.es/en** ❶ Plaza de los Naranjos (Casco Antiguo) ❶ Glorieta de la Fontanilla (Playa del Faro) 🕒 ♣ Mon–Fri: 0800–2000; Sat–Sun: 1000–1700 🕒 ☀ Mon–Fri: 0830–2030; Sat–Sun: 1000–2100

Marbella is only around an hour by bus from Málaga. Unless you hire a car, the only way to get to Marbella is by bus as it is the largest city in Spain lacking a railway station. Buses are frequent (more than hourly) and operated by **malaga.avanzagrupo.com** with the last bus back to Málaga leaving the Marbella bus station at 10.45 pm. The journey takes between 45 and 90 minutes, depending upon which bus you book.

🍴 Fine Dining

Marbella has 4 restaurants with Michelin Stars, of which three are in the town itself (🌐 **bit.ly/MarbellaMichelin**)

Messina ✿ (📍 Avenida Severo Ochoa 12 ⊘ Sun 🍴 ♣) 11 and 15-course tasting menus. *À la carte* is also available.

Nintai ✿ (📍 Calle Ramón Gómez de la Serna 18 🍴 ♣ 🌐 ☀ only) Japanese/fusion cuisine.

Skina ✿✿ (📍 Calle Aduar 12 🕒 Daily 🍴 ♣) One of the most expensive restaurants in Spain.

Affordable Eating (and Drinking)

If a Michelin-starred tasting menu is not what you're looking for, then there are plenty of places in which to find reasonably priced food and drink in Marbella. Here are a few suggestions.

🍷 🍹 🦐 🕘 🍽 **Cervecería La + Fría** (📍 Edificio Parque Marbella, Calle Alonso de Bazán 1) has a very varied and quite traditional menu, with a good choice of shellfish, fresh fish and sandwiches.

🍷 🦐 **Bar El Estrecho** (📍 Calle de San Lázaro 12) has a long history. It was founded in the fifties and it preserves its original marble tables, with fried fish still the most popular dish.

🍷 🍴 **Arco Tapas Bar** (📍 Calle Peral 14) has friendly staff and a wide variety of *tapas*.

🍷 🍴 **La Taberna del Pintxo** (📍 Avenida Miguel Cano 7) is another bar around the Parque de Alameda, near the marina. It operates in the Basque fashion — grab cold *tapas* from the bar and hot *tapas* as they pass by. You are charged when your skewers are tallied.

🍷 🍴 **Taberna Casa Curro** (📍 Calle Pantaleón 7) is a very popular bar and usually quite lively thanks to its excellent value for money and extensive menu.

🍷 🕐 🍴 **Taberna La Niña del Pisto** (📍 Calle San Lázaro 1) is a cosy *tapas* bar with an extensive menu of traditional dishes which are mostly available as *tapas*, *medias raciones* and *raciones*.

🍷 🍴 **Mia Café Tapas & Bar** (📍 Calle Remedios 7) is a friendly *tapas* bar serving well-prepared and beautifully presented food.

Estepona

🌐 turismo.estepona.es ℹ Plaza de las Flores

Of all the *soi-disant* 'former fishing towns' of the Costa del Sol, Estepona is the one that best retains its old character. There are regular bus services from Málaga with Avanza (**malaga.avanzagrupo.com/en**), with an average journey time of 1h 30m. From the *turismo*, take a leaflet outlining the '*Ruta Rincones con Encanto*' (the 'Charming Corners Route' 🌐 **bit.ly/Estepona_Corners**) — a walking route through more than two dozen of the most beautiful streets, floral displays, squares and urban gardens of the old town. Another leaflet — the '*Ruta de las Esculturas*' (Sculpture Route 🌐 **bit.ly/Estepona_Sculpture**) shows the locations of over 50 works of sculpture in Estepona, 10 of them in the old town. Another gives information about the '*Ruta de la Poesía*' (Poetry Route 🌐 **bit.ly/Estepona_Poetry**) — a route taking you past 47 poems and extracts of poems (in various languages, though mostly in Spanish) dotted around the old town on glazed ceramic tile displays. The poems are by local poets, about Estepona, or appropriate to Estepona in some way.

The fourth route is the '*Ruta de los Murales*' (Murals Route 🌐 **bit.ly/Estepona_Murals**) — a map and guide to 62 (and counting) urban murals all over the city, quite a few of them in the old town. Many people, when they hear 'urban murals' might nod politely as they imagine a few walls daubed with 'street art' of questionable quality (and I would usually be one of them). But the murals of Estepona are dramatic, impressive, beautiful and frankly, in some

cases breathtaking. In many cases, they are also vast. For anyone with an interest in contemporary art, especially as it relates to urban spaces, they are not to be missed, and many are close to the Orchidarium:

 ♘ Parque–Botánico Orquidario ⚑ Calle Terraza 86 🌐 Ⓜ orchidariumestepona.com 🕒 Tue–Sat: 1000–1330, 1500–1800; Sun 1000–1400 ⊘ Mon €

Gibraltar

🌐 visitgibraltar.gi ℹ Customs Building, Winston Churchill Avenue ℹ Gibraltar Heritage Trust, The Main Guard, 13 John Mackintosh Square (The Piazza)

The bus (again, there is no train) from Málaga to La Línea de la Concepción takes between 2h 15m and 2h 45m. When it comes to the question of how to get to Gibraltar you might be considering driving. This is probably not the best idea. Gibraltar occasionally gets into disputes with Spain that can lead to delays at the border. Further delays are probably quite likely due to added friction following the UK's withdrawal from membership of the European Union.

🗞 Practicalities

You need your passport (or EU identity card) to enter Gibraltar, and you will need it to re-enter Spain. The currency of Gibraltar is the Gibraltar Pound (GIP) which is pegged to sterling at par value. Pound Sterling is accepted everywhere in Gibraltar, but GIP is not legal tender in the UK. So do not withdraw cash from an ATM unless you are going to spend it in Gibraltar. Take some £5 Sterling notes and some coin with you if can (for small purchases and tips).

I would also advise taking the earliest bus that you can manage from Málaga, especially in the summer, so that you can explore the Rock before the heat of the day becomes unbearable (though be warned — Gibraltar is often shrouded in low cloud while Algeciras and La Línea on either side are bathed in sunshine). Have a hearty *desayuno* or *almuerzo* in La Línea and then walk across the border. When you arrive in Gibraltar, cross the runway and, if you wish, pick up a bus (🚌 **2, 3 or 10**) to the lower cable car station. There are three options: Cable Car Return (if you just want to go up and down); Cable Car Return + Nature Reserve (to explore the rock a bit before taking the car down); and Cable Car Single + Nature Reserve (if you plan to walk down). To visit three or four attractions (and to walk down into town) you ought to allow **at least** three hours.

East of Málaga (*Costa del Sol Oriental*)

Nerja

⊕ nerja-turismo.com ❶ Calle Carmen 1 🕐 Mon–Fri 1000–1400, 1700–2030; Sat 1000–1330

Don't be misled by the tourist brochure descriptions of Nerja as a 'fishing village'. Tourism is now this town's main industry and the few fishermen still to be seen along the beach provide a picturesque scene for visitors and a slim livelihood for local families. Nerja is still very much worth a visit, though.

Cuevas De Nerja

⊕ ⓔ cuevadenerja.es 🕐 ☀ 0930–1630 🕐 ☀ 0930–1900 ❶❷❸
(✿ Under 5 years old) ⊕ ✎ entradas.cuevadenerja.es

The main reason to make a day trip from Málaga is to visit the Caves of Nerja. The caves are not a suitable place if you have mobility problems as there are 458 steps to go up and down. There are no ramps. Flash photography is not allowed inside the caves. The admission price is good value for such a spectacular attraction.

The bus company ALSA (⊕ alsa.com) operates a regular service between Málaga and Nerja. The service from Málaga to Maro will drop you at the Caves — search for '**Nerja (Cuevas)**' as the destination. This will enable you to book a timed entrance ticket for the caves online: ⊕ entradas.cuevadenerja.es. The Caves open at 0930 with the last entry at 1530 (1800 in the Summer). Most people take about an hour to tour the cave. To return to Nerja city centre, the times of ALSA buses are liable to change seasonally, so use the ALSA website to plan your return journey carefully. You can buy a ticket between Nerja (Cuevas) and Nerja on the bus and the journey takes about 10 minutes. The ALSA bus will drop you at the Nerja **Estación de Autobuses** (basically a handful of bus shelters with a sporadically open ticket kiosk). From here, it's a short walk into the main part of the old town. The Balcón de Europa is 1 km to the south.

Another option to return to the city centre from the Caves is to pre-book or call a taxi. A number of taxis have their contact numbers on display outside the ticket office, but a large and reliable taxi firm is Nerja Taxi ☎ +34 952 520 537. The taxi drivers in Nerja all speak good English due to the large number of British people (and English-speaking Germans) who live and holiday in the area.

🚂 The Tourist Train (*Cuevatren*)

This is a fun option if you are visiting the caves with children. Up-to-date timetable information can be found on this page: ⊕ **cuevadenerja.es/tren-a-la-cueva-de-nerja** (in *castellano* with occasional sentences in English). The train takes 30 minutes from Nerja to the Caves. The stop in Nerja is in the **Plaza de Los Cangrejos** (marked on the companion Google map). You can book a combined caves/train ticket on the website of the Caves. Reading the timetable can seem a little confusing at first, but it is simple once you get the hang of it.

Frigiliana

⊕ **turismofrigiliana.es/en** ❶ Calle Cuesta del Apero 10 🕐 🏖 Mon—Fri 1000–1800; Sat–Sun 1000–1400; Sat 1600–2000 🕐 ☀ Mon–Sat 1000–1430, 1730–2100; Sun 1000–1430 ✉ **oficinadeturismo@frigiliana.es**

The *pueblo blanco* (white village) of Frigiliana is included as a post-script to Nerja because it's a 15-minute bus ride north. However, if you want to make a day trip, you will probably have to choose between Nerja and Frigiliana. Bus times between Nerja and Frigiliana can be found here: ⊕ **grupofajardo.es/horarios/frigiliana-nerja**

There are a couple of taxi firms (by which I mean a couple of taxis) operating in Frigiliana: Taxi Frigiliana ☎ **+34 696 969 469** and Frigiliana Taxi ☎ **+34 625 288 811**

🚶 Walking: Nerja and Frigiliana

There are fabulous walking routes throughout the Province of Málaga thanks to the large number of National Parks and Protected Natural Areas. Nerja makes an ideal starting point for walks because of the frequent buses to and from Málaga that run from the early morning until the very late evening. If you're a serious walker then useful guidebooks to the area are: *The Mountains of Nerja: Sierras Tejeda, Almijara Y Alhama* by Jim

Ryan (⊕ amzn.to/3ojJSOw), and *Walking in Andalucia: 36 routes in An-dalucia's Natural Parks* by Guy Hunter–Watts (⊕ amzn.to/403TQks), both in the Cicerone Walking Guides series. Another excellent guide is *Walk! Costa del Sol* by Charles Davis (⊕ amzn.to/41bi8dy) and the companion map (⊕ amzn.to/3MFGOGQ). You can also search for departure points (Nerja, Frigiliana, etc.) on walking route sites like **komoot**, **alltrails**, **wikloc**, etc. Steve planned his own walking holiday in the Province of Málaga and has blogged about it at 'Untravelled World' ⊕ bit.ly/UTW_Axarquia.

If you're an experienced hiker, then planning your own route is probably half the fun, but for most of us, joining a planned walk with an experienced guide is a much more attractive proposition. It is also a far more sensible option for single travellers.

John Keogh ⊕ hikingwalkingspain.com ⊗ +34 647 273 502
✉ john@hikingwalkingspain.com

John is a registered walking guide based in Nerja. He organizes short/easy (3-hour), moderate (5-hour) and serious/hard (7-hour or more) hikes in the Axarquía region. His prices are extremely reasonable and almost all hikes include lunch or dinner. Most important of all, however, is that all walks include transport from a meeting point in Nerja.

Torrox and Rincón de la Victoria

⊕ turismotorrox.es ❶ Avenida de Competa ⏱ Mon–Fri 1030–1430, 1600–2000

A few miles west of Nerja, Torrox Pueblo is also a *pueblo blanco*, and a beautiful place to visit, though it is not quite as tourism-savvy as Frigiliana. Its origins are Phoenician, it has some interesting buildings and, like every small town in Spain, some lovely bars and restaurants.

⊕ turismoenrincon.es ❶ Avenida del Mediterráneo 140 (Antigua Estación de Ferrocarril, Paseo Marítimo Virgen del Carmen)

Rincón de la Victoria ('Corner of Our Lady of the Victory') is part of the greater Málaga conurbation. It's the most prosperous municipality in the Málaga metropolitan area and is a commuter town with few foreign tourists. It also has two cave complexes — the **Cueva del Higuerón** (or **del Tesoro**) and the **Cueva de la Victoria**. There is no shortage of places to eat and drink.

North of Málaga
Álora

🌐 alora.es ❶ Plaza Fuente de Arriba 15 ⏰ Mon 0900–1500; Tue–Fri 0900–1800; Sat–Sun 1000–1300, 1500–1800

The *pueblo blanco* of Álora is a great day trip destination because it is very easy to get to by train. It's the penultimate stop on the ◉ C-2 *Cercanías* line, with around 14 trains per day. The journey from Málaga–María Zambrano takes around 35 to 39 minutes. The railway station is down in the valley, beneath the village, but Monday to Saturday there is a local (mini) bus that will take you up to the main town square (◉ **Fuente Arriba**) where the *turismo* is located. The buses are timed to coincide with the arrival and departure of the trains, and you can check the timetable here: 🌐 ctmam.es/lineas/M-341. This bus service does not run on a Sunday, so if that is the only day you are able to visit, it would be better to take the bus all the way from Málaga; although please note that the bus stop (◉ **Piscina**) is 700 m from the main square: 🌐 ctmam.es/lineas/M-235.

There is also a well-regarded *bodega* (winery) in Álora called **Bodegas Pérez Hidalgo** founded by local brothers Francisco and José Miguel Pérez Hidalgo in 2000. They produce white and red wines under the Sierras de Málaga DOP and, when booked ahead, you can enjoy a tasting of their wines accompanied by local *chorizo*, cheese and olives.

Antequera

🌐 turismo.antequera.es ❶ Calle Encarnación 4A ⏰ Mon–Fri 0900–1830; Sat 0900–2200; Sun 1000–1400

If you tell your friends you are visiting Málaga, there will almost certainly be a flash of recognition (possibly mixed with incomprehension), and that would be the case even for less well-known Spanish destinations like Ronda. Mention Antequera, however, and you are likely to be met with blank stares. Despite playing host to thousands of overnight tourists, it is not well-developed as a tourist destination in its own right, which is a great pity, because it has a great deal to offer.

It is an ideal day trip destination from Málaga as it is only an hour's journey by train. It is true that if you consult the RENFE website, you will find frequent trains to and from Antequera that take either a fraction over an hour or as little as 25 minutes on the AVE. But beware! These trains mainly stop at the new high-speed station 'Antequera–Santa Ana', 20 km outside Antequera. There is no local bus service between the city and Santa Ana, which means relying upon taxis, adding cost and losing time.

However, in 2023 a new, subterranean railway station opened in Antequera (city) allowing some AVE and AVANT (high-speed medium distance) trains between Málaga and Granada to stop in the city centre. This has made travel between Málaga and Antequera much more straightforward and convenient. There are also plans to construct a rail link between Antequera Ciudad (*i.e.* the city centre) and Antequera–Santa Ana. It seems that the practice of building high-speed stations several miles from city centres, something repeated all over Spain, while it may have lowered initial costs for Adif (the Spanish equivalent of Network Rail) has turned out to be impractical for, and unpopular with, travellers.

Another way to reach Antequera is by bus, with ALSA (⊕ **bit.ly/ALSABus**) operating frequent services of around one hour's duration. Antequera has a good urban bus network (⊕ **urbanoantequera.es**) that covers the entire city (and all the main tourist sights) in spite of there being only two bus routes. Single tickets are inexpensive (around a euro in 2023) so travellers with mobility issues can easily use buses to reach the places they wish to visit.

The Moovit App does not yet cover Antequera, so planning journeys in the city will require some old-fashioned skills, like studying timetables. There is a local bus app (for Android only) and the download link is at the bottom of the ⊕ **urbanoantequera.es** website homepage. However, it is a basic timetable and map app, not a route planner. Even so, if you use the app (or the '**Localizar Bus**' link on the website) you will at least be able to locate the bus stops.

⛪ Some Visitable Churches and Convents

Entrance is free unless indicated otherwise. Some churches are only open during mass which, except on Sunday mornings, tends to be celebrated in the early morning or in the evening: not much use to a day tripper.

⚠ Smaller churches and religious houses rely upon volunteers to remain open for tourist visits, so they may not be open when advertised. Opening times change frequently, so you may simply need to cross your fingers. Even the official Antequera *turismo* website seems confused.

Church/Convent	Address	Sun	M	T	W	Th	Fri	Sat
Santa María La Mayor ⊕	Calle San Salvador 2	1000–1800						
Iglesia Del Carmen ⊕	Plaza del Carmen	11–14	⊘	1100–1330, 1630–1745				11–14
Parroquia San Sebastián	Plaza San Sebastián	0900–1300, 1800–2000						
Madre de Dios de Monteagudo	Calle Lucena 39	(exterior only)						
Convento de Belén	Calle Belén 6	0800–1730 (church), 0930–1330, 1600–1830 (*dulces*)						
Convento de la Victoria	Carrera Madre Carmen	10–1330 17–19	0900–1400, 1630–1900					10–1330 17–19
Convento de la Victoria *museo*	Carrera Madre Carmen	1630–1900						
Convento de La Encarnación	Calle los Tintes 1	0800–0900 (during mass)						
Convento de San Augustín	C/ Infante Don Fernando 11	1100–1330	⊘					1100–1330
Convento de La Trinidad	Calle Cruz Blanca 25	0930–1300	1830–1930					
Convento de los Remedios	C/ Infante Don Fernando 72	1230–1400 1930–2030	1900–2000					1930–2030
Convento de Santo Domingo	cuesta de la Paz 16	⊘						1200–1400
Convento de San José	Plaza de las Descalzas	1300–1400	⊘					1300–1400
Museo de las Descalzas	Plaza de las Descalzas	0900–1230	⊘	1000–1330, 1700–1930				0900–1230 1700–1900
Convento Sta Catalina de Siena	Plaza Coso Viejo 3	0730–1830 (Wed 0730–1300)						
Convento de Santa Eufemía	Calle Belén 4	1100–1330	⊘					1100–1330
Real Monasterio de San Zoilo	Plaza San Francisco	⊘						1100–1400
Iglesia de San Pedro	Calle San Pedro 10	1200–1300, 1700–1900 (☀1800–2000)						
Iglesia de Santa María de Jesús	Plaza del Portichuelo 14	⊘	1100–1300					⊘
Iglesia de Santiago Apóstol	Plaza Santiago	check at *turismo*						
Iglesia de San Juan de Dios	C/ Infante Don Fernando 65	10–14, 16–18	⊘	1000–1400, 1600–1800				
Iglesia de San Miguel	Calle San Miguel 49	⊘	18–19	⊘	18–19	⊘		1930–2030
Convento de los Capuchinos	Plaza Capuchinos	1230–1330 1800–1900	1800–1900					

245

🏛 Other Monuments and Attractions

🏛 **Alcazaba** 📍 Plaza de los Escribanos 🕐 Daily 1000–1800 💶💶

The Alcazaba of Antequera is neither as complete nor as extensive as that of Málaga, let alone those of Granada and Sevilla, and really only consists of the fortified walls. However its size and position, to say nothing of the wonderful views, make it well worth a visit.

🖼🏛 **Museo de la Ciudad De Antequera** 📍 Palacio de Nájera, Plaza del Coso Viejo 🕐 Tue–Sat 0900–1400, 1600–1800; Sun 1000–1400 💶

The Museum of the City of Antequera is attractively housed in the handsome 18th-century Palacio de Nájera and contains something for everyone. The star exhibit is the **Efebo de Antequera**, a first-century AD Roman bronze discovered by chance in a nearby farmhouse in 1955.

🖼🏛 **Museo De Arte De La Diputación (MAD) Antequera** 📍 Calle Diego Ponce 12 🕐 Tue–Sun 1000–1400, 1700–2030 💶

The Art Collection of the *Diputación* is a permanent collection of (mostly modern) artworks owned by the Provincial Government. Use this link to see what the current exhibitions are: 🌐 **bit.ly/MAD_Antequera** (there is a translation link at the top of the page).

🏛 **Menga and Viera Dolmens** 📍 Carretera de Málaga 5 🕐 Tue–Sat 0900–1800; Sun 0900–1500 💶 (💶 citizens of EU member states)

The Dolmen group is formed by three megalithic monuments (the **Tholos del Romeral** and the two Dolmens of **Menga** and **Viera**). Built in the Neolithic period, the oldest of them (and the third largest such structure in Europe) is El Dolmen de Menga, which is almost 6000 years old.

🍴 Eating and Drinking

Because tourism in Antequera is relatively undeveloped, you can be reasonably certain that the bars and restaurants are of good quality. In other words, there are unlikely to be establishments kept afloat by serving substandard food to gullible tourists. The **Plaza Portichuelo** is an excellent spot for *tapas* with a good choice of places. **Bar Socorrilla** has several outdoor tables and more inside. A specialist in *carrillada* (braised pork cheek), this friendly *tapas* bar is often the first stopping point in Antequera for pilgrims walking the *Camino Mozárabe* which starts in Málaga and leads all the way to Santiago de Compostela in Galicia.

It's a bit of a climb (unless you take the bus) but the **Plaza Espíritu Santo** is a pretty square where children play football and adults chat by the fountain. Drinks and *tapas* at the friendly **Bar La Perdiz** are cheap, even by Antequera's standards, and are best enjoyed out on the square.

Antequera's **municipal food market** is situated on **Plaza San Francisco**, where in addition to **El Bar de La Plaza**, you'll also find **El Mercado**, a popular restaurant with a large terrace and varied menu. Standout dishes include a wonderfully tender *carrillada* (again) and the *bacalao mozárabe* — a tasty cod dish reputedly devised by *mozárabes* (Christians who lived under Moorish rule in medieval Spain). Just down the road, on **Calle Obispo**, is **Bar La Paz**, a venerable establishment plastered with Holy Week images of Jesus and the Virgin Mary.

Reckoned to be Antequera's top 'fine dining' restaurant, I should mention **Arte de Cozin** where owner and head chef Charo Carmona specializes in rediscovering and reinterpreting ancient *andaluz* recipes, all of which are prepared in a kitchen visible from the dining room. Charo's menu changes in rhythm with seasonal ingredients but it's often focused on hearty broths and stews known as *caldosos*, *sopas* (soups) and *cazuelas* (casseroles). Next door to the restaurant, there's a smart *tapas* bar where you can enjoy smaller bites and superb wines.

As always, follow your nose and you are sure to find a great bar or restaurant almost anywhere in Antequera but other bars and restaurants I would recommend include:

Bar Machuca (Plaza Santiago 4)

Bar Carrera (Carrera de Madre Carmen 18)

Baraka (Plaza de las Descalzas)

Abrasador Bodegas Triana (Calle Infante Don Fernando 20)

Restaurante Mesón Juan Manuel (Calle San Agustín 1)

La Cantina Antequera (Alameda de Andalucía 14)

Restaurante A Mi Manera (Calle Diego Ponce 6)

Casa Memé – Mesón La Bombonera (Calle Bombeo)

Bar–Restaurante Pizarro (Calle Pizarro 32)

Bar Chicón (Calle Infante Don Fernando 1)

Bar Toral (Calle Diego Ponce 27)

El Caminito del Rey

🌐 ✒ caminitodelrey.info

The 'Little Way of the King' is a 7.7 km trail through the narrow Gaitanes Gorge north of Málaga, which for around three kilometres consists of boardwalks positioned 100 metres over the river below. The route was originally constructed between 1901 and 1905 to facilitate the movement of workers between the hydroelectric power plants at either end of the gorge. It got its name after King Alfonso XIII walked it on the occasion of the inauguration of the Conde de Guadalhorce Dam (the río Guadalhorce is the river that flows, or now trickles, into the sea near Málaga Airport).

It is also possible, and fairly easy, to get there on public transport. Take an early train (mainline or *Cercanías*) from Málaga–María Zambrano Station to El Chorro. Take the shuttle bus to the northern 'entrance' to begin the route. Allow at least three hours to complete your walk and take the train from El Chorro back to Málaga.

You can choose between a 'general' ticket and a 'guided tour' ticket. While the guide will provide interesting information about flora, fauna, geology and history, a guided group can only go as fast as its slowest member, so bear this in mind. However, 'general' slots are booked up far in advance (three months ahead in high season).

To take the hassle out of organizing transport and tickets, and to remove the worry that you may miss a connection, another option is to book through an agency. Some online travel sites will charge the earth for a 'day trip' to the Caminito, but a reliable local agency well worth considering is **Áloratur**, based in the *malagueño* town of Álora (**aloratur.com**). Their day tours are reasonably priced, leave María Zambrano station (outside the side entrance on Avenida Héroe de Sostoa) in the morning and include entry to the Caminito. The same company also offers excursions to the Torcal National Park and Dolmens of Antequera, and to Ronda, both including transport from Málaga.

Ronda

⊕ **turismoderonda.es ❶** Paseo Blas Infante
🕐☁ Mon–Fri 1000–1800 ☀ 1000–1900; Sat 1000–1700;
Sun 1000–1430

Ronda is one of the most stunning locations in Spain and a 'city built on a hilltop', or rather two hilltops. But whereas most hilltop towns involve a great deal of climbing, Ronda is more or less flat, having been built on the *mesas* of promontories either side of a deep gorge. A monumental bridge joins the older part (*la ciudad*) with the 17th-century expansion of the town where the railway station is situated.

At the time of publication at least, the best way to get to and from Ronda is by bus. If one travels by bus the journey time is greater than the fastest train, but there are more options. There is nothing to prevent your travelling one way by train and one way by bus. However, by bus you can leave Málaga at 8 am (arriving around 10.40 am), and then return late afternoon or early evening. Though the journey is long (1¾ to 2½ hours), it is through beautiful countryside. One of the bus companies serving the Málaga–Ronda route is ⊕ **avanzabus.com** which acquired the previous operator, Portillo, a few years ago. The Damas company (⊕ **damas-sa.es**) run a more frequent service. Lastly, Autocares Sierra de las Nieves (⊕ **grupopacopepe.com/horarios**) operates two or three services a day (buy tickets for this company at the bus station rather than online).

Ronda has a small urban bus network (**urbanoronda.com**) and the same smartphone app that works in Antequera also works in Ronda. The download link is at the bottom of the homepage of the bus website. Be aware, however, that although the buses are comprehensive for a small town, the service tends to be more or less hourly. As all three buses service the Bus Station (◉ **Calle Commandante Salvador Carrasco**), you shouldn't have to wait long if you want to take the bus into town. There are always taxis for hire around the railway and bus stations.

When you arrive, head for the *turismo*, either directly by bus or walk through the town centre if you want to stop for refreshments. In Ronda, an 'access all areas' ticket is called the '*Bono Turístico*' and it gets you into a fair few of the main visitor sites in Ronda. It saves you a few euros, but you also get a map that suggests a pleasant, walkable route around the most noteworthy parts of the city. The website of the Ronda *turismo* is sleek, but not terribly user-friendly (*i.e.* it has plenty of information but sometimes presents it poorly, trying to be a bit too clever, perhaps), though the *Bono Turístico* route and map are excellent. .

🍴 Eating and Drinking

Ronda has a justly deserved reputation for the quality not only of its wines but of its food. There are myriad specialities and typical dishes of the Ronda region. Many incorporate local products like chestnuts from the Valle del Genal, pumpkin, broad beans, almonds, artichokes, goat's cheese, etc. Game is plentiful, so in season you might see rabbit, hare, partridge and other game birds on menus. Typical dishes are *migas* (fried breadcrumbs) with *chorizo*, a local *gazpacho* ('*a la serrana*'), served hot and more like an unblended *sofrito*, and a local variety of *tortilla* containing black pudding. There is also a local version of black pudding (*morcilla rondeña*) that finds its way into many dishes. Whereas to the east of Málaga, *chivo* (kid) is popular, in Ronda it is *cordero* (lamb) that is served more often, usually as '*cochifrito*' (fried with garlic). Like most mountainous regions in Spain, stews are a firm favourite. Local wine is typically red and gutsy.

🍽 Winemakers' Picks

The following restaurants and bar-restaurants have been recommended by local winemakers exclusively for this book as establishments where the best wines of the region can be enjoyed.

🍴📖⬩☰🌐♨ Sensur (◉ Calle Marina 5 ⊕ sensurgastrobar.com)

A fairly new gastrobar serving fabulous food from *tapas* and sharing plates (*raciones*) all the way up to substantial main course dishes.

🍴🍲⬩☰ Restaurante Pedro Romero (◉ Calle Virgen de la Paz 18 ⊕ rpedroromero.com)

A very traditional *rondeño* restaurant with an extensive cellar. Higher end price-wise, but they often offer a lunchtime *menú del día*.

Taberna El Almacén (Calle Virgen de los Remedios 7)

An excellent *tapas* bar with lots of dishes available as both *tapas* and *raciones*, plus daily specials. They carry a large selection of wines from Ronda, about half a dozen by the glass.

Tabanco Los Arcos (Calle Armiñán 6 **Tabanco Los Ar**)

An informal wine bar with a huge selection of *tapas* alongside more substantial dishes. An excellent place to try Ronda wines.

Bardal ✿✿ (Calle José Aparicio 1 **restaurantebardal.com**)

This Michelin-starred restaurant is the '*más alta*' of '*alta cocina*' in Ronda, with prices to match.

Tragatá (Calle Nueva 4 **tragata.com**)

This is the *tapas* bar of Benito Gómez (chef patron of Bardal), providing an opportunity to sample the dishes of a Michelin starred chef in more relaxed surroundings at more reasonable prices. The food here is pricey, but no more expensive than in many old-style '*mesón*'-type restaurants.

Restaurante Tropicana (Calle Virgen de los Dolores 11 **tropicanaronda.negocio.site**)

One of Ronda's most popular restaurants, and for good reason. 'Elevated classics' would be a good description.

Bar–Restaurante Almocábar (Plaza Ruedo Alameda 5)

An unassuming café-bar in the San Francisco *barrio* serving a good range of *tapas* in the bar and traditional dishes in the restaurant, accompanied by a very good wine list.

Restaurante Casa Mateos (Calle Jerez 6 **casamateos.com**)

A modern, friendly bar-restaurant serving top-notch *tapas* and main dishes.

Mesón Carmen la de Ronda (Plaza Duquesa de Parcent 10)

A traditional and always justly popular restaurant serving classic Spanish dishes.

✗ ♟ ✦ ⊙ ✎ ☎ 🌐 Restaurante Doña PaKita (📍 Plaza Carmen Abela 🌐 dona-pakita.negocio.site)

A traditional Spanish menu with some international riffs and influences here and there. Excellent food and a friendly vibe.

♟ ✦ ⊙ ✎ ☎ ✎ ☞ ✎ ✎ ✎ ● ☞ ☞ Bar La Taberna ('del Socorro') (📍 Plaza del Socorro 8 🌐 latabernaderonda.es)

A busy and popular bar that has a good wine list and, as far as food is concerned, covers all the bases — *tapas*, *raciones*, *ĉhacinas* (cold cuts and cheese), *revueltos* (egg dishes), fish, meat, and puddings. Something for everyone at great prices.

♟ ✦ ✎ ☎ Entre Vinos (📍 Calle Pozo 2 📘 entrevinosronda)

One of my favourite bars in Ronda, this is a tiny wine bar that serves a huge selection of *tapas* alongside a selection of *raciones*. There are a couple of tables and a few stools, but if you come here at busy times, expect to eat standing up. The *tapas* are excellent, and they know their wines, offering almost two dozen by the glass.

♟ ✦ ⊙ ✎ ☎ ✎ Gastrobar Camelot (📍 Calle Comandante Salvador Carrasco 2)

Another genuine *tapas* bar with an extensive *carta* of well-priced options, usually with a number of daily specials.

Córdoba

🌐 **turismodecordoba.org** ℹ️ Plaza de las Tendillas
🕐 0900–1430 ℹ️ Plaza del Triunfo 🕐 0900–1900 (Sun 0900–1430)

Córdoba was founded by the Romans in 206 BC, soon becoming the capital of Hispania Ulterior with fine buildings and imposing fortifications. Seneca the Elder, Seneca the Younger, and the poet Lucan were all born in '*Corduba*'. In the 6th century, with the crumbling of the Roman Empire, the city fell to the Visigoths who ruled until the beginning of the 8th century when it was conquered by the Moors. Unlike other cities, it was taken by force and no deed of capitulation was signed. In 716, Córdoba became a provincial capital and, in 766, capital of the Muslim emirate of Al-Andalus which at its height (c.1000 AD) controlled two-thirds of the Iberian Peninsula.

Most visitors come principally to see the Cathedral (or '*Mezquita-Catedral*' as it seems to be mainly known). The wonder of the building (it is a UNESCO world heritage site; actually the entire historic city centre is) is less about statues, art and decoration (because it has little of any), and more about the simplicity of the geometric forms of the Islamic architecture. On a visit, one has to 'zoom out' rather than 'zoom in' to appreciate it best. It is undeniable that this architectural monument to Moorish rule is stunning; one of the oldest mosques in the world and, when it was built, the second largest. It was, probably, built on top of a Visigothic church (dedicated to Saint Vincent, protomartyr of Spain) that was, in all likelihood, constructed on top of a Roman temple. Other Visigothic churches were plundered for stone. It was converted into a church in 1236 and was pretty much used as it was until a Renaissance chapel was constructed at its centre in the early 16th century.

By far the easiest way to travel from Málaga is by train. There is a high-speed line between Málaga and Córdoba and the journey time is between 50 and 65 minutes. (There are a few buses operated by ALSA, but the journey takes 2½–3 hours.) Once you reach Córdoba, the most practical way to get around is on foot. The city centre is compact, but if you have mobility issues then you may need to take a taxi or bus. Although Córdoba has a good urban bus network, the centre of the city and the Judería are bus-free lacunæ (the streets are too narrow, though the useful 🚍3 has a route circling the old city and will get you pretty near to the Cathedral). On the other hand, most of the sites you want to see are very close to the Cathedral and the streets are either pedestrianized or low-traffic.

All of the places mentioned below are shown on the companion Google map. Select the '**NORTH OF MÁLAGA**' layer in order to see them. The map also shows a walking route, beginning and ending at the railway station.

My general advice is to get to the Cathedral as early as possible, before it's overrun with coach parties (any time before noon should be okay, but the earlier the better). The walk from the railway station to the Cathedral is about 1.5 km (or 2 km via the *turismo*) about 30 to 45 minutes' gentle walk. A good option is a train that leaves Málaga around 9 am. That allows 45 minutes to an hour to walk from the station to the Cathedral for entry at 11 am, before it becomes too busy.

🕍 Mezquita-Catedral de Córdoba

📍 Calle Cardenal Herrero 1
🌐 **mezquita-catedraldecordoba.es** 🕐 Mon–Sun 1000–1900 🔵🟢

As mentioned above, it's a good idea to book your tickets online in advance as some time slots fill up a few days ahead. Also, having a ticket will save having to queue at the ticket office. Multiple websites are authorized to sell tickets, but it's best to use the official site to ensure that you're getting the best price (some of the others are very skilled at getting you to pay for guided tours that you may not want). The entrance ticket to the Cathedral includes admission to the Fernandina Churches, which are mostly found in the western part of the city ('Axerquía'): for more details and links to smartphone apps visit **bit.ly/RutaFernandina**. Most of the churches on the route close at 2 pm (3 pm in summer) and reopen at 3 pm (5 pm in summer), so if you want to visit them you'll need to plan carefully.

🏠 Fiesta de los Patios

In the first half of May (usually the first two full weeks of May) around 50 private *patios* (courtyards) of houses in Córdoba take part in a competition. During this time all these *patios* are open to the public to visit for free. This is a rare opportunity to see the inside of *cordobés* homes, so if your visit to Córdoba coincides with this festival I recommend that after visiting the Cathedral, you visit a few *patios*. Those north-east of the Cathedral are likely to be less busy than those in the heart of the Judería, so these are probably the best to visit — bearing in mind that they will close for lunch and siesta. Details of the festival, and a map, can be found here: **patios.cordoba.es**. If you visit outside the Fiesta de los Patios, there are still a number that may be visited all year round (mostly on the Calle Basilio). The list of attractions that you can download from the *turismo* website (or pick up from the *turismo*) tells you where they are.

Córdoba with Kids — The Zoo

⊙Avenida Linneo ⊕ **zoo.cordoba.es** ⊙ Tue–Sun 0930–2000 ⊜

If you are visiting Córdoba with children then this may be of interest, especially if they need a little reward after visiting a medieval mosque-cathedral. The zoo is only 15 minutes' walk from the Cathedral (and it is next to a large children's playground). It is small, but it has a collection of around 100 species. The animals all appear to be in good health and well cared for. Best of all, though, the ticket price is very reasonable.

Synagogue

The **Sinagoga de Córdoba** (⊙ 0900–1500 ⊘ Mon ⊜) was built after the *reconquista* in 1314 and is one of only four extant medieval synagogues in Spain (the others are in Utrera in the Province of Sevilla, and in Toledo). Recently re-opened after works to deal with damp, it is open Tue–Sun and is the second most-visited attraction in Córdoba. Although the building is over 700 years old, it functioned as a Jewish place of worship for less than 177.

✕ Some Places to Eat

Like any other Spanish city, there are decent places to eat everywhere. In this section I have avoided the main hotspots around the Cathedral so these suggestions, which barely scratch the surface, are mostly in the eastern part of the city. But if your exploration of Córdoba takes you to a different *barrio*, you'll have no shortage of options.

✕ 🎣 ⊙ ⊒ 🐚 ✎ 🍷 ● **Taberna Los Plateros** ⊙ Calle San Francisco 6 ⊕ **tabernaplateros.com**

A cavern of place, serving traditional *andaluz* fare.

✕ 🦪 📖 ⊒ 🌍 🐚 ✎ 🍷 🍸 **La Taberna del Río** ⊙ Calle Enrique Romero de Torres 7 ⊕ **latabernadelrio.com**

Excellent food in a beautiful restaurant with a terrace overlooking the river. It is reasonably priced given the location and quality of the cooking, and there are some delicious dishes on offer ranging from very traditional (*e.g. salmorejo* and *rabo de toro*) to 'updated' versions of these dishes, like a toasted oxtail brioche with goat butter, smoked soy mayonnaise and sweet-and-sour peppers.

✕ 🎐 🕐 ⌥ 🌍 🐚 💈 🍢 **Restaurante La Boca** 📍 Calle San Fernando 39

A lovely restaurant with an interesting menu with plenty of vegetarian options. They usually offer an inexpensive weekday *menú del día*.

✕ 📖 🕐 🍶 🥘 ⌥ 🐚 🍢 🌮 🌐 ☕ **Bodegas Campos** 📍 Calle Lineros 32
🌐 **bodegascampos.com**

This venerable temple of gastronomy began its existence as a wine cellar for Montilla-Moriles wines and is formed of two old *bodegas*, part of a former convent and a private house. It consists of a number of spaces and rooms and offers an extensive menu of excellent dishes. Bodegas Campos were a driving force behind the establishment of a cookery and hospitality school in Córdoba, and the high quality of the service here reflects that commitment and interest. Their puddings, including a stunning olive oil and Pedro Ximénez orange ice cream, are sensational.

🍷 💈 🕐 ⌥ 🐚 🍖 🍢 🍹 ☕ **Taberna Regina** 📍 Plaza de Regina

This friendly little bar has plenty of tables in the square outside, beneath the orange trees. The *carta* could almost be the dictionary definition of 'typical' with all the *andaluz* favourites on offer (*salmorejo*, *croquetas*, aubergines with cane honey, *flamenquín*, *revueltos*, fried fish, etc.). Most dishes are available as *tapas*, *medias raciones* and *raciones*.

🍷 💈 🕐 ⌥ 🍺 **Bar los Mosquitos** 📍 Calle Carlos Rubio 24

This is a real 'back street bar' popular with locals. The *carta* is short and simple, featuring well-known classics. Everything is available as a *tapa*, *media* or *ración*. The service can be a bit gruff, but it's efficient and courteous.

✕ ⌥ 🌍 🐚 💈 🍢 🌐 ☕ **Cocina 33 Restaurante** 📍 Paseo de la Ribera 24

A small bistro that specializes in Spanish dishes enlivened by Asian fusion elements.

✕ 📖 🍶 🥘 ⌥ 🐚 💈 🍢 ☕ **El Patio de María** 📍 Calle Don Rodrigo 7
🌐 **elpatiodemaria.com**

This lovely restaurant (and the head chef really is called María) has indoor seating though dining extends into a beautiful small patio hidden at the rear. The *carta* is small but offers a varied selection of dishes, including a decent choice for vegetarians. Puddings are all homemade (often a reliable sign of a great kitchen).

The Alhambra (Granada)

🌐 **turgranada.com** ❶ Plaza del Carmen 9
🕐 🌙 0830–1800 🕐 ☀ 0830–2000

This section is entitled 'The Alhambra' rather than 'Granada' for a couple of reasons. First, the main reason that most people visit Granada is to see the Alhambra. To go to the city without visiting it would be as contrary as visiting Córdoba without seeing the *Mezquita-Catedral*, or visiting Madrid and ignoring the Prado. Second, the Alhambra is a huge complex and to do it justice one needs to spend a few hours there (the average time spent there is three hours, according to its website), leaving little time for other sightseeing, at least on a day trip. Córdoba can comfortably be 'done' in a day, making it an ideal day trip from either Málaga or Sevilla. Granada, on the other hand, has enough to keep a visitor occupied for at least two or three days. But if your main aim is to 'do' the Alhambra, then a day trip will just about suffice.

The first thing you must do, as soon as you can, is buy your ticket(s) for the **Alhambra**! Two million people visit annually and numbers are strictly limited and controlled in order to protect the fabric of the site. During the summer season, many of the slots are booked weeks ahead. The Alhambra is open every day except Christmas Day and New Year's Day. 🌐 alhambra-patronato.es

The entry slot that you book for the Alhambra does not determine the time you enter the Alhambra complex itself, but the time of entry to the **Palacios Nazaríes** (Nasrid Palaces), which are just one element of a complex, albeit the most famous. So, if you think that you will get to the Alhambra at 11 am, I would advise booking a ticket for 11.30 am (or even later), to build in some latitude.

A new high-speed train route between Málaga and Granada entered into service in 2022, with the fastest trains taking just over an hour. When the trains are operating to schedule, this is the best way to travel. In the event of delays due to maintenance, the next best way to travel to Granada is by ALSA bus (journey time: 1hr 15m to 2h).

To book your travel between Málaga and Granada, consult: ⊕ **renfe.es** (trains), ⊕ **alsa.com** (buses), ⊕ **omio.co.uk** or ⊕ **budbud.com** (trains, buses and rideshares), or ⊕ **thetrainline.com** (trains and buses). I have used all five sites to search for sample journeys and the most surprising finding was that the most comprehensive results overall came from **thetrainline**. However, websites change all the time, so I'd advise the belt-and-braces approach of searching a handful of sites. To plan your visit and your booking the following table showing roughly how long it takes to get to the Alhambra may be helpful.

Point of Arrival	Taxi	Bus	Bus & Walk	Walk
Railway Station	15 mins	30 mins	35–45 mins	45–55 mins
Bus Station	20 mins	35–40 mins	40–50 mins	60 mins+

These are very approximate times which can of course change considerably if the taxi rank is empty, or you have to wait a long time for a bus. If you decide to walk part of the route, how long it takes depends not only upon your walking speed, but how often you want to stop and look at points of interest en route. To take the bus, use the Moovit app to plan your journey. If you take the bus all the way from either the bus or rail station, you will need to take two buses (changing, usually, at the stop opposite the Cathedral), so keep your first bus ticket because it includes a free '*transbordo*' (transfer) to your second bus.

🏰 The Alhambra

The Alhambra is not merely a citadel, or a fort, or a palace. Nor is it merely a collection of palaces (though it contains such a collection). It is more like a self-contained city, consisting of palaces, defences, forts, gardens, dwellings, baths, and mosques. It was where the royalty of Moorish Granada resided, in splendid isolation from the populace in the city below. When Washington Irving visited in 1828, it was a crumbling ruin occupied by poor families (70 years later, the first edition of the *Spain and Portugal* Baedeker guide reported that the Alcazaba of Málaga was 'a confusing medley of houses, ruins and Gypsy huts').

Unlike the Alcázar of Sevilla, which is still a royal palace, and the Alcazaba of Málaga which served as an official residence for a very short time following the *reconquista*, the Alhambra was set to become the monarch's main palace in Andalucía. Indeed, one of the largest structures in the complex is the Palace of Carlos V (Carlos I of Spain). Work on this building was interrupted by the Moorish uprising in the Alpujarras in 1572 and it was never completed. So as well as the Moorish period buildings for which the Alhambra is known, in the same complex there are later additions, including a church and a convent (the latter now converted into Granada's *Parador* hotel). Visiting the Alhambra, then, is more like visiting a town than a castle or a palace and one can feel quite lost exploring 14 hectares covering several centuries of history.

Alhambra means 'the red one' and during the 'golden hour' before sunset it certainly appears to have a reddish hue. But things may not be quite this simple especially if, as many historians insist, the walls were probably whitewashed in Moorish times. There are two other theories for the name. The first is that because construction largely took place at night (the daytime summer temperature in Granada is regularly over 30° Celsius and occasionally surpasses 40°C), people in the city below would have seen the red-hued fire of torches above them. Another possibility is that the name is connected to the founder of the Nasrid dynasty who ruled as Muhammad I (1238–1273). He was known as 'al-Hamar' ('the Red') on account of the colour of his beard.

To simplify matters somewhat, the complex has four main parts. The most famous are the **Nasrid palaces**, the best-preserved Moorish buildings with their peaceful patios and fountains. The **Alcazaba** is the military zone (and the oldest part of the complex, constructed in the 11th century. The **Medina**, which is now composed of a number of buildings constructed after the *reconquista*, is the site of the old 'city' of the Alhambra complex that would have been at the service of the court. Finally, the **Generalife** was a retreat for the Nasrid royal family surrounded by orchards and gardens.

The Alhambra is a place where following some sort of guided tour is probably a good idea, if only to help make sense of such a vast complex that spans such a long sweep of history. Availability of guided tours is limited, so search online to see what's on offer (there are a few companies offering this service, one being ⊕ **alhambradegranada.org**). When booking, Check to see if the tour includes a ticket to the Nasrid Palaces (some do not). A cheaper option is to use an audio guide. Indeed, if you are able to install the app on your smartphone, then it's free. You can also prebook a handheld set to pick up on arrival: ⊕ **bit.ly/AlhambraGuias**.

ACCESSIBILITY: Wheelchair users can access the Generalife (though there are steep inclines) and the Nasrid Palace complex, but not the Alcazaba nor most of the Medina/Partal. On the other hand, tickets are available at a 33% discount. For more information visit ⊕ **bit.ly/AlhambraFAQ**

🍴 Restaurants

🍴🦞📖🍸🍲🔪🎝🌍🐚🗲🍗🍷 **Parador** 📍 Calle Real de la Alhambra
🕐 Lunch: 1300–1600, Dinner 2000–2300 ⊕ **bit.ly/MenuNazari**

The restaurant of the *Parador* has a good reputation if you want to treat yourself to a meal in a stunning setting (especially if you can sit on the terrace). It is inside the Alhambra precincts so you will need to show your restaurant reservation email on your phone to be given access, unless you combine it with a visit to the Alhambra. The *Parador* serves a *menú del día* called the '*Menú Nazari*' which you can book online.

🍴📖🍲🌍🐚🗲🔪 **Restaurante Jardines Alberto** 📍 Paseo de la Sabica 1 🕐 Tue–Sat 1130–2300; Sun–Mon 1130-1730
⊕ **jardinesalberto.es**

This restaurant, with three shady terraces, is located directly opposite the main ticket office, or 'Access Pavilion' of the Alhambra. Normally, this would set alarm bells ringing, but the quality is actually very good. The food is freshly cooked and the serving staff, ably presided over by the affable and experienced Sergio Arcas, are friendly and efficient.

🍴📖🔪🍲🌍🐚🍷 **Negro Cárbon** 📍 Puente Cabrera 9 🕐 1300–1630, 1900–2330 ⊕ **negrocarbon.es**

Negro Carbón is an excellent restaurant, though it is not cheap. It is also not suitable for vegetarians as it not only specializes in perfectly cooked, delicious steaks, but in large steaks.

🍴🦞🔪🍲🐚🔪🍵🍷 **Asador Contrapunto** 📍 Gran Vía de Colón 20 🕐 1300–1600, 2000–2300 ⊕ **asadorcontrapunto.com**

For a top-end meal in Granada, this would probably be my recommendation, though it has very little to offer to vegetarians. Contrapunto is a beautiful, modern restaurant serving well-executed Spanish dishes from a thoughtfully planned menu. The 6-course tasting menu is good value.

🍴📖🔪🍲🐚🗲🍲🔪🍶🍵🍷 **La Cuchara de Carmela** 📍 Paseo de los Basilios 1⊕ **restaurantescarmela.com** 🕐 1300–0000

Just the other side of the bridge across the River Genil, this is a traditional restaurant founded in 1955, but recently updated with modern twists in the kitchen too. '*Cuchara*' means 'spoon' and stews and casseroles are a speciality of the house.

✖ ✎ ☰ ✆ ✎ ✍ El Mercader ⚲ Calle Imprenta 2 ☉ Mon–Tue Closed; Wed 1930–2300; Thu–Sat 1330–1530, 2000–2300 ☎ +34 633 790 440

Run by husband and wife team Cristóbal and Nuria, the food is wonderful here; very traditionally Spanish with a touch of modern panache featuring dishes like lamb sweetbreads (with black garlic cream and prawns) and veal tongue (slow cooked with pumpkin puree and prunes). For the quality, it is excellent value. Bookings by telephone or in-person.

✖ ⛻ ☰ ✆ ✎ Restaurante Albahaca ⚲ Plaza Campillo Bajo 5 ⊕ restaurantealbahaca.es ☉ 1330–1530, 2030–2230

Albahaca ('basil') is a decent, traditional and reasonably priced restaurant at any time, but I include it here because they do a reasonably priced, filling and delicious *menú del día* Tuesday to Friday (including evenings Tue-Thu). It's rather old-fashioned in its décor but it has a lovely atmosphere.

✖ ⛶ ▣ ⛻ ✄ ☉ ✎ ☰ ✆ ✦ ✎ ✍ La Vinoteca ⚲ Calle Almireceros 5 ⊕ lavinotecagranada.es ☉ 1300–1630, 1930–2330

As the name suggests, La Vinoteca is primarily a wine bar, but the food stands out for its quality. The *menú del día* is good value and filling.

✖ ✿ ⛶ ✎ Damasqueros ⚲ Calle Damasqueros 3 ☉ Tue–Sat 1300–1500, 2030–2230; Sun 1300–1500 ⊕ damasqueros.com

In the Realejo district, this one makes the cut on account of their well-balanced and delicious tasting menu ('*Menu Degustación Semanal*') which changes weekly to reflect seasonal produce.

✖ ✄ ☉ ☰ ⊕ ✆ ✦ ✎ Casa Colón ⚲ Calle Ribera del Genil 2 ☉ 1300–0000

Strictly speaking, Casa Colón is probably a *tapas* bar, but the quality of the *tapas* makes it more of a gourmet experience than your average bar. Casa Colón is also in a lovely spot down by the River Genil, with a terrace.

✖ ⛶ ◑ ▣ ☉ ✎ ☰ ✆ ✎ ✍ Vino y Rosas ⚲ Calle Álvaro de Bazán 12 ⊕ bit.ly/VyRGran ☉ Tue–Sat 1300–1700, 2000–0000; Sun 1300–1700 ☎ +34 958 036 520

You could easily walk straight past this little place, assuming it to be a rather twee café. 'Wine and Roses', however, serves some of the best food in Granada and is one of the city's gastronomic highlights. It's extremely good value given the quality of the cooking, and it is one of the cosiest places to enjoy a meal.

✄ ♟ Bars

Remember that in Granada all bars hand out a free *tapa* with every drink ordered. The only exception to this rule are establishments that are primarily restaurants but which have a small bar area. As *tapas granadinas* are all free, the portions are modest. The modest sample of bars listed below serve *tapas* (everywhere in Granada does) and many have *comedores* (restaurant sections).

Plaza Nueva

Bodegas Castañeda ♀ Calle de Almireceros 1

Los Manueles ♀ Calle Reyes Católicos 61 ♀ Calle Monjas del Carmen 1

Casa Julio ♀ Calle Hermosa 5

Los Diamantes ♀ Plaza Nueva 13 (fabulous, but always packed)

Bar el León ♀ Calle Pan 1

Cathedral

Bar Soria ♀ Calle Laurel de las Tablas 3

Bar Provincias ♀ Calle Provincias 4

Más que Vinos ♀ Calle Tundidores 10

Bar Poë ♀ Calle Verónica de la Magdalena 40

Calle Navas

Almost everywhere on this narrow street is excellent

Albaicín

Casa Torcuato ♀ Calle Pagés 31

Bar los Mascarones ♀ Calle Pagés 20

Bar Aliatar 'Los Caracoles' ♀ Plaza Aliatar 4

Reina Mónica ♀ Calle Panaderos 20

Horno de Paquito ♀ Calle San Buenaventura (Plaza Aliatar)

Bar Aixa ♀ Plaza Larga 5

🔭 Other Sights in Granada

If you leave Málaga early and return late (or if you decide to stay overnight in Granada; there is no shortage of cheap and basic accommodation if all you need is a bed), then you will have time to see something more than the Alhambra. Here are a few suggestions.

Monastery of San Jerónimo

♀ Calle Rector López Argueta 9 ⏰ Mon–Sun 1000–1330, 1600–1930
🌐 realmonasteriosanjeronimogranada.com €

The Royal Monastery of St. Jerome is a former Hieronymite monastery in the Renaissance style. The church, famous for its architecture, was the first in the world consecrated to the Immaculate Conception of Mary. The star attraction is the baroque monastic church, which is breathtaking.

The Barrio of Albaicín (alto)

🌐 **bit.ly/AlbaicinGranada**

The upper part of the Albaicín district is picturesque and fun to explore (though, be warned — it is perched on a hill and, although one can get to and from it by bus, there is a lot of walking up and down hill required).

El Bañuelo (Moorish Baths)

📍 **Carrera del Darro 31** 🕙 **Mon–Sun 1000–1700** 💶💶

Though fascinating and, unlike the modern 'Granada Hammam', a genuine Arab bathhouse (once part of the complex of the 'Mosque of the Walnut'), you might baulk at the entrance price, but the ticket will allow you to visit (on the same day) the *bañuelo* and three other historic sites: the Dar al-Horra Palace, the Casa Horno de Oro and the Corral del Carbón.

Palacio Dar al-Horra

📍 **Callejón de las Monjas** 🕙 ☀️**0900–1430, 1700–2030;** 🌰**1000–1700 (combined** 🏷️ **)**

A Nazari palace located in the Albaicín neighbourhood and built in the fourteenth century on a former Zirid palace of the eleventh century, which was the first residence of the founder of the Nasrid dynasty, Muhammad I.

Casa Horno de Oro

📍 **Calle Horno del Oro 14** 🕙 ☀️ **0900–1430, 1700–2030;** 🌰 **1000–1700 (combined** 🏷️ **)**

The *Casa Morisca de la Calle Horno de Oro* ('The Moorish House of Golden Oven Street') is located near the River Darro.

Corral del Carbón

📍 **Calle Mariana Pineda** 🕙 **0900–2000 (combined** 🏷️ **)**

The Corral del Carbón or Correo de los Moros is a 14th-century Nasrid '*alhóndiga*' (corn exchange) preserved almost in its entirety.

Casa de Zafra

📍 **Calle Portería Concepción 8** 🕙 **Mon–Sun 0900–1430** 💶

This Hispanic-Moorish house, like others in the city, has survived because it was joined to a religious building, in this case to the convent of Santa Catalina de Zafra. It now houses the 'Centro de Interpretación' for the Albaicín district.

Convento de Santa Catalina de Zafra

◉ Carrera del Darro 39 🕐 Mon–Sun 0900–1430 € (donation)

A monastery of Dominican nuns ('*monjas*' in Spanish) founded in 1540. The church may be visited and the sisters sell their homemade *dulces* from the convent door (**0900–1230, 1600–1800**).

Casa de Castril

◉ Carrera del Darro 41–43 €

This grand house with its beautiful plateresque doorway takes its name from the Manor of Castril granted by the *Reyes Católicos* to their Secretary, Hernando de Zafra. It was built in 1539 by his grandson. It now houses the Archaeological Museum of Granada.

Cuarto Real de Santo Domingo

◉ Plaza de los Campos 6 ⊘ Mon €

The 13th century 'Royal Room of St Dominic', is what remains of an Almohad Palace of Moorish Granada, located in the heart of the city, next to what was the *barrio* of Alfareros.

Casa de los Tiros

◉ Calle Pavaneras 19 ⊘ Mon €

The Casa de los Tiros was built between 1530 and 1540 and is similar to other palaces of Granada at the time. It is named after the cannon ('*tiro*' means 'shot') once positioned on its battlements. It is currently a museum with a fine collection of painting and sculpture.

Capilla Real (Chapel Royal)

◉ Calle Oficios ⊕ capillarealgranada.com 🕐 Mon–Sat 1000–1830; Sun 1100–1800 €€

The final resting place of Fernando and Isabel, this chapel is somewhat like a 'Royal Peculiar' in the UK and is not part of the Cathedral.

Catedral de Granada

◉ Plaza de las Pasiegas 🕐 Mon–Sat 1000–1815; Sun 1100–1815 ⊕ catedraldegranada.com €€

Like the Cathedral of Málaga, Granada's cathedral is also unfinished.

Hospital de San Juan de Dios

◉ Calle San Juan de Dios 19 ⊕ basilicasanjuandedios.es 🕐 Mon–Sat 1000–1900; Sun 1000–1200, 1330–1900 €€

Now a private hospital run by the Order of St John of God, but it is possible to visit the chapel (a minor basilica), which is stunning and richly decorated and gilded.

Afterword

I really hope you have found this book useful. I began work on the more comprehensive version (*Málaga: A Comprehensive Guide to Spain's Most Hospitable City*) during the COVID lockdown, having failed to find any adequate guidebook to Málaga available in English. This volume is a condensed version of that book, and is aimed at first-time visitors to Málaga and those visiting for a short break.

If you've found it useful, I'd really appreciate your leaving a brief review (if you bought it online). If you have any corrections, suggestions, questions or criticisms, you can get in touch at ✉ **farolabooks@gmail.com**.

 If, having discovered Málaga, you are keen to visit again and you would like to learn more about its history, culture, gastronomy, winemaking and traditions, then you will find much more information in my more detailed guide, which is three times the length of this one. You could then give this book as a gift to a friend to encourage them to discover one of Spain's loveliest, yet least well-known, city destinations!

The longer version of the guide also contains detailed sections about gastronomy and local wines, *Semana Santa*, the *feria* and the bulls, among other topics.

There is plenty to see in Málaga. One would need two or three weeks just to visit the museums and galleries. On a return visit, having ticked off the 'main attractions', you will still find plenty to explore and discover. First time visitors often tend to stay around the *centro histórico*. More time is required to do justice to the *barrios* that surround it. Why not seek out that fantastic local restaurant or charming neighbourhood bar that hasn't yet appeared in any guidebook?

Travel an hour or so outside the city limits and you can discover an entire province. This brief guide provides a number of suggestions, but the in-depth version of the guide includes more destinations as well as giving travel information and suggestions of attractions and options for dining.

Málaga is also a convenient point of entry and/or departure for visits to other destinations. Few regional UK airports operate regular flights to Sevilla or Granada, yet there is often a choice of flights to Málaga, only 1-2 hours away by train. Even Madrid is less than 3 hours from Málaga by train (with average fares costing around ⅓ as much as for comparable journeys in the UK). At the time of publication, a ticket from Málaga to Madrid on a high speed train (the same distance as Edinburgh to London) was, on average, £1 cheaper than a ticket from Reading to London.

¡Buen Viaje!

📷 Picture Credits

Original diagrams are the work of the author and published under a ©①② licence (**creativecommons.org/licenses/by-sa/4.0**).

Creative Commons symbols are used under a ©① licence (**creativecommons.org/licenses/by/4.0**). Other fonts used in this book are issued under the Open Font Licence (**scripts.sil.org/OFL**).

The 'Málaga' Symbol Font (created using FontForge) makes use of glyphs created by the author, henceforth licensed under a ©①② licence; SVG vectors issued under an open licence (**svgrepo.com/page/licensing**); SVG vectors from **fontawesome.com** issued under a ©① licence; icons made from **onlinewebfonts.com/icon**, Icon Fonts licensed by a ©① licence; and glyphs from **thenounproject.com** users: Adrià Sánchez Aran (**/Siqmundo**), Linseed Studio (**/linseedstudio**) infinit.space (**/infinit**), Andrew Doane (**/andydoane**), Ann Artemova (**/sunnyicons**), Lars Meiertoberens (**/lars.online**), Kick (**/kickg**), Valter Bispo (**/valterbispo**), Adrien Coquet (**/coquet_adrien**), and Abu (**/jamainabusanin7**), all licensed under a ©① licence.

Unless otherwise attributed, all maps (and graphics with map content) were created by the author using MapOSMatic/OCitySMap (March–June 2023) with map data © 2023 OpenStreetMap contributors (**openstreetmap.org/copyright**), used here under an Open Data Commons licence (**opendatacommons.org/licenses/odbl**).

With the exception of those listed below, all other graphics and photographs in this book are either in the ⓟ public domain or the work of the author published under a ©①② licence. The remainder are published under © and 📷 (Unsplash) licences:

1	©①	Paolo Trabattoni flickr.com/photos/mctraba/9636914400
6	©①②	Real Academia Española, https://commons.wikimedia.org/w/index.php?curid=50839196
10	©①	Magnus Akselvoll, https://flickr.com/photos/magnus_akselvoll/24327343590
12	©①	Martin Ultsch, https://flickr.com/photos/149503730@N03/31189268981
13	©①②	Dr Bob Hall, https://flickr.com/photos/houseofhall/48710757593/
14	©①	Aapo Haapanen https://flickr.com/photos/decade_null/5275644988
22	ⓟ	Universitätsbibliothek Heidelberg http://diglit.ub.uni-heidelberg.de/diglit/braun1582bd1
28	©①②	HansenBCN, https://commons.wikimedia.org/w/index.php?curid=3784036
31	©①②	Hoteles Santos https://commons.wikimedia.org/w/index.php?curid=122609699
41	©①	Ruben Holthuijsen, https://flickr.com/photos/rubenholthuijsen/36879245103/
45	©①	Mike McBey, https://flickr.com/photos/158652122@N02/50628079421
45	©①②	Tyk – Own work, https://commons.wikimedia.org/w/index.php?cu-

rid=5134379

47	©①②	The author, created using MapOSMatic/OCitySMap 03/02/2023 with map data © 2023 OpenStreetMap contributors
48	©①②	Mstyslav Chernov - Self-photographed, http://mstyslav-chernov.com https://commons.wikimedia.org/w/index.php?curid=25938269
50-56	©①②	The author 2023, created using MapOSMatic/OCitySMap 03/02/2023 with map data © 2023 OpenStreetMap contributors
57	©①②	Tyk, https://es.m.wikipedia.org/wiki/Archivo:Ermita_de_Zamarrilla2.jpg
58-61	©①②	The author, created using MapOSMatic/OCitySMap 03/02/2023 with map data © 2023 OpenStreetMap contributors)
65	⚓	Quino Al, https://unsplash.com/photos/hnlu7XOzPcU
72	⚓	Veronika Hradilová, https://unsplash.com/fr/@vrsh
73	©①②	Steph Gray, https://flickr.com/photos/lesteph/4023045288/
76	©①②	Katina Rogers, https://flickr.com/photos/katinalynn/9697412702
77	©①	Conall, https://flickr.com/photos/conall/52417502739
105	©①	Jorge Franganillo, https://flickr.com/photos/franganillo/51901162598
148	©①②	Lisa Risager, https://flickr.com/photos/risager/4009451418
150	©①	Nick Kenrick. https://flickr.com/photos/zedzap/14921834904
154	©①	35mmMan, https://flickr.com/photos/35mmman/15410849595/
155	©①②	Jfernandorosas, https://commons.wikimedia.org/w/index.php?curid=17363746
157	©①②	Emilio, https://flickr.com/photos/emijrp/9033255944/
183	⚓	Quino Al under the Unsplash license https://unsplash.com/@quinoal
189	⚓	QuinoAl, https://unsplash.com/@quinoal
193	©①	Olga Berrios, https://flickr.com/photos/ofernandezberrios/450692908/
193	ⓟ	Gilles Roy, https://flickr.com/photos/yorsellig/32658258783
202	©①②	mertxe iturrioz, https://flickr.com/photos/moxola/32367882976
213	©	Una Voce Málaga
214	ⓟ	By Unknown author - British Library, https://commons.wikimedia.org/w/index.php?curid=76798779
217	©①②	amata_es https://flickr.com/photos/amata_es/1353978599
228	©①②	Ángel de los Ríos, https://flickr.com/photos/diocrio/38979583474/
233	⚓	Amos from Stockphotos.com, https://unsplash.com/@stockphotos_com
235	©①②	Hernán Piñera,https://flickr.com/photos/hernanpc/16326686375
240	©①	Wolfgang Manousek, https://flickr.com/photos/manousek/10949357945
243	©①	Weldon Kennedy, https://flickr.com/photos/99123936@N00/4260153563/
252	⚓	Hasmik Ghazaryan Olson, https://unsplash.com/@find_something_pretty_everyday
253	⚓	Saad Chaudhry, https://unsplash.com/photos/uYMyUKL1QSU
257	©①②	The Very Honest Man, https://flickr.com/photos/14183788@N00/9018554311

Printed in Great Britain
by Amazon